THE
KISSING
SAILOR

The Mystery Behind the Photo that Ended World War II

THE
KISSING
SAILOR

Lawrence Verria & George Galdorisi

Foreword by David Hartman

Naval Institute Press
Annapolis, MD

Naval Institute Press
291 Wood Road
Annapolis, MD 21402

First Naval Institute Press paperback edition published in 2023.
ISBN: 978-1-68247-902-5 (paperback)
ISBN: 978-1-61251-127-6 (eBook)

**The Library of Congress has cataloged the hardcover edition as
follows:**

Verria, Lawrence.
  The kissing sailor : the mystery behind the photo that ended World
War II / by Lawrence Verria and George Galdorisi.
    p. cm.
  Includes bibliographical references and index.
  ISBN 978-1-61251-078-1 (hbk. : alk. paper) 1. World War, 1939–
1945—Peace—New York (State)—New York. 2. V-J Day, 1945—New
York (State)—New York. 3. Mendonsa, George. 4. Sailors—New York
(State)—New York—Pictorial works. 5. Nurses—New York (State)—
New York—Pictorial works. 6. Photographs—Political aspects—United
States—History—20th century. 7. Friedman, Greta. 8. Sailors—United
States—Biography. 9. Eisenstaedt, Alfred. 10. Times Square (New
York, N.Y.)—History—20th century. I. Verria, Lawrence. II. Galdorisi,
George, 1948- III. Title.
  D816.V47 2012
  940.54'5973092—dc23

                                                    2012007542

♾ Print editions meet the requirements of ANSI/NISO z39.48-1992
(Permanence of Paper).
Printed in the United States of America.

31 30 29 28 27 26 25 24 23   9 8 7 6 5 4 3 2 1
First printing

To my wife, Celeste, and our daughters, Chelsea, Britney, and Simone, for encouraging a high school history teacher to give chase.

Lawrence Verria

This book is dedicated to my wife, Becky, and our adult son and daughter, Brian and Laura, for their infinite patience and understanding throughout all my writing pursuits and especially for their gentle encouragement in the process of producing this book.

George Galdorisi

CONTENTS

ILLUSTRATIONS

A book? An entire *book*? About a black-and-white still photograph? Must be some picture! Indeed, it's one of the most memorable and beloved photos ever taken, and this book about it is masterful storytelling, a super detective story that solves a sixty-five-year-old mystery. Who were the sailor and nurse, in a passionate kiss, in *LIFE* magazine's photo taken in Times Square, New York City, on August 14, 1945, the day that World War II ended? What made this one photo worth not only a thousand words, but millions of words over decades? Because it makes us actually *feel* like we were there experiencing the exultation of the war's end with millions of others around America.

Who were the players in this tale? Three people from different worlds who had never met each other came together, purely by chance, for just a few seconds at 44th Street and Broadway at a historic moment in time. They were the great photographer, Alfred Eisenstaedt (Eisie), the Father of Photojournalism, who was on assignment for *LIFE* in Times Square trying to capture, on film, the wild emotions of that day; an American sailor who was on leave after two years serving on board ship in the Pacific War; and a young woman in a nurse's uniform who was on lunch break from her job in midtown Manhattan. She had strolled to Times Square to learn for herself what patients had been telling her all morning, that the war might be over.

World War II was the most widespread and destructive conflict in history. Fifty million to seventy million people died. Tens of millions more were injured, many for life. Every person and nation on the planet was affected in some way by the horrendous war. America was directly involved in combat for three years and nine months. It was the last time in America that every man, woman, and child, along with all business and government leaders, were totally committed to a common goal. The announcement that Japan had surrendered on August 14, 1945, unleashed a volcanic eruption of excitement not seen before or since—spontaneous parades, singing, dancing in the streets, and uninhibited hugging and kissing, including by total strangers. In New York City, Times Square is where people go to celebrate, then and now, and it was a magnet for New Yorkers who wanted to share their exhilaration that day. People by the tens of thousands poured into the Square from apartment buildings, offices, theaters, and restaurants. Booze was flowing at bars across the city, mostly for free. By seven that evening there were half a million people in Times Square. The world could breathe again. The war had finally ended. That day has been called "the happiest day in the history of America."

The sailor and his very new girlfriend were spending his last day of leave going to the one-o'clock movie at Radio City Music Hall. Someone pounded on the theater door and yelled, "The war is over!" Radio City emptied. The couple left the theater, stopped at a bar and had a few quick drinks (at least, *he* did), then headed into Times Square. Pandemonium broke out. In his joyous state, the sailor spotted a nurse in white, walked up to her and, without so much as saying "Hello," grabbed her, bent her back, and kissed her hard, her body shaking in submission. The girlfriend looked on. (It's a good sign that the sailor and his girlfriend have now been married for more than sixty years.)

From its first issue in 1936, *LIFE* was the most influential picture magazine in the country and had been telling the story of the war in all of its horror and emotion. Each week *LIFE* reached some seventy-five million reader-viewers with extraordinary photographs that made us laugh, cry, curse, and weep. In the magazine's forty-two-year life, Eisie photographed eighty-six of its cover images. When he arrived in Times Square that afternoon, the place was already coming unhinged. With his Leica 35mm camera, he spotted numerous targets of opportunity, including that sailor in a passionate embrace and kiss. It lasted just a few seconds; the sailor and nurse parted, never introduced. Eisie took four pictures, then moved on quickly to find new "photo ops" without interviewing the couple or learning their names.

That photo has allowed millions to "be there" in Times Square at that moment, to feel the emotions of that day in America. The sailor and nurse never saw the picture until 1980, thirty-five years after their chance meeting in Times Square. They did meet again, several times, over the next thirty years. Only now, more than sixty-five years after that photo was taken, have their identities been uncovered by a Rhode Island high school history teacher, Larry Verria, and a retired U.S. naval aviator, Captain George Galdorisi. Many pretenders came forward to say that *they* were in that photo, but Verria and Galdorisi's ten years of sleuthing and master detective work have finally revealed, with certainty, what millions have wanted to know for decades. Who were and are the "sailor" and "nurse" in the iconic photo? Verria and Galdorisi's investigative team included, among others, photo analysis experts, forensic anthropologists, facial recognition specialists, and cutting-edge techno-wizards from Cambridge, Massachusetts. Sherlock Holmes and Watson would applaud.

Oh! Who are the "sailor" and "nurse"? Continue, intrepid readers, and join detectives Verria and Galdorisi for a mystery solved and an emotional journey, a trip back in time to a few moments of joy and exultation in America.

David Hartman

Note: Hartman interviewed Eisenstaedt on network television in 1987. Eisie confirmed that neither he nor *LIFE* knew the true identities of the sailor and nurse. Hartman met with the "real" sailor in Jamestown, Rhode Island, in October 2011.

David Hartman was the original, and for more than eleven years, host of *Good Morning America*. He writes and produces numerous programs about the history of military aviation and space, and he has earned two national News and Documentary Emmys for writing, as well as the Aviation/Space Writers Association Journalism Award.

ACKNOWLEDGMENTS

From the outset, this project knew no greater friend than Capt. Gerald O'Donnell, USN (Ret.). He is a selfless champion of the truth. His stewardship, support, and watchful eye made this book possible.

Early on Dr. John Walsh, Lynda Tisdell, Denise Arsenault, Brigitte Martino, Maryann Vollaro, and Jacques Arsenault provided constructive criticism, but more important, energetic encouragement for a work in its infancy. Their influence can be detected even in the final manuscript. Stephen Power, senior editor at John Wiley Publishing, provided early enthusiasm for this project and gentle coaching along the way. Dr. Helen Anderson-Cruz's superlative efforts editing this book's final manuscript cannot be overstated. And at the end of the long journey, copy editor Wendy Bolton's concluding look and commentary of our work proved most helpful.

We are indebted to Brown University librarian Carina Cournoyer, Anne Clifford and her team at the Coronado Public Library, Cheryl Stein and staff members at Rogers Free Library in Bristol, Rhode Island, and the librarians at the Providence Public Library and the New York Public Library. Your tolerance for two patrons who collectively made use of almost every research service you offered is most appreciated.

Russell Burrows and Rob Silviera shared their expertise and exercised great patience while preparing the book's photographs.

Norman Polmar offered insightful advice regarding the best way to share this engaging story with the U.S. Naval Institute's readers.

Marcel Arsenault, development coordinator at Sharp Enterprise, saved the authors several long-distance trips to New York by double- and triple-checking Times Square's configuration and landmarks.

Without the generous assistance of Professor Richard Benson; Baback Moghadam, PhD; Hanspeter Pfister, PhD; and Dr. Norman Sauer, we never could have proven the real kissing sailor's identity. Each of you made a significant contribution to history.

While Lois Gibson and Chris Palmer recognize a different kissing sailor than did the authors of this work, their worthy challenge and generous sharing of evidence informed our work. Glenn McDuffie and Ken McNeel, both good men, were fortunate to have Gibson and Palmer in their respective corners.

John Silbersack, our superb agent at Trident Media Group, demonstrated infinite patience and above-and-beyond efforts to enable this book to reach fruition and ultimate publication.

Even with all the evidence and arguments in support of this book's conclusion, closure could not have been realized without the cooperation of Bobbi Baker Burrows at *LIFE*. Her skillful eye, principled conscience, and courageous voice raised our work to new heights.

This book may never have been written if it were not for Anthony Restivo, a wisecracking student who always gravitated to the back of his U.S. history class. He knew the kissing sailor all along.

INTRODUCTION

They were supposed to be dead. Enemy bullets wiped out the photographer's World War I regiment at Flanders. Nazis exterminated the Jewish woman's family in the Auschwitz concentration camp. Typhoon Cobra drowned the sailor's World War II mates in the Pacific Ocean. Despite forces that schemed to kill them all, somehow the German photographer, the Austrian Jew, and the American sailor lived to cross paths in Times Square, New York, on the day Japan surrendered to the United States.

On that V-J Day (Victory over Japan Day), in the nation's crossroads, the assertive sailor did not properly introduce himself to a woman he assumed to be a nurse. She did not invite his approach. None of that mattered. The Navy man swooped in and kissed her anyway. He held her tight for several seconds, as if not wanting to let a hard-earned victory slip away. Before he released her, many people surrounded the couple and took notice of the sailor's stylish caress and the nurse's flexible torso. One person in that crowd had a Leica camera hanging from his neck. Without conscious thought or a second's hesitation, he lifted the camera to eye level and directed the lens at the entwined couple. He clicked the shutter closed four consecutive times. One of these pictures came to epitomize World War II's triumphant end.

For years people gazed at the V-J Day photo and marveled at what they saw. But they didn't all see the same thing. Many people were reminded of war and peace. Some imagined love or lust. Still others sensed relief and exhilaration. No matter how the photograph affected them, as time passed admirers grew increasingly curious about the sailor's and nurse's identities. For years no caption ever mentioned either's name, and a decades-long mystery was the result. While many people tried to crack the case, most investigations concluded with something along the lines of, "I'm the sailor."

Adding to the kissers' anonymity, for sixty-three years the photographer's iconic picture went untitled. Though often referenced as "The Kiss," "The Sailor and the Nurse," or "The Kissing Sailor," not until 2008 did *LIFE: The Classic Collection* christen its aged offspring. The informal blessing amounted to, "Best to just call it, *V-J Day, 1945, Times Square*."[1] The unceremonious anointing did not extend to the photographed sailor and the woman dressed in white. Even after sixty-five years, both remained nameless. *LIFE* never shared publicly who they thought might be their kissing sailor.

To be fair, executives at *LIFE* could argue persuasively they had no responsibility to tag their famous photograph's paramours. But their contention ignores the essence of the whole mission. Naming the sailor and nurse is not so much a line of reasoning, but rather a matter of soul. *LIFE* had an obligation to the historical record, as well as to the two national treasures in their cherished photo. It turned its back on both history and the photo's principals. Perhaps worse, it neglected its sacred mission. It was the magazine that promised to show the world. And almost always, it did that. But with *V-J Day, 1945, Times Square*, it lost sight of its charge. Instead of showing and sharing, for years it buried a story most worthy of the celebrated image.

In 1986, news anchor Ted Koppel unearthed and shared what he believed to be the long, lost account of *LIFE*'s famous photograph. In the documentary *45/85: America and the World since World War II*, Koppel proclaimed Marvin Kingsbury *the* kissing sailor. The segment's short clip shows Kingsbury pointing up to the news ticker in Times Square, declaring, "The Japs have surrendered . . . flashed on there." Kingsbury then explained, "I met the girl coming across the street right here, grabbed her, put my foot before her. Right down." Kingsbury's delivery convinced Koppel that the former sailor's claim rang true.

No doubt, thousands of Americans trusted the popular news commentator's declared opinion. Still, something about Kingsbury's story just didn't seem right. As Kingsbury demonstrated his technique for putting the nurse "right down," his mannerisms better suited a construction worker digging a ditch, rather than a sailor embracing the woman in the famed celebratory hold and kiss. At best, his explanation of the lead-up emphasized the predictable. At worst, his rendition came across as a concocted story from more than forty years ago. *V-J Day, 1945, Times Square* deserved a better story.

As it turned out, Kingsbury had a lot of competition. Years earlier, many World War II sailors, a Coast Guard seaman, two home-front nurses, and a dental assistant claimed key roles in the famous photograph. Their campaigns for recognition had turned contentious. Exchanges got ugly. Controversy brewed. And the battling had just begun. Later, more contenders entered the fray.

Most of the campaigning sailors and home-front women had convincing proof to back up their claims. But *LIFE* had the power. And without *LIFE*'s blessing, no kissing sailor or nurse could hope to win over the masses to their version of that V-J Day from so long ago. As the years passed, arguments in favor of one kissing sailor candidate over another succeeded only in knotting the mystery tighter. For more than sixty-five years the mystery remained, while *LIFE* watched.

The search for the kissing sailor is not an exclusive undertaking. Some of the forthcoming findings have existed for consideration for years. And most of the determinations unique to this book could have been discovered decades earlier. Well over a half century ago, a photographer and his Leica camera made plainly visible almost everything needed to make a positive identification of the kissing sailor and offer a convincing take on the nurse he kissed. All one had to do was look—really look— not just watch.

The kissing sailor and the woman dressed in white in Eisenstaedt's *V-J Day, 1945, Times Square* still walk among us. And while the scene they created appears so familiar to most, we know far too little. Against all the odds, and maybe with fate's forces at their backs, two strangers traversed the world's most popular square on the day history's most destructive war ended. Without rehearsal or intent, they communicated what the climax of a victorious war *felt* like. The particulars of that saga inspire the human spirit. Proof of their part in that iconic photo persuades the inquisitive. Treatment of their claims upsets the fair-minded. Forces beyond their control have denied them their due far too long. Their story, most worthy of the celebrated image, will finally be told.

PART 1

PRACTICALLY PICTURE-PERFECT

The impulse to shoot is an instant reflex from the brain to the fingertip, bypassing the thinking stage. Often when you start to do that—think—it is too late, because thinking causes a tiny fraction of delay.

ALFRED EISENSTAEDT
Eisenstaedt's Guide to Photography

THE PHOTO

On Tuesday afternoon, August 14, 1945, Americans could practically taste the victory over the Japanese Empire. But that wasn't enough. They wanted to see it and never forget what it looked like. They needed a picture—one so sensational that those yet to be born could experience the same exhilaration and always remember what the end of World War II *felt* like.

While many newspapers and magazines hunted for such an image, the expectation of one publication far exceeded the others. Subscribers of that leading photo journal had come to expect captivating photographs, especially during World War II. Now, with victory in their grasp, the magazine's subscribers looked for a one-in-a-million photo to mark the occasion.

In pursuit of this image, the photo journal's most prominent photographer searched the streets of Times Square. He understood his charge. The magazine that employed him had earned a reputation for always getting *the* picture. So had he—and today his reputation was once again on the line. On this day, he looked for a picture that would epitomize the American victory.

Finding such an image grew increasingly challenging. As the early afternoon progressed, the nation's most famous square filled with celebrants. The photographer's field of vision narrowed. Keeping track of people's movements bordered on the impossible. Focusing on any one person proved especially futile. The noise of clacking feet, laughing voices, and escalating commotion added multiple layers of distraction. Despite the mounting obstacles, the photographer persisted in his search for *the* photo.

Suddenly, at the extremity of his peripheral vision, he noticed a tall sailor swooping in on a shorter woman dressed in white. Without conscious thought, he acted quickly. Spinning around, he raised his Leica camera and took a photo of what appeared to be a sailor and nurse kissing. He had taken thousands of pictures during his celebrated career. Many commanded the world's attention. None looked like this one. Ultimately, that photo came to epitomize the victorious end of World War II.

While in the future many would marvel at the sailor's and nurse's captured pose, in truth the shoot required no posing or fussing. In fact, the photographer exercised no role in bringing the moment about. However, his contribution proved enormous. He acted impulsively, aimed accurately, and commanded that the camera's shutter close at the most poignant moment. The image he captured allows one to see the exhilaration, taste the kiss, smell the perfume and cologne, hear the bustling streets, and feel victory.

V-J Day, 1945, Times Square struck a powerful chord in 1945 and continued to play well with future onlookers years and even decades later. The photo grabs the viewer's attention and, like the pictured sailor, never seems to let go. All the photo's features compete for the eye's focus. The sailor's massive right hand cups the woman's waist and holds on tightly. She sways her left hip out lazily. His left arm supports her upper torso, which might otherwise collapse toward Times Square's pavement. Her right leg bends slightly upward, propped by a downward, pointed high-heeled white shoe. With their lips pressed tightly together and his nose compressing her left cheek, she closes her eyes, ostensibly content to remain unaware of her pursuer's identity. Their uniforms' colors, dark navy blue and bleached white, offer the only contrast between their two melded bodies. Those gathered around the victory celebrants focus attention on the captured moment. Grins and smiles indicate they approve. At last the conquering hero and his obliging maiden are together, safe and sound.

Over the ensuing years millions stared at or studied the anonymous sailor and nurse. Each viewing ignited their imagination. They devised story lines to complement what they saw, but they never knew the truth. Instead, like a 1940s movie, surmised plots glossed over the war's miseries and romanticized life in general. Predictably, the stories climaxed either with the couple parting and never speaking to each another again, but wondering what ever happened to each other, or the photo's principals married, and hung Eisenstaedt's famous photograph in the living room of the Cape they bought after the war. And, of course, they spawned a boatload of children. While corny and clichéd, such scenarios sit well with a sentimental public.

Often people's fictional plots surrendered to fantasy. And who can blame them? The photograph brims with perceived unbridled passion and sexual tension. *V-J Day, 1945, Times Square* invites viewers to participate in the frolic. Many cannot resist the temptation.

Even without such enticement, other less readily observable considerations give people cause to stare at the photo longer. One might argue that Times Square's suspended instance marks the pinnacle of America's narrative. America defeated its demons, Adolph Hitler, Benito Mussolini, and Emperor Hirohito and the Japanese military. A victor nation celebrates gleefully. Prosperity, security, and confidence await the entwined couple. There will be marriages and a baby boom, creating a common experience that continues to characterize America's preferred vision of itself. *V-J Day, 1945, Times Square* marks the starting line of a sprint toward a more prosperous standard of living and an inventive ideal family life. One can assume the sailor and nurse will go on to purchase a split-level home, live in suburbia, drive big cars, watch television shows, and produce children—lots of children. Life will be good. No one foresees the Korean or Vietnam conflicts, the civil rights struggles, Watergate, terrorist attacks, or today's concerns of "America's decline." Nothing distracts us from the bliss. In fact, in that moment, everybody longs to *be* an American. And on this glorious day, at that precious moment, regardless of their birth nation, everyone waves the Red, White, and Blue.

Though most photographs fade with the passing years, the black-and-white photo of a sailor and nurse kissing on V-J Day sharpens and raises its voice. Taken in the planet's most popular meeting place and printed in the magazine known around the world for its captivating photographs, the image reminds us of a time when we felt better as a nation and as individuals than we ever had before and we ever have since. Like a fond memory, no one wants to turn away. And for more than sixty-five years, almost no one did.

THE PLACE WHERE PEOPLE MEET

Just the mention of its name conjures imagery of glaring lights, crowded streets, huge billboards, and outrageous scenes. People from around the world can speak to the location with so much familiarity that one might think the place exists no farther away than their backyard. The area is so well known that no matter how people reference the location, everyone knows of where they speak. *The nation's square, the crossroads of the world*, and *the meeting place* all call attention to the same prized real estate—Times Square. And through the years, whether cheering to celebrate the end of a long world war, bundling up to watch a lighted ball drop from a skyscraper on a frigid night, or peeking at a peep show in the early morning hours, people rush to Times Square to see and give witness.

Despite its historic standing in the nation's psyche, Times Square's fabled past runs just over one century. Fewer than five decades before a sailor kissed a nurse on V-J Day, and a few years prior to the time when Time Square's first multicolored lights glittered, people met at Longacre Square. Outlined more in the shape of a woman's accented figure than a square, Longacre enticed patrons to New York City's 7th Avenue and Broadway intersection. Though in the 1800s visitors typically met at stalls and talked about horses, as the nearby theater district's lights shone closer, the venue and topics of conversation changed. By the late 1800s the area's country feel could only be found farther north. The urbanization took on greater momentum in 1902 when the *New York Times* set up shop at the intersection of 7th Avenue and 42nd Street.

The *New York Times* constructed its new building, the Times Building, on a triangular landmass that looked over the square. The newspaper's executives chose the location wisely. Not only did the *New York Times,* 375-foot-high tower look over the entire square, but in 1904 the world's second tallest building sat directly over the city's newly constructed 42nd Street subway station. That stop proved to be the busiest hub in New York's underground transportation system. From that time forward, the 42nd Street subway exit funneled people from all points of origin and every walk of life into Times Square.

In 1904 the area's new inhabitant petitioned for a name change. They succeeded. Longacre became Times Square. The paper that printed "All the News That's Fit to Print" wasted no time making *their* square the nation's most important civic meeting place. As early as 1904, the Times Tower's powerful searchlight signaled Theodore Roosevelt's election to the presidency. The spectacle drew a fascinated audience. The stream of light from atop the building could be seen for at least thirty miles.[1] That light show, impressive for its time, would prove primitive compared to what was ahead.

While no sole source can be credited for the dazzling light spectacle that came to epitomize the area, Oscar J. Gude, a German-born entrepreneur, might account more than any other individual for the sea of brightly lit advertising signs. Gude saw Times Square's phenomenal advertising potential soon after first surveying the locale.[2] Not only did the area draw increasing numbers of businessmen and visitors, but its low roofs and wide-open spaces created a visual bonanza.[3] In 1904, his first sign for Trimble Whiskey proved an overwhelming success. Propped at 47th Street, right before Broadway and 7th Avenue intersected, its moving light forms amazed Times Square's pedestrians. Other companies soon approached Gude to enlist his services. By 1912 his signs dominated the Times Square nightscape.[4] Advertisements that blinked, imitated movement, and spilled beyond rectangular confines commanded attention. Soon the lit billboards of Times Square competed with the Statue of Liberty and other city attractions for the tourist's eye.[5]

Through 1945 Times Square's fame and popularity grew, undaunted by those who questioned the area's moral standing, or lack thereof. Over the years live theater, vaudeville acts, and movie houses took turns beckoning crowds to the square. Some motion pictures even advertised Times Square to the nation. In 1942, *Yankee Doodle Dandy* featured James Cagney singing "Give My Regards to Broadway." Cagney won an Academy Award for his performance. Thousands followed the Oscar-winning actor's example and made the pilgrimage to pay their respects to the street that ran through the world's most recognized intersection.

Three years after the Times Building dropped its first lighted ball on New Year's Eve, the *New York Times* added another reason to gather in *the* square. In 1910 they provided round-by-round bulletins of the Jim Jeffries–Jack Johnson boxing match. The fight's reporting drew about 30,000 interested followers to the 42nd Street end of Times Square. People liked this immediacy of learning about the news in real time. The news agency took note and built on that notion. In 1919 they constructed an electric scoreboard to report in real time the Cincinnati Reds–Chicago White Sox World Series games. On October 2, 1919, as Belgium's King Albert I and Queen Elizabeth arrived in New York, men and boys in black and grey top hats and caps congregated around the Times Building to watch play-by-play bulletins.[6] In 1928 the instant reporting of news took on greater permanency. In that year the *Times* invested in an electric board that flashed the news in moving type around the building's perimeter. The scroll— variously called a news ticker, ribbon, or zipper—became a fixture around the Times building, where for fifty years people gathered to learn about the world beyond the nation's square.

People continued to gather in Times Square despite developments that could have potentially curbed such behavior. In 1937 Americans spent $900 million on radios. As a result, many thought people would stay home on New Year's Eve rather than trudge out in the cold to witness another dropping of the ball in Times Square. The odds-setters were in error. Like years before and those to follow, people mobbed the nation's crossroads.

While the day's news often drew people to the intersection of Broadway and 7th Avenue, Times Square's greatest attraction had nothing to do with headlines. More than anything else, the area's free and dazzling light show lured visitors. Continuing the tradition of the square's theater entrances on The Great White Way, storefront signs and advertising billboards lit the area with a spectacular colorized glare. Prior to World War II, signs such as the Bond clothing store's large neon lettering stood out as recognizable landmarks. Throughout Times Square, visitors of all ages gaped at the carnival of lights and special effects. The manifestations never got old, and never remained exactly the same. As early as 1906, atop the Knickerbocker Hotel, advertisers erected electric spectacles that drew world attention.[7] From 1916 to 1921, lower energy costs and new technology encouraged Times Square businesses to install bigger and higher-wattage signs.[8] In 1933, visitors to the nation's meeting place came to see Douglas Leigh's enormous, *steaming* cup of A&P coffee. In 1942 Leigh added the Camel man, puffing cigarette smoke rings.

Up until World War II the light show grew larger and brighter. However, in the early 1940s, the war's effect on the home front extended to Times Square. During those years the square's luminosity dimmed. Defense necessitated the darkening. Even miles out at sea, Times Square's glow outlined ships against the skyline. The background light made American Navy ships easier targets for German submarines. After the sinking of several Navy ships, in April 1942 the U.S. government ordered the lights above street level turned off in Times Square for most of the war.[9] Even the *Times* ribbon had to sit still and dark until 1945.

But the dimmed skyline did not deter crowds from gathering in the world's meeting place during the early 1940s. In fact, just the opposite occurred. In a similar fashion to what happened during World War I, people flocked to Times Square during World War II. Throughout the war Times Square was the center of the world's most popular liberty port.[10] New York's vast harbor, the Brooklyn Navy Yard (the nation's largest),[11] and military training posts along the Northeast coast provided an ever-replenishing source of servicemen. And whether they anticipated their fighting days apprehensively or enjoyed their long-delayed and deserved leave, Times Square's free public shows, often attended by celebrities to sell war bonds, created an irresistible attraction. In 1944 approximately 25,000 scream-ing fans stormed the Paramount Theater to see Frank Sinatra.[12] Other excited visitors during that same year came to see mov-ies such as, *Our Hearts Were Young and Gay.* During the war, Times Square gained a reputation as a B-movie paradise.[13] In the warehouse of attractions, no single draw stood out among others. As one visiting soldier's *New York Post* itinerary testified, the nation's square brimmed with a litany of enticements: "I'll go to Times Square and stand there practically all day smelling the frankfurters and breathing in the cold air from all those air-conditioned movie houses. And one of the things I want to do is yoo hoo at every pretty girl who passes by."[14] Rather than declining, Times Square's crowds rose to unprecedented levels during the war years.[15]

While the growth in servicemen traffic created a local eco-nomic boom in New York, arriving sailors and soldiers taxed business facilities. To meet the demand, 200 military service centers of one kind or another sprang up to feed or otherwise meet the needs of the 93,700 servicemen and women who cir-culated through New York every week.[16] In Times Square, sailors dropped into the Pepsi Cola Service Center to shave, shower, or write letters. New York became a home away from home for many servicemen.[17]

During the war, Times Square functioned as the thump-ing heart of the nation's war bond drive. In fact, in 1943 Times Square was temporarily renamed "Bondway" to promote war bond drives.[18] Government-sponsored radio broadcasts from

Times Square encouraged war bond sales and metal scrap drives. In 1944 President Franklin Roosevelt lighted a six-floor-high Statue of Liberty replica that sat on an oversized cash register, located about a hundred feet from the 42nd Street subway entrance. For the seventh war bond drive, a statue depicting the famous flag-raising photo at Iwo Jima was erected in front of the 43rd Street war bond station. That famous scene stood proudly in front of Childs Resturant until after the war ended.

On August 14, 1945, what turned out to be the last day of World War II, Times Square anticipated good news. Business owners, residents, and visitors readied for the biggest celebration in the square's history. New York had lifted the restrictions on lights. The *Times* ribbon, again operational, informed onlookers of the day's news. Activity at the crossroads carried on briskly. Handsome servicemen and pretty girls filled the streets. Shows and spectacles invited every passerby to have a look. As the day progressed, anticipation of the war's end built. Holding back became increasingly difficult. With Japan's imminent surrender still unannounced, New Yorkers and visitors in Times Square wanted to let loose. They waited anxiously for word of victory.

That day, postcards for sale in many of the square's stores depicted the area's past and hinted at its future. Most shone brilliantly and colorfully, but none captured the square's infectious spirit and effervescent soul. They couldn't. Up to that moment, no image taken in Times Square could make the heart race. There was, as of yet, no defining kiss.

3

THE PUBLICATION

Time, Inc., founder Henry Luce had an idea for a new magazine. From his office, a short walk from New York's Times Square, it occurred to him that photos printed on large pages could tell stories as well as, maybe even better than, words. Rather than read, subscribers could watch, witness, and wonder. Of course, by the 1930s other magazines had already upped the number of photographs on their pages, but Luce intended to take the concept to a new level.

He thought some more and conferred with others about his ideas for the new publication. In 1936 he articulated his vision: "To see life; to see the world; to eyewitness great events; to watch the faces of the poor and the gestures of the proud; to see strange things . . . the women that men love and many children; to see and take pleasure in seeing; to see and be amazed; to see and be instructed; thus to see and to be shown is now the will and new expectancy of mankind."[1] Luce's brainchild, *LIFE* magazine, "The Show-Book of the World," freed their photographers to pursue and picture subjects as they found them. Loosely composed directions and a few editors' notes made up the full complement of directions for *LIFE*'s cameramen.[2] Uninhibited, photographers could surprise, even shock, the viewer.[3] Just like life itself, the new magazine strove to be varied, unpredictable, and adventurous.

Of course, in addition to publishing pictures, *LIFE* printed letters. But photos always eclipsed words. During the magazine's weekly layout sessions, *LIFE* editors first spread out and arranged

numerous pictures, and then added words sparingly.[4] *LIFE* introduced the photo essay to Americans. Pictures told the story. Words
clarified the meaning. And usually just a few words sufficed.

In some respects the magazine's images printed bigger than
life, or at least larger than anything appearing on the pages
of other publications. Most other magazines had miniature
images on noticeably smaller pages. Newspapers turned out a
few grainy pictures on pulp newspaper stock. To publish more
photos proved cost prohibitive. Consequently, text continued its
dominance of most publications—but not *LIFE*.

Several factors converged to fertilize *LIFE*'s propagation of
the visual. For one, technological innovations supported the
production of more photos. Roll film replaced photographic
plates, freeing photographers from laborious preparations and
transitions.[5] The new film formats enabled the wide use of
modern, small-format cameras like the Leica, which could take
pictures in rapid sequence. By1936 *LIFE* was able to print more
pictures more economically by developing cheaper forms of
coated stock.[6] With Time, Inc.'s advanced distribution capabilities and ongoing improvements in transportation, more photos
could be dispersed to more subscribers.

But paper, technology, and cost factors don't take pictures.
Photographers do. And *LIFE* hired the world's best. In the early
years the new hires included Margaret Bourke-White, Peter
Stackpole, and Alfred Eisenstaedt. Later, *LIFE* photographer giants
included Rex Hardy, Gordon Parks, Bill Eppridge, and Larry
Burrows, among numerous others. Collectively, their portfolios
chronicle the world's history from the 1930s through the 1970s.

Luce introduced *Time* magazine's new sister on November
23, 1936. Even at conception the siblings acted differently. "LIFE
was more fun."[7] And their father knew it. Pictures in black and
white or in color invited interpretation. Rather than producing posed and stoic portraits, *LIFE* photographers sought individuals where they labored, loved, and lived. Often they did so
without the subject's knowledge. To create a natural feel in their
pictures, *LIFE* photographers got out of the way. They climbed

trees and poles, mixed in with the subject's peers, or became lost in large crowds. Only the pictures mattered—and, of course, people's responses to those images.

Margaret Bourke-White's picture of a dam under construction at Fort Peck, Montana, graced *LIFE*'s first cover. A picture on the inside cover showed an anonymous child's birth, with the caption "*Life* Begins." It would not be the last time *LIFE* printed a picture of an unidentified person.

Considering the magazine sold out of all its 250,000 newsstand copies on the first day,[8] and commanded an overriding presence throughout the midcentury, one might assume *LIFE* cornered the market for photo journals. It did not. Many other publications competed for the public's viewing eye. In Europe, the French *Vu*, the German *Berliner Illustrierte Zietung*, and the British *Weekly Illustrated* captivated the public. In the United States, rivals included *National Geographic*, *Vanity Fair*, *Collier's*, *Liberty*, *Saturday Evening Post*, and *Look*. In this competitive market, not everyone read, or looked, at *LIFE*. In fact, only one out of every four Americans "read" *LIFE* regularly.[9] Newspapers and some magazines had greater circulation and a more diverse readership than *LIFE*. Those who did subscribe to *LIFE* typically stood on the upper rungs of the socioeconomic ladder.[10] The farmer in Montana with dirty fingernails or the fisherman in Rhode Island with sunburned knuckles were less likely to pick up *LIFE* than the dentist who handled sterilized instruments in Chicago or New York.

But number crunching can mislead. Much of *LIFE*'s draw, success, and impact defied direct quantification. A single photograph can influence a viewer far more than a "formula driven" newspaper piece.[11] While more people might have viewed other media sources, those daily papers and periodicals would be hard, pressed to match *LIFE*'s eternal imprint on the events and times they depicted. Further, *LIFE* had a greater "pass-along factor" than other publications.[12] After a customer finished his *LIFE*, he typically didn't throw it away. Instead, a neighbor or a colleague was given a look. One market survey estimated that each copy of

LIFE was seen by seventeen people.[13] By 1956, at its peak, *LIFE*'s pass-along factor numbered seventy-five million or more.[14] Also, though not everyone subscribed to *LIFE*, those who did—lawyers, politicians, and educators—enjoyed considerable influence. Given their professions, they were likely to share what they *saw* with many people. *LIFE* subscribers often opened conversations with, "Did you see that picture in *LIFE*?" Further still, the *keeper factor* enhanced *LIFE*'s standing among other publications. Unlike newspapers, people did not throw out their *LIFE* magazines at the end of every week. Even forty years after the last *LIFE* entered circulation, the photo journal continues to sell on eBay, in yard sales, and in consignment shops. Many continue to collect *LIFE* magazines. All these factors demonstrate *LIFE*'s reach stretched far beyond its subscription rates, which numbered respectably in the millions nationwide.

Those who viewed *LIFE*'s pictures did not always see the pictures the same way. Their vantage point determined their interpretation. Sometimes they spied the photo as if from behind a distant window with no connection to the subject. Such viewings tended to amuse. At other times, up close, the subscriber saw hauntingly familiar images. And at special times, a published still photo conveyed motion and froze the viewer. Though rare, those printed pages caused the spectator to *feel*. And whether he laughed, wept, cursed, or just gazed, he never forgot what he saw. For thirty-six years and through 1,864 consecutive issues, purchasers turned *LIFE*'s pages in search of such images.

As early as the Great Depression, *LIFE* established an "iconic presence and cultural prestige."[15] The "Show-Book of the World" stitched itself into the fabric of the times it photographed. *LIFE* fortified that standing during World War II. During that war the photo journal's willing cooperation with the national government's war efforts, including censorship, bordered on collaboration. Ten days after the Japanese bombed Pearl Harbor, Henry Luce communicated to President Roosevelt, "In the days to come—far beyond strict compliance with whatever rules may be laid down for us by the necessities of war—we can think of no greater happiness than to be of service to any branch of our government and to its armed forces. For the dearest wish of all of us is to tell the story of absolute victory under your leadership."[16] Accordingly, *LIFE* obliged the Office of War Information's prohibition of published pictures of American war dead until 1943. Afterward, they agreed to show dead Americans (but not their faces) to help jump-start the waning war bond drive.[17]

Cooperation with the government proved good for business at *LIFE*. During Word War II the magazine's circulation boomed. One might say, "World War II was made for *LIFE*."[18] At the very least, they enjoyed a fruitful marriage. During the war, *LIFE* became the era's most important picture magazine.[19] Many of the publication's photographs depicted women— mothers, wives, and girlfriends—waiting anxiously for their courageous men to return from war. Interspersed with patriotic photographs, stories, and advertisements, the propaganda heightened the anticipation of the soldiers' and sailors' return to America. As 1945 progressed, many imagined what that reunion might *feel* like.

Of course, in addition to propaganda and patriotism, *LIFE* photographed the most upsetting aspects of war, producing images that affected people deeply. In 1995 Frederick Ivor-Campbell of Warren, Rhode Island, attributed his "lifelong abhorrence of cruelty and violence" to his "early exposure" to *LIFE*'s published photographs of the Bataan Death March fifty years earlier.[20] Another viewer, Gordon Liddy, credited *LIFE*'s full-page photo of three dead American soldiers on the beach at Buna, New Guinea, printed in September 1943, for "hardening the wartime resolve of the American people."[21] *LIFE*'s World War II photos informed and affected people's remembrances of the era.

During the postwar period, which commenced on August 14, 1945, *LIFE*'s reach lengthened further still. The published pictures of the era chronicled the political, sports, and entertainment worlds, and the American family's backyards. According to John Loengard, a former *LIFE* photographer, "By 1960 it seemed that almost everyone had been photographed by *LIFE* at least once. Anyone at the time might know somebody who knew somebody else—whose face had actually appeared in the magazine."[22] And so it was.

Arguably, *LIFE* sometimes went over the top to get *everyone's* picture. In one particularly controversial piece, *LIFE* instructed wives how to undress in front of their husbands. And, yes, of course, pictures told the story. Another, interestingly, less-upsetting feature for *LIFE* readers celebrated the power of the A-bomb and warned of the dangerous new world that lay ahead. Between photo essays on women undressing and bombs dropping, *LIFE* sold Cadillac cars, Camel cigarettes, and Coca-Cola. Like the magazine's stories, the advertisements enticed viewers with pictures.

It seemed *LIFE* appeared everywhere, but not forever. By the time John F. Kennedy became president the media market had changed. Instead of subjects wondering, "Will the picture be in next week?" they were increasingly more interested in knowing, "Will we be on at 5 or 11?"[23] By 1960, television established itself in households across the United States. The magazine market, later to be followed by the newspaper beat, lost subscribers. But *LIFE* went down swinging. Remaining more popular than many of its competitors, *LIFE* never succumbed to TV. When *LIFE* ceased weekly publication in 1972, the magazine bowed to niche publication markets, not the boob tube.[24] But, of course, the passing of the thirty-six-year-old publication giant gave cause for sad reflection. At the news conference announcing the end, Andrew Heiskell, *LIFE*'s chairman of the board, fought tears and offered, "I'm only sad that with such a record of achievement *LIFE* should have such a short life."[25]

During the years that followed, efforts to resurrect *LIFE* paid the former publication the ultimate compliment. In 1978 the photo journal reappeared as a smaller-sized monthly maga-zine, which ran through March 2000. Later, *LIFE* reappeared as a newspaper insert. Over the years, Time Life published special-edition magazines and books. Many of those publi-cations reprinted older photos from *LIFE* magazine. Some of those photographs reappeared often. One photo of a sailor kissing a nurse at the end of World War II graced the pages of those publications more than any other. Most recently, starting in March 2009, *LIFE* published a large interactive website, hosted and promoted by Google. Once again, the publication remains all about the pictures.

But *LIFE* as Americans once knew it no longer exists. Even though no one wanted the old publication to go, even *LIFE* can't be raised from the dead. So remembering must do. Thanks to old copies stored in people's attics, and pictures that are republished to this day, we can still see what Henry Luce envisioned almost a century ago. And whether the image captures children watching a puppet show, a marching band leader kicking up his leg with an impromptu parade behind him, or a sailor kissing a "nurse" on the day World War II ended, because of *LIFE* we can always visit a time and place preserved forever by a sharp-eyed photographer.

PART 2

THE TRUE STORY OF THE KISS

Some argue that the couple in LIFE's most popular photo should remain anonymous. They contend that anonymity adds to the photograph's appeal. But such proponents do not know the story of the duck, the saved, the model, and the father of photojournalism.

THE DUCK FROM
PORTUGUEE ISLAND

Arsenio and Maria Mendonsa lived nine months per year on Portuguee Island, a rocky landmass off Newport, Rhode Island's scenic Ten Mile Drive. The time the Mendonsas spent on their stone-laden and treeless lot correlated directly with the fishing season, which lasted from early spring to late fall. The quarter-acre island got its name from the men and women who worked, lived, or fished off the isle. Every person had either emigrated from Portugal or was born to parents from Portugal's Madeira Island. Portuguee Island's one substantial structure served as the family's home, as well as the sleeping quarters for six Portuguese fishermen. Four-foot cement blocks raised the building above the sand and rocks, allowing water to flow underneath the house during particularly high tides.

Despite Portuguee Island's spartan accommodations, the Mendonsas lived healthy and fertile lives. On February 19, 1923, Maria Mendonsa gave birth to Arsenio's fourth child, George. By her own admission, Maria raised her son as a duck. Children's play on Portuguee Island consisted of splashing around inlets, skipping rocks between cresting waves, and swimming and fishing in the harbor. The surrounding water aptly substituted for a playground.

By the time George turned twelve, Arsenio had turned Portuguee Island's playground into a training camp for a life at sea. He taught his sons how to find the best fishing spots, fix ripped fishing nets, and navigate the local waters. George proved a quick study. He learned to navigate by dead reckoning (making use of a watch and familiar locations), and by reading a compass. While the plotting did not rival the sophistication of the U.S. Navy's celestial navigation, by age eighteen George could find his way around Rhode Island's Narragansett Bay with great confidence.

4-1. Arsenio Mendonsa's fishing crew makes its way past Portuguee Island (in background with buildings) in approximately 1930. George, seven years old, is navigating the last boat. (*Permission granted by George Mendonsa*)

Rhode Island's East Bay waters also provided the Mendonsas with steady employment and financial security, even during the Great Depression. But there were exceptions. On September 21, 1938, the same waters that provided a bounty of scup, bass, and tuna, laid out a welcome mat for the Long Island Express, a mon-ster hurricane of almost biblical proportions. Mimicking a Nazi blitzkrieg that would wreak havoc in Europe a year later, the Hurricane of '38 slammed the southern New England coast with wind gusts exceeding 186 miles per hour.[1] Portuguee Island's raised structures never stood a chance. By the time the hurricane rushed through, the only thing left on Portuguee Island were rocks, and even they had been moved about from

long-established resting places. Though the Mendonsas'
fishing village lay in ruin, George's family fared better than
others. They survived. More than six hundred others did not.[2]

With the passing of the worst storm in Rhode Island's history, Newport and other surrounding seaside communities
buzzed with word of a war that President Roosevelt promised
would not involve America's sons. At first the Mendonsas did
not heed the talk about faraway lands. Instead, they concerned
themselves with the day's catch from nearby waters. But as the
decade progressed, developments in Europe and the Pacific
drew their attention. In the late 1930s German submarines
patrolling the Rhode Island coast brought the war's realities
to their doorstep. The Japanese bombing of Pearl Harbor on
December 7, 1941, broke down that door as the nation plunged
into a war that would change America forever.

George first heard of the Pearl Harbor attack when
leav-ing the Capital Restaurant in Newport's Lawson Square.
Like most Americans he promised to get even with "the
bastards." But vengeance did not translate into immediate
military service. His father still needed his navigator, and the
U.S. government granted draft deferments to fishermen and
other food produc-ers. But within a year the call to serve
became too persistent to ignore. In November 1942 George
enlisted in the U.S. Navy and attended boot camp in Newport,
Rhode Island, approximately a mile from his home.

At boot camp, Navy officials were impressed with
George's navigation experience and expertise. They asked
him to give up his boatswain's mate rank and attend
quartermaster school. George learned that Navy
quartermasters stand watch on the ship's bridge as assistants
to the officers of the deck control-ling the ship, and that,
further, they performed other important duties such as
conducting weather observations and keeping logs and
records. Although George was initially hesitant, as he did not
fully understand all of the quartermaster's duties, he agreed
to the training upon learning the offer came with better pay.
Being raised as a duck had its benefits.

In late summer 1943, George reported to Treasure Island in San Francisco with thousands of other enlistees awaiting assignment. He was not prepared for what he witnessed in the city by the bay. Sailors in uniform outnumbered civilians. Many of those sailors were missing one leg or one arm and made their way around on crutches or in wheelchairs. George thought, *Holy Christ . . . what the Hell is going on in the Pacific?* The Navy brochures he had thumbed through before enlisting emphasized clean linens and delicious food, not the fallout of battles at sea. George never forgot San Francisco's crash course on war's reality.

The Navy assigned George to the USS *The Sullivans* (DD-537), a Fletcher-class destroyer honoring the five Sullivan brothers

4-2. George Mendonsa, 1945. (*Permission granted by George Mendonsa*)

killed at the Battle of Guadalcanal. George was one of only three quartermasters (all third-class rate) on the destroyer. By the time he returned from the Pacific in July 1945, George would have two more chevrons sewn on his uniform, indicating he had been advanced to petty officer first class.

The Sullivans left San Francisco Bay on December 23, 1943. Dispatched to be part of Task Group 38.2 for most of the Pacific campaign, *The Sullivans'* mission was to bombard islands the Japanese had captured to "soften up" the Japanese defenders before Marine Corps landing forces assaulted the islands. Once the Marines' land invasion commenced, *The Sullivans'* mission changed to attacking Japanese airstrips on nearby islands so the Japanese couldn't launch aircraft from these airfields to attack the Marine Corps' landing forces. After the Marines established control of the objective location, *The Sullivans* waited for orders to bombard the next invasion site.

Similar to many sailors' experiences during war, George's time in the Pacific proved a medley of extremes. Monotonous routine contrasted starkly with the intensity of life-and-death struggles. The former proved more familiar. The latter proved most memorable. The Japanese Imperial Navy made sure of that. So did the Pacific Ocean.

George had learned at a young age to listen to the Atlantic Ocean and watch the sky. Those sounds and sights imparted warnings that sometimes required quick action. In 1938 when the Long Island Express rushed toward Narragansett Bay, sudden seas and fast-forming clouds indicated trouble.[3] George and his father pulled in nets, motored boats to safer harbors, and ordered everyone to evacuate Portuguee Island for safer ground. Those actions saved the lives of his family and fishing crew.

During World War II George tried to learn the Pacific Ocean's language. And while he started to understand her ways, in the end the effort was for naught. The Navy empowered others to assess developments and make determinations. George had to follow their commands.

Adm. William Frederick "Bull" Halsey Jr., the Task Group 38.2 commander, gave orders in the Pacific. But the Pacific still wielded tremendous power, though deceivingly so. The world's largest ocean never agreed to host a manmade conflict that commenced on dry soil. Her cooperation was not to be taken for granted. Admiral Halsey didn't respect that, at least not enough.[4] The slight proved tragic.

In December 1944 a typhoon bullied the U.S. Navy east of Luzon. But the terrible storm had not always been a bully. Typhoon Cobra reportedly started on the morning of December 11, 1944, on the edge of a Caroline island's coastline. At that location, three Japanese soldiers fishing in a primitive canoe witnessed the formation of an expanding whirlpool.[5] While it is unverifiable whether the three fishermen observed the typhoon's creation, nearby at that approximate time Typhoon Cobra made its debut, causing little more than a ripple in the water. As she embarked on a northwestward path, Admiral Halsey didn't give the Long Island Express' distant cousin a cursory look. Though she splashed loudly, owing to a series of undelivered or unread messages, and perhaps Admiral Halsey's misinterpretation or outright denial of the obvious, Typhoon Cobra pulled off a sneak attack on the U.S. Navy.[6]

On December 17, 1944, George and *The Sullivans*' crew took notice of worsening conditions. As the barometer started to fall, cresting waves rose. *The Sullivans* "rolled terrifyingly."[7] Spiraling winds hurled pelletized raindrops horizontally, temporarily blinding sailors standing watch outside the skin of the destroyer. Ordered precautions on some nearby ships included having seamen topside roped to a shipmate. These precautions extended to Task Group 38.2's aircraft, where crews had to re-lash planes with triple-steel cables.[8]

As conditions worsened, Admiral Halsey ordered ships to refuel. He issued the orders from USS *New Jersey*, a massive battleship that could absorb the impact of pounding seas much better than destroyers like *The Sullivans*. After experiencing seventy-foot seas smashing against all sides of his battleship, Halsey recorded: "What it was like on a destroyer one-twentieth *New Jersey*'s size I can only imagine."⁹

George Mendonsa did not have to exercise his imagination, but he did have to carry out Halsey's commands. That proved problematic. Even during calm seas the responsibility of maneuvering a vessel during refueling fell to the most experienced helmsman.¹⁰ Refueling alongside the massive tanker assigned to Task Group 38.2 in the middle of a typhoon heightened the call for experience and expertise. As *The Sullivans'* senior quartermaster, George had both. Accordingly, Capt. Ralph Jacob Baum assigned George to steer the destroyer during battle operations and refueling. Steering *The Sullivans* during Typhoon Cobra proved more challenging for George than any other assignment during the war.

Typhoon Cobra engulfed destroyers with waves larger than Lt. Gerald R. Ford, future president of the United States, on the USS *Monterey* (CVL-26) had ever seen.¹¹ Those waves played *The Sullivans* like a yo-yo. Thirty-five-foot drops displaced large volumes of water that compromised *The Sullivans'* steering capabilities. Refueling became almost impossible. Quartermaster Mendonsa could see that, even before steering *The Sullivans* alongside the tanker. Admiral Halsey saw only the need to refuel his force. And his view of the operation mattered far more than George's or any other subordinate who had to carry out orders amidst Typhoon Cobra's soaking rains, punishing winds, and hurling waves.

What also mattered was George's ability to steer his destroyer alongside the tanker without smashing against its side. To maintain a distance of approximately forty feet between the fueling tanker and his destroyer, George steered *The Sullivans'* rudder fifteen degrees inward. In effect this was like having no rudder angle at all. While the destroyer fought against the forces of nature, Captain Baum continually yelled out conflicting commands to his quartermaster, ordering: "Take her in! Take her out! Out! Out! . . . Take her in!" At some point Captain Baum's orders became more consistent. "Take her out! Take her out! Take her out!"

While George knew that Baum wanted to avoid getting too close to the tanker, the quartermaster also understood that the sea's driving strength would push *The Sullivans* too far from the tanker. The fueling line could not hold against such great force. As soon as Baum realized this, too, he yelled, "Bring her in! Bring her in!" Despite George's attempts to change *The Sullivans'* direction, this time the ship did not answer. Running at twelve knots in billowing seas, the rudder commanded limited control of the ship. While the tanker rose and fell in perfect rhythm with *The Sullivans*, the movement in and out from the tanker proved unmanageable. Distressed over the worsening predicament, Captain Baum yelled loudly at George, "Full Rudder!" "Full Rudder!" George shouted back. "I got full rudder, Captain! Full Rudder!" Finally, the two oil hoses snapped. Shortly afterward, with winds well over one hundred knots, Halsey cancelled refueling efforts for the day.[12] *The Sullivans* was filled to only half capacity. Other ships were worse off. They had to brave Typhoon Cobra with a fighting spirit, but little more than fumes for fuel.

As ships buckled down to weather the storm's forces, some destroyers struggled more than other ships. USS *Dewey* rolled 84 degrees, lost her smokestack, flooded her boiler, and lay dead in the water. Somehow, against seemingly insurmountable odds, she righted herself and survived the typhoon's wrath. Three other destroyers, *Hull*, *Monaghan*, and *Spence* did not. Before Typhoon Cobra ran into a cold front on December 19 and lost its tropical airflow, it claimed the lives of 790 men.[13] In its wake, *The Sullivans* rounded up survivors and mourned the senseless loss of life—but they could not mourn for long. Soon, an even more lethal foe drew their attention to the sky.

As George learned in a string of hotly contested battles at Truk, the Marshall Islands, and Leyte Gulf, the Japanese military yielded nothing to the Americans' superior firepower. The enemy reinforced that notion with a ninth-inning scheme that shocked Americans' sense of "fair" play.[14] Though by late 1944

Japan's military had lost most of its skilled pilots and managed a vastly depleted military arsenal, their high command devised a secret and shocking strategy to defend their homeland: the Kamikaze Special Attack Corps. The plan called for young Japanese pilots to dive-bomb American aircraft carriers, hurling themselves and their doomed aircraft into flight decks and island structures. While the Kamikaze Special Attack Corps persisted for a relatively short portion of the war, and in only one theater of a worldwide conflict, it is difficult to overstate the impact of this Japanese tactic. The samurai of old Japan re-emerged in October 1944. By July 1945 the kamikazes made 2,550 attacks, claiming 12,000 American lives, 36,000 wounded sailors, and 74 sunk or damaged ships.[15] But the kamikazes' success cannot be explained by numbers alone. The sound and sight of plummeting planes produced terror at sea and, by extension, throughout the American homeland.

On May 11, 1945, kamikaze aircraft took aim at the USS *Bunker Hill*, an Essex-class aircraft carrier, while it operated off Okinawa. Sailors on surrounding destroyers, including *The Sullivans*, demonstrated exceptional marksmanship, hitting many suicide dive-bombers and causing them to drop into the Pacific Ocean.[16] But some did not. Two Japanese Zeros found their target, igniting a firestorm and an eruption of thick black smoke. A total of 393 *Bunker Hill* sailors perished, either being consumed by the flames, succumbing to smoke inhalation, or drowning.[17]

The kamikazes had targeted the perfect ship for their destructive purposes. USS *Bunker Hill*'s deck spanned 128,620 square feet.[18] Even Japan's young, inexperienced pilots flying poorly maintained Zeros couldn't miss the mark. Tragically, *Bunker Hill* might as well have been a powder keg. After planes returned from their sunrise bombing raids, the aircraft's capable deck crew refueled and rearmed planes with .30- and .50-caliber shells, bombs, air-to-air rockets, and napalm.[19] A spark could have ignited a bonfire—the kamikazes flew in with a blowtorch.

4-3. *The Sullivans* approaches the burning *Bunker Hill* after two kamikazes crash-landed into the carrier in May 1945. (*National Archives photo #80-G-274264*)

Shortly after the kamikazes' attacks, *The Sullivans*, with George Mendonsa at the helm, approached *Bunker Hill*'s port side. The wounded carrier had maneuvered into a high-speed turn. As she heeled to her side, blazing oil ran off the flight deck, creating a curtain of flames that descended toward the ocean. Some who escaped did so via uncoiled ratlines that hung from the ship like rosary beads. A number of fleeing sailors couldn't maintain a grip on the slick lines. The force of their fall scraped others off the line, too. Together they plunged into blackening waters.

Most *Bunker Hill* sailors did not know how to swim.[20] All were terrified. As the sailors fell into the ocean, *Bunker Hill* continued to move at approximately ten knots. The overboard sailors' survival fell to the graces of a higher power, and the approaching *The Sullivans* (along with other U.S. Navy ships). Arriving close behind the smoking carrier, *The Sullivans'* crew pulled men from the ocean, some soon after they dropped into the Pacific. At several points, the responsibilities almost overwhelmed

Quartermaster Mendonsa. Blazing sun, scorching flames, and billowing black smoke generated nervous energy and a racing heart, pouring sweat, and dizzying fatigue. George wanted to locate and rescue every floating *Bunker Hill* survivor—thankfully many other Navy ships took part in the rescue mission.

George remembered: "We did everything we could to find those poor bastards." And the poor bastards knew it. Rich Lillie, a torpedoman second class on *Bunker Hill*, jumped from the carrier at 11:00 AM with several other sailors. As soon as they entered the water, *Wilkes-Barre*, a light cruiser that pulled along *Bunker Hill*'s starboard side, almost ran over them.[21] In addition to covering *Bunker Hill* from another anticipated kamikaze attack, *Wilkes-Barre* took on many *Bunker Hill* survivors via mail sacks that the crews attached to guy wires between the two ships.[22] Lillie did not make it into one of those blood-soaked bags. Shortly after diving into the Pacific, Lillie and company floated well behind *Bunker Hill*'s and *Wilkes-Barre*'s course lines. After a half-hour they could no longer identify the *Wilkes-Barre*, or any other ship, on the expansive horizon. As they drifted, survivors of the smoldering aircraft carrier worried that rescue might never arrive.

After two hours drifting aimlessly, Lillie saw a ship approaching on the horizon. Shortly after determining it was a destroyer, he could discern the number 537 on the ship's port side. *The Sullivans* had come back to save their comrades. While many of *The Sullivans*' earlier rescues had been undertaken via lowered whale boats, this time the destroyer's crew threw out lines to the fatigued and floating sailors. Once the sailors secured themselves to the feeder line's belts, *The Sullivans*' crew pulled them in and up to safety. Lillie later offered: "I don't care what anybody says. We wasn't the heroes. George was the hero. I don't know how he got to us, but he did. Probably understood drift. He saved my life."[23]

The Sullivans also saved 166 other *Bunker Hill* sailors.[24] Many of those rescued sailors came on board seriously injured or traumatized. While George and the other *The Sullivans*' sailors did what they could to help their mates, many *Bunker Hill* survivors were transferred to hospital ships. On one of those ships, USS *Bountiful,* nurses scrambled to care for wounded sailors. George's vantage point on *The Sullivans*' bridge provided a clear view of what was occurring. He never forgot what he saw.

The sight of U.S. Navy nurses caring for the badly burned and severely injured sailors contrasted sharply with almost everything George had witnessed earlier that day, and what he had observed throughout most of the war. Nurses tended to sailors with twisted limbs, fractured bones, bleeding wounds, and horrible burns.[25] Some sailors suffered from smoke inhalation. Others were traumatized from seeing too much suffering and human destruction. And still others must have felt guilty about their random survival. Whatever their medical needs, the nurses rushed from patient to patient to administer whatever treatment they could. With medical supplies wanting, a compassionate facial expression or a held hand sometimes provided ample service, at least for the time being. As George surveyed activity on *Bountiful,* he paused and absorbed the softer side of life that endures even during war's darkest moments. After more than two years at sea away from the gentler sex, this contrast between war and nurture in such a sort time span seemed surreal. But the distinction was real, rare, and soon, over.

The war raged on, and by late spring 1945 the Japanese Navy had been decimated as a fighting force and no longer presented a serious threat to U.S. and Allied naval forces. An invasion of Japan loomed, but not immediately. Even though much of the world celebrated Victory in Europe (V-E Day) on May 8, 1945, the transfer of U.S. soldiers, sailors, airmen, and Marines from the European theater to the Pacific would take months. Because the Japanese presented virtually no offensive threat, and many U.S. Navy ships had been at sea for more than two years without any substantial time in port, in mid-1945 many U.S. Navy ships received orders to return to the States for repairs of one sort or another. *The Sullivans* was one of those ships. On June 20, 1945, *The Sullivans*' sailors left the Philippines bound for California to begin a thirty-six-day leave.

On their way to San Francisco *The Sullivans* once again refueled alongside USS *Essex*, and this time for the last time of the war. During earlier refueling operations, *Essex*'s band played music for sailors on the smaller ships they refueled (destroyers like *The Sullivans* did not have bands). At the end of such sessions, the band performed "California Here I Come." Selected as a good-natured joke, the band knew full well the departing ship did not push off toward the Bear Flag state. *The Sullivans'* sailors added to the ritual by offering their refueling host a middle finger salute. *Essex* sailors returned the gesture in kind. Both crews enjoyed the routine.

But on this last refueling mission, *Essex*'s band altered the ritual. Perhaps realizing that on this occasion many sailors' extended shore leaves would take them all the way across the United States, *Essex*'s band played "Give My Regards to Broadway." While George's destination was well northeast of Broadway, he had long since learned that forces beyond his control could alter chartered courses. As a smile came across his face, George nodded in acknowledgment of the *Essex* crew's good wishes. If the opportunity should present itself, he promised to extend their best wishes to the most famous street in the nation's largest city.

5

THE SAVED

Buildings stood taller than mountains. The sky never darkened. The inhabitants never slept. There, possibilities knew no limit. Greta Zimmer wondered if what she had heard about New York City was true. As a child, Greta never thought she would visit such a magnificent place.

Greta was born far from Times Square's bright lights. During her idyllic childhood, Austria's blue lakes, white-capped peaks, and green valleys surrounded her. Classical symphonies, Renaissance paintings, and live theater were featured in city centers. Even at a young age, she cherished her country's stunning beauty and creative voice.

Greta's mother and father treasured Austria, too. In their beloved country they raised their three daughters with a deep understanding of the Jewish faith and a rich appreciation for the arts. Greta learned to play violin and piano at a young age. She performed in concerts, or at least that is how she saw them during an innocent time. At the end of each performance, her mother, father, aunts, and uncles stood to applaud Greta. They adored their musician.

During the early 1930s money was hard to come by in Austria. But the Zimmers could have been worse off. Accustomed to difficult times, Jews in Austria supported one another. They communicated, networked, and prayed. Neighboring non-Jewish communities took notice. What they saw—Jews struggling to rise above economic hardship—bothered them. They wondered at what expense to themselves did their Semite neighbors make do.[1]

People wondered in Germany, also, and rushed to judgment. Nazi leader Adolph Hitler pushed forward a solution to
"the Jewish problem." The plan did not bode well for Jews. The
Nazis set out to brutalize and humiliate a proud and industrious
people. Their scheme spread quickly to nearby nations.

In March 1938 Hitler invaded Austria, his birthplace. The
Austrians did not resist.[2] The Anschluss, a union of Austria
and Germany, pleased Hitler. Many Austrians welcomed the
arrangement. Most Austrian Jews did not.

Hitler wasted no time demanding an immediate and bru-
tal crackdown on Austrian Jews. As *LIFE* magazine reported,
regarding the Nazis' actions in Austria, "Jews were beaten, spat
on, ejected from theaters, stores, all in accordance with the Nazi
explanation that the Jews had ruined the Germans."[3] No doubt
the persecution of Jews bothered many outside the Jewish community. However, fear or disbelief stopped open opposition to
the Nazi regime. The treatment of Jews worsened.

In Greta's homeland, anti-Semites forced well-dressed Jews
to perform menial labor in public forums. Her people were
made to wash streets, scour sidewalks, and scrub buildings,
sometimes with tiny brushes they had to dip in burning acid
and water.[4] These locations and structures were already clean.
The Nazi orders had another, sinister, purpose. Locals gathered
to heckle, taunt, and laugh at the humiliated Jews. Even Jewish
women and their children were forced to perform this menial
labor. In at least one instance, Nazis ordered Jewish women in
fur coats to scrub Vienna's streets while German soldiers uri-
nated on their heads.[5] As the Nazis forced the Jews to perform
these acts, Austrian civilians gleefully smiled in the background,
heightening the Jews' degradation.[6]

By 1938, Austrian Jews sought shelter from the looming slaughter. For most, their efforts proved futile. The Nazis
hunted them down. Almost everyone who could have helped
the Jews either looked away or froze. Horrible stories of mis-
treatment drew the international community's attention, but
not their assistance. The community of nations, including the

United States, refused to ease immigration quotas. Many Jews took flight anyhow. By 1939, 20,000 Austrian Jews had fled their homeland.[7] The Zimmers stayed in Austria.

As conditions worsened and opportunities to flee began to evaporate, Greta's family worried more. Why worry did not result in the immediate relocation of the Zimmer daughters perplexes the logical thinker. But logic did not govern the Zimmers' thought process. Paralyzing fright did. Other factors may have delayed the Zimmer girls' departure. Up until 1939, the Nazis fanatical forces had not yet inflicted as much cruelty toward the Zimmers as they had on other less-fortunate Jews. Not all of Austria's Jews washed Vienna's streets. Also, the Zimmers underestimated the degree to which Hitler would go to solve the Jewish problem. Even today, despite clear photographic evidence, the extent to which the Nazis carried out the final solution remains unfathomable. Whatever reasoning impacted their decision most, the Zimmer matriarch and patriarch hoped for the best and opted to keep the family together and in familiar territory.

In 1939 the Zimmers' thinking changed. As atrocities mounted, opportunities to leave Austria dwindled. Soon, those opportunities would vanish. Greta's parents knew they had to act before it was too late. They recognized that conditions for Jews in Austria had deteriorated to appalling levels, and perhaps they had yet to experience the worst. The Zimmers made the fateful decision that security for their girls was paramount. Though they would be separated from their daughters, their girls would be safe and that was what mattered most to them. One daughter found haven in British Palestine. The Zimmers secured passage to New York for their other two daughters, Jo and Greta.

At fifteen years old, Greta understood why she and her sister needed to make their way to a foreign nation still struggling through the Great Depression. Everything she loved in Austria had either been destroyed, or soon would be. Fanatical forces greater than her family's capability to fend them off made grim forecasts painfully predictable. Her mother and father had no choice but to break up the family. Greta comforted herself that the parting would be short. Certainly, she trusted the separation would be temporary.

Greta took little more than fond memories on her journey to the United States. She left much behind in her beloved Austria. She longed for her youthful days spent singing and playing for an appreciative audience. Most painfully, she dreaded leaving her parents. Tragically, 1939 proved to be the last year Greta's relatives heard her perform. Shortly after Greta and her sisters left their homeland, Nazis rounded up her parents and aunts and uncles like cattle bound for the slaughterhouse. After the war, Greta learned that the Nazis had transported her mother and father to the Auschwitz concentration camp in Poland. Though she never investigated the particulars of her parents' fate, Greta knew they would remain beyond her embrace forever. She never returned to Austria.

In 1939 Greta's New York relatives welcomed their cherished nieces. An expansive ocean, a powerful country, and a nation's largest city protected them from Adolph Hitler's reach. But the Atlantic did not insulate Greta entirely from Europe's miseries. The war that had engulfed her homeland soon drew in the United States. Once again she endured good-byes, as friends turned soldiers and sailors left to do battle with the Germans and Japanese.

During the ensuing years, Greta thought often of those New York friends who had left to fight in Europe or in the island-hopping campaigns in the Pacific theater. During their absence, she and her sister pinned troop locations on a large world map that hung in their bedroom. The accuracy of the pin placement was completely dependent on these friends' letters, but the exercise provided them with some comfort. A soldier's or sailor's written communication meant that they had survived the war—at least up to the date of the postmark on the envelope. Those letters heartened Greta, who anxiously awaited her friends' return to what was now her home, too.[8]

As the war raged on, Greta and Jo shared memories, told secrets, and competed with one another. Rivalries arose over matters of all sorts. Even their respective heights generated contests. Almost every morning the sisters measured one another down to the fraction of an inch. At sixteen, Greta reached her adult height—five feet, four, and, three-quarters inches. While she had not attained the standing of a basketball center, with a little help from heels she could garner attention in a crowd. A smile that made her eyes twinkle, as well as a slim and attractive figure, enhanced her good looks. No doubt World War II servicemen who flocked to New York took notice.

As the war progressed, Greta volunteered as an air-raid warden in her aunt's neighborhood. During blackouts Greta walked along nearby streets looking for the slightest sliver of light. When stillness and a moonless night accompanied the blackness, an eerie serenity settled in. She knew this tranquility amidst a terrible war could not last for long. The two conditions were incompatible. One had to prevail. On those dark nights when Greta looked for light behind black-painted windows, thoughts of distant battles triumphed over peace. She longed for the day when the outcome would be different and those who had gone to fight could return home.

During the war's final years, Greta graduated from the Central Needle Trade School in New York, a predecessor of the Fashion Institute of Technology. Shortly afterward, a friend who worked at a New York City dentist's office informed Greta about a job opening for a dental assistant. Even though this vocation would sidetrack Greta temporarily from her passions, including the theater and painting, she thought this line of work would at least help pay the bills and might even prove interesting in the short run. After Greta followed her friend's lead, a dental practice in Manhattan hired her to clean teeth and prepare patients for fillings and tooth extractions. The office was located a short walk from Times Square.

At about the same time she started working as a dental assistant at the office of J. L. Berke, a woman who made it her business to look after young working girls rented Greta a room in Manhattan. The move brought her closer to her work and the heart of the city. She shared the apartment's living space with several other girls. Greta had her own bedroom and a mother figure to look after her. She appreciated both.

Within weeks of moving to her new residence, Greta knew her way around the city almost as well as a native New Yorker. She learned to navigate complicated subway connections, rush through crowded streets, and find some refuge among skyscrapers. One such place, close to Times Square, served the best lemon meringue pie in the city. There, with a cup of boiling black tea in hand, she escaped from the war, if only for a few moments.

But the fantasy of forgetting about the war always expired quickly. Signs and symbols throughout the U.S. home front ensured that thoughts of war were ever present. Gold star windows, news about atrocities in Europe, and pictures of kamikaze attacks in the Pacific reminded everyone that war raged on. Only victory could end these constant reminders. Greta yearned for that day.

With the Allies' triumph in Europe on May 8, 1945, Greta waited expectantly, and not at all patiently, for news of the Pacific theater's victorious conclusion. The next three months continued with reports of harrowing battle scenes, dashing hopes for a quick Allied triumph. Though news agencies promised the war would end victoriously for the United States and its allies, Greta worried more than she hoped. Almost every news bulletin reinforced her anxiety. News reports on August 6 heightened her angst to new levels. The atomic bomb's detonation over a Japanese city ushered in a new and uncertain era. Restless nights followed. Greta's bouts of broken sleep continued despite a *New York Times* article that assured readers the atomic bomb caused limited human destruction.[9] Greta could still trust, but she was not naive. The sight of mushroom clouds over Hiroshima and Nagasaki told her a new and dangerous time had descended upon the world. She knew, too, that dropping a bomb that was capable of wiping out a major city meant that thousands of civilians must have been killed. There had already been too many American, Austrian, and Asian deaths.

Sometimes the sense of loss overtook Greta. To cope, at night she prayed for peace. Weekday mornings she hurriedly prepped for work. Her morning routine included a quick shower, a short make-up session, and a light breakfast that she ate rushing out the door: just over a half-hour. Afterward, a subway fare and short walk brought her to the dentists' office at 305 Lexington Avenue, near 38th Street. There, Greta changed into her uniform, which consisted of a white dress, white shoes, and white stockings. Rarely did she go out in public wearing her dental assistant uniform.

When Greta arrived at the dentists' office, she passed through a waiting room where numerous publications covered tables. Throughout the day, patients thumbed through the strewn newspapers and magazines. The practice killed time and often distracted them from the purpose of their visit. By early August 1945, many headlines practically predicted the day and time of the Japanese surrender. Afraid of disappointment, Greta tried to ignore these promising articles and darted into the office to prepare for the day's work.

As the warm days of August 1945 wore on, Greta tried to focus more on her responsibilities at Dr. J. L. Berke's dentist office than on a prolonged war over which she had no control. She arrived at work by nine o'clock on most mornings, took lunch after both dentists did, and left for home around five o'clock But even with the consuming duties of each day, like most Americans, the Austrian dental assistant tried to picture that moment when the war would become part of a painful past. She thought the celebration would outdo any that New York had ever experienced. The unleashing of pent-up emotions might even overshadow the revelry of V-E Day months earlier. Her wish encouraged an unrealistic expectation, one whose fantasy paled compared to what was ahead.

6

THE MODEL

The Sullivans arrived in San Francisco Bay on July 9, 1945. Shortly after docking, George received orders that could have been no better received had he written them himself. "Mendonsa! Get your blues on! You're getting a flight to New York."

Over the past year and a half George had worn his working uniform while carrying out his duties on board ship. That ensemble consisted of dungaree pants and a light blue shirt. During the interim, his formal blues had remained cooped up in his locker. When George went to put on the dress uniform, the outfit appeared tattered to him. In addition, the government-issued uniform hung loosely on George's body. Though the sloppy appearance bothered George, he laughed when first putting on the úniform. He thought, "After two years on this tin can, we must both be a sight for sore eyes." For the short term, George figured he and his uniform made a perfect match.

George took a bus to the San Francisco Municipal Airport to catch a plane heading northeast. During the bus ride he sat beside a woman for the first time since *The Sullivans* set out on its deployment to the Pacific in December 1943. Ironically, being confined in a tin can while a fanatical enemy was hell-bent to ensure his destruction caused George'less apprehension than the bus ride with a strange woman by his side. Still, despite the momentary awkwardness, the homesick sailor welcomed a female's sweet scent and soft voice. "We must have talked about the weather," he reminisced years later.

When George returned to Newport, he found that circumstances had changed from two years prior. For one, while George had fought for his country, a Newport girlfriend he left behind in 1943 found time to talk about more than the weather with male civilians. While the relationship with his boyhood sweetheart had not been very serious, news of her activities over the past two years disappointed the returning sailor. She had never mentioned the other men in her letters to George. The discovery of his old girlfriend's activities bothered him for the early part of his military leave.

In addition to his old girlfriend's new status, his father, the family's strong-willed disciplinarian, had aged beyond two years. Working without the help of his sons had taken a toll on the fishing boat captain. His back ached, his hands cramped, and he moved slower. But the father's compromised state did yield some positive results. The old workhorse found time to relax with his son. He and George fished the familiar spots and talked about the past. Narragansett Bay's lapping waters proved the perfect venue for the father and son reunion.

George's father was not the only family member who changed during the war. George's younger sister, Hilda, had married a Navy chief boatswain's mate from Long Island. With George on leave in July 1945, Hilda visited with the family. The Petrys, Hilda's in-laws, joined her. "They came to get a good feed," George remembered. And no doubt the Portuguese food and his mother's lack of portion control contributed to the draw. The menu included linguica, chourico, blade meat, Portuguese rolls, sweet bread, and kale soup. While not supportive of a healthy cardiovascular system, the pleasures of the palate outweighed such concerns.

When they made this journey for their "feed," as George described it, the Petrys brought their niece Rita with them. Rita had planned to visit her grandmother in Merrick, Long Island, but at her aunt's urging, and her grandmother's good wishes, she decided to make the jaunt with her uncle and aunt to Newport, Rhode Island.

Rita, reserved and attractive, grew up among a close-knit family, in Forest Hills, New York, a suburban area on the western part of Long Island. Days spent playing hopscotch with girls from down the street and being home a half-hour after the street lights came on made up the tapestry of her childhood. However, similar to many girls and boys of her generation, the whirlwind that emanated from Japanese propeller planes suctioned a portion of that childhood innocence from her grasp.

In 1941 Rita attended the Academy of St. Joseph, a Catholic boarding high school. At 5:00 PM on December 7 of that year, a nun announced over the loudspeaker that the Japanese had attacked the United States. However, even with this intrusion from the outside world, Rita and the other girls did not understand the full ramifications of what had happened. And owing to fortunate circumstances, she remained protected from some the war's most painful consequences. Rita's brother, three years younger than she, could not enlist until near the war's end. He never saw combat. Her father was too old for the draft. Rita's connection to the fighting overseas remained relatively limited for most of the war.

Her only direct link to the war turned out to be a Portuguese American sailor from Newport, Rhode Island. Rita met him at the Mendonsa-Petry cookout in July 1945. He arrived late but entered the family gathering in grand fashion. Carrying a bag of clams and lobsters he had caught that day, George Mendonsa was noticed by every Petry in attendance. One of those Petrys drew his attention. He couldn't look away. Rita Petry's wavy, dirty-blond hair framed an attractive smile and wide, blue eyes. He thought, "My God, she looks like a model." Others had thought so, too. A year earlier when Rita visited family in Florida, an area businessman asked her to model swimsuits for a local advertising campaign. Against her grandfather's protestations, she took the shop owner up on his offer. At her grandfather's insistence, she turned down future photo shoot opportunities.

George was not a model, but the look of a tall, fit fisherman with the bounty from his labors swung over his shoulder must have had its appeal. When George asked Rita to go bowling the next night, she accepted the invitation. During the next few days the Navy quartermaster first class introduced Rita to many of Newport's attractions: the mansions, the coastline, and, apparently, George. The introduction went well. When Rita returned to Long Island, she and George remained in touch. During one of their frequent phone conversations they made plans to get together for a few days on Long Island, just before George's return to San Francisco.

As the last week of George's leave approached, on August 6, 1945, the United States dropped an atomic bomb, "Little Boy," over Hiroshima, Japan. The new weapon had far greater destructive capabilities than its nickname suggested. Though the bomb killed thousands of civilians instantly, and committed many others to a miserable and slow death, most U.S. citizens expressed no remorse. In fact, most Americans relished the news, including President Harry Truman. The new president had assumed the nation's highest office in April 1945, upon President Franklin Roosevelt's death. Truman's reaction to the atomic bomb's detonation bordered on gleeful. After reading the news, the president grabbed a nearby officer and said, "This is the greatest thing in history."[1]

The "greatest thing in history" had a limited impact on Rita and George. Neither knew what to make of it. President Truman's announcement did not describe the awesome devastation or speculate on the future ramifications of a weapon seemingly more suited for 1950s science fiction movies than 1945's sobering realities. All George knew was that if the Japanese did not surrender soon, he would likely take part in some aspect of the dreaded invasion of mainland Japan. That concerned him more than the type of bombs U.S. planes dropped from the sky. As he and other servicemen noticed, the closer American forces approached to the enemy's home turf, the more desperate and formidable the Japanese defenses became. The extent to which the enemy would go to save their motherland had become frighteningly clear in the battles at Leyte Gulf, Iwo Jima, and Okinawa.

As George prepared for his trip to New York to see Rita, on August 9, 1945, Japan's Supreme Council for the Direction of the War met to consider surrendering to the United States. After intense deliberation, the six-member body was deadlocked. During that meeting, they learned that the United States had dropped the next greatest thing in history, "Fat Man," another atomic bomb, on Nagasaki. That explosion had even more force than "Little Boy." Soon thereafter the group adjourned.[2] They had reached no definitive position on whether or not to continue the war against the United States.

While Japan's high command continued to weigh their options in secret, George bid his father farewell. Arsenio Mendonsa was not one to succumb to emotion. In truth, as far as his son could determine, Arsenio lacked the slightest trace of sentimentality. But on this day, as George said his good-byes to family and friends and set out once again to do battle with the Japanese military, Arsenio put his arm around his fourth born, the fisherman turned sailor. Perhaps the old man contemplated the rising number of gold stars in Newport, Rhode Island, windows. Whatever prompted the father's change in temperament, the departing embrace served not only as Arsenio's first openly emotional gesture toward his son, it proved to be his last.

As George left Newport for Long Island on August 10, 1945, he worried little about the prospects for the future. He knew only two things for certain: a pretty girl waited for him in New York, and on August 14 a plane departing from LaGuardia Airport would take him back to San Francisco, where he and his shipmates would board *The Sullivans* to finish what the Japanese had started on December 7, 1941.

7

THE FATHER OF PHOTOJOURNALISM

Most people recognize the faces he immortalized. Almost no one could indentify him, even if he held up one of his famous photos. Alfred Eisenstaedt, the father of photojournalism, took pictures of the famous, infamous, and everyday people caught in fascinating daily routines. While few ever heard his voice, for much of the twentieth century they stared at the scenes he captured. The view he provided awed his audience.

Alfred Eisenstaedt specialized in suspending time. His photographs still give reason for pause. Eisenstaedt's collage of wide smiles, surprised looks, and candid expressions testify to the photographer's developed skills, inherent sense of timing, and quick reflexes. Opportunities present themselves to many. Few seize upon or even recognize the unfolding prospect. Eisenstaedt saw pictures before their conception, positioned himself inconspicuously, and at the most opportune instance pounced via the pressing of a camera's button. The take, sometimes an upsetting sight, other times a most pleasurable instance, focused millions of people's attention.

From a very young age, Eisenstaedt was called to take photographs. Born in 1898 to a Jewish family in Dirschau, West Prussia, in 1906 his family moved to Berlin, where his love of photography first took hold. In 1912 an uncle fostered that love by buying his nephew an Eastman Kodak Folding Camera No. 3.[1] Like a boy in a 1950s American town might run off to a neighborhood baseball diamond with a new bat, Eisenstaedt carried his camera to local venues in search of photographic subjects. He was not overly selective. Almost everything the young photographer saw qualified as picturesque.[2] Unmoving statues in front of old buildings, streaming light through green leaves in the spring, or old men gathered under a street lamp at night called to the young photographer. He saw the extraordinary in the ordinary. At a young age he began developing his own photos. While not yet his profession, photography was already proving to be his passion.

In 1916 events far removed from his boyhood pursuits determined Eisenstaedt's future trajectory. For this journey he carried a rifle instead of his camera. After his seventeenth birthday, the German high command drafted Eisenstaedt into the army, where he served as a cannoneer with the 55th Artillery Regiment. In that same year, a photographer took his picture in Naumburg, Germany, as he posed with eight comrades. With the exception of Eisenstaedt, everyone in the picture died in World War I,[3] or the Great War, as people called it at the time. Eisenstaedt's survival owed little to his fighting skills. During a battle at Flanders on April 9, 1918, an enemy explosion over Eisenstaedt's head shot shrapnel through his legs. As he fell, the bottom half of his body went numb. He wondered if both his legs had been shot off. With machine-gun fire ricocheting all around him, others in his regiment could not risk trying to rescue him. As Eisenstaedt lay helpless on the battlefield, he thought he would be killed.[4]

Two hours later, Red Cross personnel drove up, put Eisenstaedt in a wagon, and took him to a facility near Lille, France, for medical treatment. While there he learned that his legs could be saved. He also learned that everyone in his battery had been killed.[5] His wounds prevented him from fighting during the last months of World War I. For the next two months he walked on crutches, and for the next ten months he needed a cane to move about.

In the coming months the injury kept him out of several other potentially fatal battles. During this reprieve from the trenches he visited local museums and studied the work of great artists. Eisenstaedt took particular note of their handling of composition and lighting.[6]

Shortly after World War I ended in 1918, on the eleventh hour of the eleventh day of the eleventh month—Germany's economy spiraled downward. Inflation in the postwar economy soared. The rising cost of goods far outpaced people's incomes. Like many other Germans, Eisenstaedt's family lost the savings they had put away prior to the war. To help pay the family's bills, Alfred sold belts and buttons. Though by his own account he was not a very good salesman, his sales pitches sustained him well enough to continue buying camera equipment.[7]

Eisenstaedt's career as a photographer began with the sale of his first photo to *Der Weltspiegel* in 1927.[8] The picture focused on a woman playing tennis in Johannisbad, Bohemia. With a friend's help, Eisenstaedt cropped the picture via an enlarger to focus attention on the tennis player and her shadow. *Der Weltspiegel* published the photograph with the caption "Fall—Shadows Grow Long."[9] The editors offered to consider Eisenstaedt's other treatments, "as long as they are good ones."[10] In 1928 he became good enough for the Associated Press to hire him. While the Great Depression settled in during the late 1920s and early 1930s, Eisenstaedt expanded his portfolio of captivating images. Several respected photo journals published some of those photos. While not yet a household name, Alfred Eisenstaedt's work earned increased attention in photography circles.

As the 1930s progressed, so, too, did the political fanaticism in Europe. Surely Eisenstaedt took notice of rising tensions as he viewed increasingly disturbing developments through his camera's lens. In 1934 Eisenstaedt found himself uncomfortably close to one of those disturbances. During a shoot of Benito Mussolini, Italy's "big shot" Fascist leader, officials suspected Eisenstaedt's 90mm lens was a weapon.[11] Consequently, the Italian guard held him for approximately an hour while they checked his credentials with the Associated Press. During another photo shoot a few years later, Eisenstaedt froze Joseph Goebbels' cold stare for the camera. Despite the terror associated with photographing the ruthless Nazi propaganda minister, Eisenstaedt explained, "When I have a camera in my hand I know no fear."[12]

The suspension of fear did not affect his good judgment, at least not for a prolonged time. With Nazi fanaticism spreading, Europe proved no place for a Jewish photographer. In 1935 Eisenstaedt left Germany with his Rolleiflex camera and settled in New York City. Owing to his impressive photograph portfolio, *Time* founder Henry Luce hired Eisenstaedt and three other photographers (Margaret Bourke-White, Thomas McAvoy, and Peter Stackpole) to work on Project X, the successful start-up for the enormously popular *LIFE* magazine.

LIFE wanted to introduce Americans to a photojournalistic publication that employed numerous, large, captivating images to tell the world's story. For the West Prussian–born photographer, *LIFE*'s new approach was "old hat."[13] The photographer and the magazine proved a perfect match. *LIFE* did not hamstring their individualistic photographer, who had grown accustomed to making his own rules. As Eisenstaedt later explained, "At *LIFE* we were never told how to photograph. We were all individualists. We could do anything we wanted to do."[14] The product Eisenstaedt provided *LIFE* was the photo journal's reward for their purposeful lack of supervision. Starting with the magazine's second issue in 1936, Eisenstaedt's photos graced eighty-six of the publication's covers.

Eisenstaedt's portfolio of memorable images expanded dramatically during his *LIFE* years. He photographed scenery, animals, and people of all walks of life. He focused on athletes, artists, actors, and government officials from numerous countries. Some of his best work continued to include common folk captured in unique circumstances. These images contributed handsomely to his celebrated collection.

To capture one of his most famous pictures, in 1933 Eisenstaedt sat one seat over from a young girl during a premier at La Scala, Milan's famous opera house. While the lighting and background enhance, the photograph, the girl's focus on a friend to her left draws attention. If she had become aware of Eisenstaedt's presence the picture would likely be much less interesting.

That phenomenon, removing the photographer's presence from the photograph, characterized many of Eisenstaedt's creations. No doubt his short frame (five feet, four inches) aided this desired effect, but his stealth-like practices contributed more. Eisenstaedt's approaches included the use of natural light rather than flash photography, carrying little equipment, and inconspicuously waiting as he let the subject(s) offer him the moment worth capturing. As he once explained, "I could sit in the first row of the audience and nobody paid attention to me. Sometimes I even sat among the musicians dressed as one of them, my tripod between my legs. A little later I bought an attachable silent diaphragm shutter—it didn't make a click."[15] Eisenstaedt would go to great lengths to remain unnoticed as he captured people's natural mannerisms and movements.

Four photos he snapped for a *LIFE* series in 1944 about World War II soldiers bidding farewell, Eisenstaedt used a 2¼ Rolleiflex, "because you can hold a Rolleiflex without raising it to your eye; so they didn't see you taking the pictures."[16] In one of those photos taken at Pennsylvania Station in New York City, a tearful woman stands beside her husband, unaware of Eisenstaedt's presence. As a result, the photo maintains a moment-in-time appeal. A posed look would appear contrived and artificial, thereby of little interest to the viewer. Eisenstaedt labored to avoid both such conditions.

As World War II's end approached, many more opportunities presented themselves to the photographer whose perceptive eyes constantly looked for such offers. His subjects continued to be unaware of his attention and surprised by his captivating creations.

On the morning of August 14, 1945, George Mendonsa and Greta Zimmer knew of *LIFE* magazine, but, did not know Alfred Eisenstaedt. Eisenstaedt knew World War II but did not know George or Greta. On the day World War II ended, the *LIFE* photographer, the World War II sailor, and the Austrian, born dental assistant crossed paths in Times Square. At the time they saw nothing significant or special about their shared moment. Later, others saw their meeting differently. So did they.

8

MORNING, V-J DAY, 1945

On the morning of August 14, 1945, people across the nation hoped for an end to the war in the Pacific but faced the grim prospect that its extension might include the dreaded invasion of mainland Japan. Similar concerns weighed heavily upon Americans during most World War II mornings. But on Tuesday, August 14, optimism outweighed worry. Stories were afoot that Japan was ready to surrender. And unlike many rumors during the war, this reporting bore truth. In fact, on August 11 Emperor Hirohito had declared to Japan's Supreme Council for the Direction of the War that they must "bear the unbearable" and surrender.[1] By daybreak on August 14, Japan had sent an official surrender statement to the U.S. commander in chief. As President Truman waited for Japan's official admission of defeat, Americans across the country continued to anticipate the end of the war, listen to the news, and feed the rumor mill.

At times, the eagerness for peace tried to hurry its arrival. And on Sunday, August 12, a little persuasion almost made that possible. On that day a Washington, D.C., radio station broadcast that Japan had surrendered. A victory celebration ensued. The guilty sources later retracted their premature announcements, ending what turned out to be a victory celebration dress rehearsal throughout Washington, D.C., and the nation.[2]

By August 14, 1945, the anticipation of peace once again reached a fever pitch. That morning the *New York Times* ran the front-page headline, "An Imperial Message Is Forthcoming Soon." The accompanying story reported the following: "The Japanese Government has accepted the Allies' surrender formula embodied in the note dispatched to Tokyo by the United States, Smei, the Japanese news agency, said today (Tuesday) in a wireless dispatch recorded by the Federal Communications Commission. 'It is learned that an imperial message accepting the Potsdam proclamation is forthcoming soon,' the English language wireless dispatch said, as directed to the American zone."

The *Providence Journal* ran even more optimistic (and accurate), bold, front-page headlines. On the morning of August 14, 1945, the Rhode Island daily newspaper declared: "Tokyo Broadcast Says Japan Has Surrendered." A smaller subtitle on the same front page reported that in Times Square, "hilarious, singing crowds formed impromptu parades" to celebrate Japan's expected surrender. There, celebrants reduced the actual news of a Japanese capitulation to a formality. New Yorkers had waited long enough. More than three laborious and sacrificial years had passed since their enemy struck at Pearl Harbor. Clearly the Japanese had little left with which to attack any more.

Even without the official word, New York residents and visitors wanted a victory party. Some decided to jump-start festivities. Individual conversations that probably began with, "Did you hear?" led to higher-pitched and more confident declarations. Loud laughter, animated facial expressions, and demonstrative gestures followed. The merriment spread from tall skyscrapers down to subway stations. As the early afternoon progressed toward evening, coworkers danced in offices and strangers hugged on streets. Almost everyone got caught up in the contagious euphoria. For at least this moment in time, every American and ally was a brother, a sister, a friend, or a lover. The military man on leave and the nurse who ended her shift early fell prey to the same pervasive optimism.

While much of New York hosted early celebrations, Times Square drew the largest crowds. There, drinking establishments lined the streets to quench the city's thirst for liquor. No bar suffered from a shortage of patrons.[3] And war, with transient servicemen, proved good for commerce. On August 14, 1945, business would be particularly brisk. Like the war, peace, or the anticipation thereof, served saloons' bottom lines well.

But, of course, misleading broadcasts, premature victory parties, and swirling activity, no matter how persuasive, outrageous, or spectacular, do not equate to peace. And on that Tuesday morning, most Americans did not know that by evening the war would expire. At daybreak, August 14, 1945, most expected to wish and wait one more day.

No doubt many who made their way to New York on the last day of World War II wanted to forget the miseries of the prolonged Pacific campaign. They sought distractions, not news. Times Square proved the perfect destination. Within almost every city block a treasure chest of diversions presented themselves. People-watching offered the most readily available and cheapest pastime. The parade of inhabitants and visitors included businessmen in suits hurrying to appointments, ladies with flowers in their hair meandering about, boys in short-sleeve shirts looking for mischief, and proud sailors in uniform pursuing pretty women. On August 14, 1945, the nation's most populated square was hopping.

But even with all the neatly pressed military uniforms and festive women's outfits, the city's brilliant lights stole the show, at least for the time being. Colorful ads, oversized neon logos, and theater entrances' blinking bulbs enticed the passersby. The spectacle made it difficult to pass up seeing a play, listening to a symphony, or taking in a movie.

Of course, there were reasons to venture beyond Times Square. One of the city's most popular movie theaters, Radio City Music Hall, stood at the corner of 6th Avenue and 50th Street. On August 14, 1945, *A Bell For Adano* played at the "Showplace of the Nation." The movie starred Gene Tierney, John Hodiak, and William Bendix and took place in an Italian town recouping from World War II. The feature film ran at 10:30 AM, 1:05 PM, and 4:00 PM. In between showings, the Rockettes, Corps de Ballet, and an orchestra entertained moviegoers. The mixture of acting, dancing, and music amused audiences. Arguably, the ensemble made for the best performance in town—but not on August 14, 1945. On that day, the greatest celebration in the city's history kicked up several blocks south of Radio City Music Hall, where, as in decades past, people met.

By that morning's end, New York workers let out for lunch and visiting shoppers poured into Times Square seeking bargains. As a steady stream of pedestrians exited the 42nd Street subway station, the sidewalks became increasingly congested. Soon, so did the city's streets.

9

SHE LOOKED LIKE A NURSE

Tuesday, August 14, 1945, started off for Greta Zimmer in the same manner as did most weekdays during that year. Hurrying to get ready for work, she showered, dressed, and pinned her hair up tightly to keep her long locks from covering her ears and neck. Before leaving her Manhattan apartment she grabbed a quick bite to eat, reached for her multicolored, small purse, and rushed out the door. Running late, Greta walked briskly toward the subway station to catch a train that could get her to work on time.

Her destination was the 33rd and Lexington subway stop, approximately five blocks from Dr. J. L. Berke's dentist office. Greta had worked as a dental assistant at the Manhattan office for several months. While she hoped to someday design theater sets and pursue other vocations in the arts, work as a dental assistant bought her some independence and took her mind off a prolonged war.

When Greta arrived at the dentists' office on the morning of August 14, she changed into her working uniform. If it were not for her place of employment, she could have been easily mistaken for a nurse. Her white dress, white stockings, white shoes, and white cap did not distinguish her from thousands of other caregivers in New York.

While Greta performed her dental assistant duties that Tuesday morning, many patients burst into the office short of breath and beaming. Excitedly, they informed the staff and patients that the war with Japan had ended. Most patients and workers believed them. Greta wasn't so sure. She wanted to trust their reports, but the war had rained more than a fair share of misery upon Greta. Her defenses remained high. She opted to delay a celebratory mindset that could prove painfully premature.

During the later morning hours, patients continued to enter the dentists' office with more optimistic news. While Greta tried to ignore the positive developments, the temptation to flow with the prevailing winds challenged her reserve. As the reports became more definitive and promising, Greta found herself listening, contemplating, and growing eager. The messengers of victory sang a similar refrain. Each triumphant bearer of good news entered the dentistry office with wide-open eyes and broad smiles. Patients reported the news throughout the morning with announcements like, "Did ya hear? The Japs are surrendering!" and more confident and substantiated declarations such as, "The Japanese already gave up. It's in the papers." A few accounts did not mention the enemy, and instead jumped to the joyous punch line, "The war is over! After all this time, can you believe it? It's over!" With each animated revelation, Greta felt her heart beat faster. But still she wondered, *Can it really be true? The war is over?*

As the day ticked closer to noon, this whirlwind gained velocity with every claim of victory. By early afternoon, Greta's cautionary mindset gave way to youthful anticipation. The attractive, Austrian-born dental assistant began thinking, *Maybe the war really is over.* She reasoned that even if the stories weren't true, a crash landing was a risk she was willing to take for a flight of fantasy.

When the dentists switched off for lunch, Greta found the workplace confining. She became fidgety and increasingly preoccupied with the stream of incoming reports. Once the office's two dentists returned from their lunches after one, Greta quickly finished the business before her. Soon after, she grabbed her small hand purse with the colorful pattern, took off her white dental assistant cap (as was customary before going out in public), and set out during her lunch break for Times Square. There, the *Times* news zipper utilized lit and moving type to report the latest news. She needed to know for herself if the claims that had been tossed about over the past several hours were misleading hearsay, or if, on this day, the reports would finally be true.

The trek from the dentists' office to the square took several minutes. Traveling four blocks west on 37th Street, Greta took a right on Broadway, two blocks from 42nd Street and Times Square. As Greta drew nearer to the 7th Avenue intersection, bustling streets slowed her pace. She did not mind. The festive mood lifted her heightened spirits further. As she drew closer to her destination, her steps became shorter and more rapid. Her eyes opened wider. She was almost there.

When Greta arrived at Times Square, a holiday atmosphere was taking hold. While the celebration was subdued compared to what would follow later that night, Greta could sense a vibrant energy in the air. Suited businessmen, well-dressed women, and uniformed soldiers and sailors entered the pandemonium from all directions. Their path of travel varied. Some ran with no determined direction. Others walked with purpose. Some remained stationary, as if waiting for something big to happen. Greta paid no one particular person much attention.

As she proceeded into the square she moved by several recognizable landmarks: the 42nd Street subway stairwell, a replica of the Statue of Liberty, and a large statue of Joe Rosenthal's famous picture from a few months earlier. After walking a few paces beyond the twenty-five-foot model of the Marines raising the flag at Iwo Jima, Greta spun around and looked in the direction of the Times Building. She focused her sight just above the third-floor windows, where the scrolling lighted letters spelled out the latest headlines. Greta read the racing and succinctly worded message quickly. Now she knew the truth.

10

THE LAST DAY OF LEAVE

On the last day of his leave, George Mendonsa paid no attention to the day's newspaper headlines and worried little about his Japanese enemy. After almost two years in World War II's Pacific theater, his mindset was that the war would unfold independent of his blessing or curse. On the morning of August 14, 1945, his thoughts focused primarily on Rita Petry, an attractive Long Island girl he met a few weeks earlier in Rhode Island.

George woke up that Tuesday morning alone in a bedroom at the Petry family's Long Island home. After breakfast with Rita's family, he leafed through the *New York Times* looking for show times in New York's theaters. He and his new girlfriend decided to take in a matinee at Radio City Music Hall, the "Showplace of the Nation." They thought the 1:05 PM showing of *A Bell for Adano* would give them plenty of time to make it back to Long Island by early evening. They had promised Rita's mother and father they would be back in time for dinner.

George was scheduled to depart for San Francisco that night. In a few days he expected to board *The Sullivans* and prepare for what he hoped would be the last battles of World War II. He *knew* an invasion of the Japanese mainland was imminent. While he did not welcome the looming chain of events, he thought finishing off the Japanese in their homeland would be a fitting bookend to a war that commenced almost four years earlier with the empire's surprise bombing of Pearl Harbor. But all that was in the future. He still had one day left to enjoy in New York.

During his stay at the Petrys' home, George became better acquainted with Rita's blood relations. He discovered that a very protective mother and father had instilled a strong value system in their daughter. But just in case temptation trumped upbringing, Rita's parents chaperoned the couple at every opportunity.

Of course, some aspects of Rita's life fell beyond her parents' complete control. For one, Rita had grown into a very attractive young woman. That development interested George. Also, in general, Rita's parents had less jurisdiction over her activities now that she was a student in college. That was to George's liking, as well. Apart from Rita's parents for the afternoon, the visiting sailor from Rhode Island looked forward to the lack of supervision.

Preparing for that day, George wore a formal blue Navy uniform that he had tailor-made while on leave in Newport. Rita liked how well fitted the new uniform appeared, but she also noticed that "he didn't look like a usual sailor. He didn't have those things on his shoulder." Rita had observed "those things," or rates, on almost all other sailors' formal blues and dress whites. Although Rita offered to sew the chevron on his uniform, George insisted that he take care of the matter with a crossbow hand-stitch he had perfected affixing rates on uniforms on board *The Sullivans*. While not part of his official capacity on the destroyer, his mates had often asked him to hand-stitch rates to their uniforms. His handiwork gave the uniform a classier appearance. But George did not get around to adhering the rate to his uniform during the last week of his leave. So, in the event the shore patrol inquired as to the whereabouts of his rating badge, George made sure to carry the chevron on his person when he and Rita set out for the city.

The forecast for George's last day of leave promised no rain. Rita was happy not to have to carry along an umbrella or sweater. The sun was supposed to shine brilliantly most of the day. Only New York's skyscrapers would provide some shade. Because temperatures were supposed to rise into the low 80-degree range, Rita wore a light dress with sleeves that extended a few inches beyond the middle of her forearms.

When Rita and George arrived in Manhattan at approximately noon, the city already buzzed with rumors of Japan's anticipated surrender. However, neither Rita nor George listened much to people's conversations. Intent on getting to the theater for the 1:05 movie, they made their way from the subway directly to Radio City Music Hall.

For all their rushing, George and Rita never saw the climax of *A Bell for Adano*, the movie they had come to see. At some point during their viewing of the film, a theater employee interrupted the show by pounding on the entrance door and announcing loudly that World War II had ended. Radio City Music Hall patrons simultaneously leapt to their feet with a thunderous applause. Though President Truman had not yet received Japan's official surrender, and the White House's official announcement of Japan's capitulation was still hours away, few raised the slightest objection to the premature declaration.

Seconds after the theater attendant's announcement, George, Rita, and most other moviegoers poured out of Radio City Music Hall and into a bustling crowd at 50th Street and 6th Avenue. Concurrently, workers and visitors hurried out of other buildings throughout New York and rushed into congested streets, avenues, and boulevards. As soon as they merged into the frenzied scene, they fed off the contagious excitement that surrounded them. People yelled out news of victory and peace in high-pitched voices. They smiled and laughed. They jumped up and down with no thought of proper decorum. As if caught in a magnetic field, the historic celebration moved toward Times Square. People from other sections of the city were funneled to the same crossroads where they had gathered for celebrations in the past.

George and Rita got caught up in the undercurrent, as well. After leaving Radio City Music Hall and taking in the surrounding celebration, George and Rita made their way west on 50th Street for one block. At 7th Avenue they took a left toward Times Square. Looking south, they could see the crowd thickening. While not nearly as congested as it would become at seven that evening, their path of travel was encumbered by walkers whose movements appeared increasingly random. They stopped abruptly. They were jolted out into the street. They darted around and about other pedestrians. They had no planned path of travel. And for good reason. Their destinations were more about a frame of mind than a particular locale. As George and Rita made their way toward the 42nd Street subway station, even their movements became unpredictable. They walked on sidewalks, in the middle of streets, and they popped in and out of stores.

Just before entering the heart of Times Square, at the corner of 7th Avenue and 49th Street, George and Rita dropped into Childs Restaurant for celebratory libations. Like other watering holes in New York, people walked, skipped, and ran up to the jam-packed bar to tip a glass or two (or significantly more) to the war that they thought had finally ended. The scene at Childs looked much like that on 7th Avenue. Order and etiquette had been cast away. Rather than placing orders for a specific mug of beer or a favorite glass of wine, patrons forced their way toward the bar and reached out an arm to grab one of the shot glasses of liquor that lined the counter. After slugging down the shot, the patron's left or right forearm lowered abruptly, banging the empty glass onto the counter. A generous bartender continuously poured the contents of hard liquor bottles into waiting glasses. George grabbed whatever the server dispensed and did not ask what it was he drank. He knew the desired result would be the same whether the contributor was Jack Daniels, Jameson, or Old Grand Dad. Even Rita gave over to the reckless abandon. After several minutes and the consumption of too many drinks, George and his date made their way out of the packed restaurant.

When George and Rita left the bar, emotions and alcohol propelled them out into Times Square, where victorious World War II celebrants continued to mass. George thought, *My God, Times Square is going wild.* And at that point, so was George. He felt uncharacteristically blissful and jubilant. As George moved briskly toward the 42nd Street subway station, the sailor from *The Sullivans* outpaced his girlfriend. For the moment, no one could corral George. And no one tried—not even Rita. The realization of a triumphant war created more vigor than his large frame could hold. He needed to release the energy. As he marched down 7th Avenue, he sidestepped little boys, maneuvered around old ladies, and bumped up against other servicemen. While George was difficult to track, Rita did her best to keep up. At most points she trailed him by only a few feet. Although she enjoyed the frolic through Times Square, she wondered if George would ever stop for a breather.

IN SEARCH OF THE PICTURE

A s the spirited celebration of Japan's surrender grew, reporters from the *New York Times*, the *New York Daily News*, the Associated Press, and other well-known publications descended on Times Square to record the spontaneous merriment that was enveloping the world's most important crossroads. The publications' photographers added more bodies to a burgeoning impromptu gala. One of those photographers represented *LIFE* magazine.

LIFE had made a name for itself during the war. The magazine that set out to picture the world had done just that. British prime minister Neville Chamberlain, Italian dictator Benito Mussolini, and Japanese emperor Hirohito had appeared on the cover of *LIFE* during the 1930s and 1940s. So, too, had actress Shirley Temple, steelworker Ann Zarik, and comedian Bob Hope. Throughout the early 1940s *LIFE* subscribers saw hundreds of war photographs, many enlarged on oversized pages. From 1943 onward, those images became less posed and closer to the battle lines.[1] *LIFE* viewers saw American servicemen floating dead along European shores, lying lifeless on Pacific beaches, or scattering for cover on the deck of a burning aircraft carrier. Home front treatments included women's baseball teams filling the entertainment gap left by depleted major league teams. During the war Americans bought *LIFE* at unprecedented levels because they wanted to see the war in all its forms. The magazine rapidly became an indispensible part of American culture during the 1940s.[2]

In April 1945 *LIFE* celebrated the end of war in Europe, but the rejoicing lasted only one issue. In the coming weeks, *LIFE* focused more on Pacific theater developments, including a major piece on the United States' dropping of the atomic bomb. The published scenes of the destruction awed and shocked Americans. Some contemplated the future in the dust of such a tremendous explosion. Most were happy the Japanese fell victim to the new bomb's might.

On August 14, 1945, *LIFE* sought pictures that differed from most others printed earlier in the war. On this day, *LIFE* wanted its viewers to know what the end of the war *felt* like. They didn't know with any degree of certainty what incarnation that feeling might take, but they left it to their photographers to show them—just like they had with other events over the publication's nine-year history. Those unsupervised approaches had rarely led to disappointment in the past and *LIFE*'s editors trusted their photographers to deliver again that day.

LIFE's trust in their photographers was especially complete when Alfred Eisenstaedt was on assignment. He had photographed the people and personalities of World War II, some prior to the declaration of war and others even before *LIFE* existed. As a German Jew in the 1930s, he chronicled the developing storm, including a picture of Benito Mussolini's first meeting with Adolph Hitler in Venice, on June 13, 1934. In another shoot he photographed an Ethiopian soldier's bare, cracked feet on the eve of Fascist Italy's attack in 1935.

After the outbreak of war between Japan and the United States, Eisenstaedt focused on the American home front. In 1942 Eisenstaedt photographed a six-member Missouri draft board classifying a young farmer as 2-C, indicating draft deferment because of his occupation's importance to the nation. For another series in 1945, he visited Washington and photographed freshman senators performing comical monologues and musical numbers to entertain Capitol reporters. During World War II, Eisenstaedt showed the world what war looked like on the U.S. mainland.

On the day World War II ended, Eisenstaedt entered Times Square dressed in a tan suit, a white shirt with a lined tie, tan saddle shoes, and a Leica camera hanging from his neck. Despite his distinctive ensemble, he traveled stealthily among the kaleidoscope of moving parts, looking for *the* picture. He made sure not to call attention to himself. He was on the hunt. He knew there was a picture in the making. Kinetic energy filled the square. Eisenstaedt wished for others to *feel* it, too. To create that sense, Eisenstaedt's photo needed a tactile element. It was a tall order for the five-foot, four-inch photographer. He relished the challenge.

At some point after 1:00 PM. Eisenstaedt took a picture of several women celebrating in front of a theater across the street from the 42nd Street subway station stairwell. The picture showed ladies throwing pieces of paper into the air, creating a mini-ticker-tape parade. While the photo had its charm, it was not the defining picture Eisenstaedt was searching for that day.

Shortly after closing the shutter on that scene, Eisenstaedt turned to his left and looked up Broadway and 7th Avenue to where 43rd Street connected to Times Square's main artery. As Eisenstaedt continued to search for a photograph that would forever define the moment at hand, he peered around and beneath, but probably not over, the sea of humanity. News of the war's end had primed America's meeting place for a one-in-a-million kind of picture. A prospect would present itself soon. Eisenstaedt knew that. So he looked and waited.

THE KISS

Greta Zimmer stood motionless in Times Square near a replica of the Statue of Liberty and a model of the Marines raising the flag at Iwo Jima. To Greta's left was Childs restaurant, one of several in New York, including this establishment at 7th Avenue and 44th Street. But Greta did not come to Times Square to stare at statues or belly up to bars. She wanted to read the *Times* zipper and learn if Japan really had surrendered to the United States.

With the 44th Street sign and the Astor Hotel to her back, she looked up at the tall triangular building that divided one street into two. The lit message running around the Times Building read, "VJ, VJ, VJ, VJ . . ." Greta gazed at the moving type without blinking. A faint smile widened her lips, and narrowed her eyes. She took in the moment fully and thought, *The war is over. It's really over.*

Though Greta had arrived in Times Square by herself, she was not alone. While she continued to watch the moving "VJ" message, hundreds of people moved around her. Greta paid little attention to the swelling mass of humanity. But they were about to take notice of her, and never forget what they saw. Within a few seconds she became Times Square's nucleus. Everybody orbited around her, with one exception. He was drawn to her.

Fresh from the revelry at Childs on 49th, George Mendonsa and his new girlfriend, Rita Petry, made their way down Times Square toward the 42nd Street subway station. Rita fell behind

George by a few steps. Meanwhile, Eisenstaedt, who a short time earlier had snapped a photo of women celebrating outside a ticket office, persisted in his hunt for *the* photo. After traveling a block or so up Times Square, he took notice of a fast moving sailor he thought he saw grabbing a woman and kissing her. That sailor was heading quickly south down Broadway and 7th Avenue. Wondering what the sailor might do next, Eisenstaedt changed direction and raced ahead of the darting sailor. Doing so was not without its challenges. He had to work through and around many civilians and servicemen who moved all about Times Square. As Eisenstaedt approached the 44th Street sign, he continually scanned the scene ahead of him for the least encumbered pathway. To avoid bumping into people in the crowded street, he had to look away from the sailor he was trying to track. When glancing over his shoulder, he struggled to regain his focus on the Navy man wearing the formal Navy blue uniform. As he did so, Greta looked away from the *Times* zipper and started to turn to her right. George crossed the intersection of 44th Street and 7th Avenue, lengthening the space between him and Rita. The photographer, the sailor, and the dental assistant were on a collision course.

With a quickening pace that matched the surrounding scene's rising pulse, the sailor who served his country on board *The Sullivans* zeroed in on a woman whom he assumed to be a nurse. The liquor running through his veins transfixed his glassy stare. He remembered a war scene when he had rescued maimed sailors from a burning ship in a vast ocean of water. Afterward, gentle nurses, angels in white, tended to the injured men. From the bridge of *The Sullivans* he watched them perform miracles. Their selfless service reassured him that one day the war would end. Peace would reign again. That day had arrived.

George steamed forward several more feet. His girlfriend was now farther behind. He focused on Greta, the "nurse." She remained unaware of his advance. That served his purpose well. He sought no permission for what he was about to do. He just knew that she looked like those nurses who saved lives during the war. Their care and nurturing had provided a short and precious reprieve from kamikaze-filled skies. But that nightmare had ended. And there she stood. Before him. Far from the attacking enemy. Close to home. With background noises barely registering, he rushed toward her as if in a vacuum. The last step and the second before his encounter with the shape of a woman in white squeezed out the remaining space between them. Though George halted his steps just before running into Greta, his upper torso's momentum swept over her. The motion's force bent Greta backward and to her right. As he overtook Greta's slender frame, his right hand cupped her slim waist. He pulled her inward toward his lean and muscular body. Her initial attempt to physically separate her person from the intruder proved a futile exertion against the dark-uniformed man's strong hold. With her right arm pinned between their two bodies, she instinctively brought her left arm and clenched fist upward in defense. The effort was unnecessary. He never intended to hurt her.

As their lips locked moistly, his left arm supported her neck. His left hand, turned backward and away from her face, offered the singular gesture of restraint, caution, or doubt. The struck pose created an oddly appealing mixture of brutish force, caring embrace, and awkward hesitation. He didn't let go. As he continued to lean forward, she lowered her right arm and gave over to her pursuer—but only for three or four seconds. He tried to hold her closer, wanting the moment to last longer. And longer still. But they parted, the space between them and the moment shared ever widening, releasing the heat born from their embrace into the New York summer evening.

The encounter, brief and impromptu, transpired beyond the participants' governance. Even George, the initiator, commanded little more resolve than a floating twig in a rushing river of fate. He just had to kiss her. He didn't know why.

For that moment, George had thought Times Square's streets belonged to him, but they did not. Alfred Eisenstaedt owned them. When he was on assignment, nothing worth cap-

12-1. Alfred Eisenstaedt photographed this kissing scene in Times Square during the afternoon of V-J Day, August 14, 1945. The second photograph (top right) in the sequence became *LIFE*'s most prized photograph. (*Permission granted by Bobbi Baker Burrows at Time-Life.*)

12-2. Eisenstaedt's first photograph.

12-3. Eisenstaedt's second photograph, *V-J Day, 1945, Times Square.*

12-4. Eisenstaedt's third photograph.

12-5. Eisenstaedt's fourth photograph.

turing on film escaped his purview. Before George and Greta parted, Eisenstaedt spun around, aimed his Leica and clicked the camera's shutter release closed four times. One of those clicks produced *V-J Day, 1945, Times Square*. That photograph became his career's most famous, *LIFE* magazine's most reproduced, and one of history's most popular. The image of a sailor kissing a nurse on the day World War II ended kept company with Joe Rosenthal's photo of the flag rising at Iwo Jima. That photo proudly exemplified what a hard-fought victory *looks* like. This photo savored what a long-sought peace *feels* like.

Alfred Eisenstaedt was not the only photographer to take notice of George and Greta. Navy lieutenant Victor Jorgensen, standing to Eisenstaedt's right, fired off one shot of the entwined couple at the precise moment the *LIFE* photographer took his second picture of four. Though Jorgensen's photo did not captivate audiences to the same degree that Eisenstaedt's second photograph did, *Kissing the War Goodbye* drew many admirers as well.

And then it was over. Shortly after the taking of *V-J Day, 1945, Times Square*, Greta returned to Dr. J. L. Berke's dental office and told everyone present what was happening on New York City's streets. Dr. Berke had Greta cancel the rest of the day's appointments and closed the office. Afterward, as Greta made her way home, another sailor kissed her, but this time politely on the cheek. For this kiss Greta no longer wore her dental assistant uniform and no photographers took her picture. And as far as she could tell, she had not been photographed at any point in time during that day. She did not learn otherwise until years later, when she saw Eisenstaedt's photograph of a Times Square couple kissing in a book entitled *The Eyes of Eisenstaedt*.

George did not realize that he had been photographed, either. When George turned from the act he instigated, he smiled at Rita and offered little explanation for what transpired. As hard as it is to believe, she made no serious objection. George's actions fell within the acceptable norms of August 14, 1945, although not any other day. Actually, neither George nor Rita thought much of the episode and proceeded to Rita's par-

12-6. Lt. Victor Jorgensen snapped this photograph at the exact moment Alfred Eisenstaedt took his second photograph of the 1945 V-J Day kissing sequence. (*National Archives photo #80-G-377094*)

ent's home via a 42nd Street subway train. Later that evening, the Petrys transported George to LaGuardia Airport for a flight to San Francisco that left at approximately midnight. Neither he nor Rita discovered Eisenstaedt's *V-J Day, 1945, Times Square* until 1980.

13

PICTURES FROM V-J DAY

The same day the Father of Photojournalism took the most famous photo of his illustrious career, all of New York went wild. Celebrants set off 377 fire alarms[1] and covered New York City streets with more than 4,863 tons of paper.[2] That August 14—noisy, messy, and full of life—rolled on without inhibition into the next morning. On August 15, New Yorkers ventured a repeat performance. Of the thousands of people who posed before a stranger's camera on V-J Day, 1945, many wore a formal, blue, Navy uniform. Years later some of those sailors thought Alfred Eisenstaedt took their picture. And though that is not possible, their actions and activities on that victorious day matter. Their celebrations contribute significantly to the story of V-J Day, 1945, the happiest day in American history.[3]

Though New York may have had the largest celebration, every city and town across the United States and around much of the world had just as much reason to celebrate. People throughout the nation shouted, kissed, and danced into the night. While all those festivities resulted from the same announcement, the parties, merriment, and commemorations differed considerably. In Columbus, Ohio, a bartender mixed "Atomic Cocktails."[4] In the nation's capital, churches rang their bells and celebrants sang "The Star-Spangled Banner."[5] In San Francisco they lit bonfires in the streets, danced on top of vehicles, and otherwise engaged in rowdy and destructive behavior that resulted in several deaths.[6] At the opposite extreme, some celebrants just talked. Mrs. Ira Eaker, who maintained five pairs of nylon stockings throughout the entire war, said, "Do you know, in army circles on V-J Day there was more talk about nylons than anything else?"[7] But regardless of how people commemorated that moment, everyone rejoiced in the news. Well, almost everyone.

Some frowned upon the celebrations' superficiality. Simon Greco, a conscientious and disappointed war objector, lamented: "When the war ended, I expected some great religious feeling to take over. In other words, I really expected all the wheels to stop, theaters to close, bars to close, trains to stop running. Something irrational. Nothing happened. A bunch of people gathered in Times Square, some gals getting laid. And that was the end of it. The wheels were going, the bars were open, the pool halls were open, the factories were running, almost as if nothing had happened."[8]

But something had happened, as all of Japan soon learned. Kept in the dark as to their nation's hopeless predicament during the last months of the war, Japanese citizens did not receive the news of their defeat well. Many who listened to their emperor's voice for the first time sobbed when he conceded to the United States' terms of surrender. Thirty people in a crowd that gathered outside the Imperial Palace to hear the emperor's announcement committed suicide.[9] Even Americans in a Japanese prisoner-of-war camp took in the news in silence. They were stunned. One American prisoner, Anton Bilek, recalled, "Nobody said a damn word. It was quiet, quiet, just the shuffling of feet. I went behind the first barracks and cried like a baby."[10] And, undoubtedly, no Japanese sailors joyfully kissed nurses outside the palace or, for that matter, anywhere else in Japan.

But in the United States they couldn't stop kissing. In Chicago, thirty sailors formed a line and kissed every woman who passed. In New York, "One sailor firmly took hold of a girl and as he gave her a longer-than-movie kiss a shipmate jokingly fanned him."[11] As was reported in the *Rocky Mountain News*, "Servicemen kissed their girls and then they kissed somebody else's girls, and pretty soon everybody was kissing everybody else and nobody was complaining."[12] Keeping track of who

kissed whom on August 14, 1945, became impossible and seemingly pointless.

On the same August 14 that a photographer captured a
sailor kissing a nurse in Times Square, Betsy Ross Austin kissed
Dominick Bruno. The schoolgirl and soldier had already established a relationship, of sorts. In 1941, at age fifteen, Betsy
noticed a handsome serviceman driving in a jeep several feet
behind her school bus. On an impulse she wrote her name and
address on a piece of paper and threw it out the window with
the hope that the trailing soldier would pick it up. Not only did
he scoop up the note, he started writing the assertive fifteen-
year-old two weeks later. He continued writing her throughout
the war. On August 12, 1945, nineteen-year-old Betsy met her
long-distance boyfriend for the first time in Charlotte, North
Carolina. On the second day of their relationship, Japan surrendered to the United States. To celebrate they went to the
square—in Charlotte. There, a sharp-eyed newspaper photographer captured for the ages their passionate kiss. The
next day the *Charlotte Observer* published their picture. Less
than a month later, Betsy and Dominick moved to New York,
where Betsy got a job as an office manager at Macy's, within
walking distance of Times Square. Though Eisenstaedt's captured Manhattan embrace forever overshadowed Betsy and
Dominick's Charlotte kiss, no one ever wondered about the
North Carolina couple's identities. Their marriage lasted more
than sixty years.[13]

Not all who celebrated V-J Day in Times Square pulled off
kissing a strange woman. Sixteen-year-old Gerard Meister spent
the morning of August 14 at a city swimming pool in the Bronx.
That afternoon, the loudspeaker blared out that the Japanese had
surrendered. Shortly afterward, Gerard set out to 7th Avenue and
Broadway in Manhattan with Mae, a young girl he barely knew.
Arriving in Times Square, Gerard noticed "soldiers and sailors were climbing the lampposts, shouting, throwing their hats
in the air. Everyone was hugging and kissing."[14] Overcome with
the power of suggestion, patriotism, and pumped-up hormones,

Gerard attempted his own version of George and Greta's Times Square act with his young companion:

> "Mae!" I exclaimed breathlessly, embracing her. "It's over, the war is over!" I leaned forward to kiss her.
> "I don't kiss on the first date," she said firmly. "We won't have anything to look forward to."
> "But this isn't a date," I countered. "It's an event, a celebration!"
> "Please," she said, "what kind of girl do you think I am?"[15]

Despite Gerard's repeated advances, Mae never succumbed to V-J Day's relaxed mores. Instead of trying to kiss Mae, Gerard should have jump-started an impromptu parade. Thousands across the nation did. In New Orleans, Melba Lusse grabbed a flag she had mounted on a fishing pole and led a procession down Saint Roch Avenue. Her eight-year-old daughter followed suit, tooting a tin horn. Not far behind came Lusse's son, carrying a bottle of Dixie Beer. Other neighborhood families couldn't help but fall into line, too, hollering and singing loudly.[16] Out in the Pacific, the *Honolulu Advertiser* reported, "We watched a soldier and a sailor dance on top of a moving car. Sailors piggybacked on each other, sun-browned kids piggybacked on sailors, and a gang of barefoot youngsters came from nowhere, holding crab nets and bamboo fishing poles and danced into the parade on Alaska St."[17]

When celebrants didn't form parades, they most often made noise. Their joyous racket could be heard in towns and cities throughout the United States. As the *San Francisco Chronicle* reported, "The air raid sirens sounded first. Then automobile horns, factory whistles and ship whistles—and church bells."[18] In New York's Times Square, for twenty minutes "the victory roar . . . numbed the senses."[19] Even many who had lost loved ones to the long war screamed and shouted to fill the void.

Across the nation countrymen and women saluted the war's passing with a celebratory libation. And they often drank for free. In Boston's North End, women served free wine. And as the

Boston Globe reported, "On the streets it seemed everyone had a bottle. And these bottles were freely handed around among persons who were total strangers a moment before."[20]

When August 14, 1945, ended, soon, too, did the parties, parades, and pomp and ceremony. But thanks in large part to a photo in Times Square, New York, and another in Charlotte, North Carolina, the world will always remember the day a long war ended and a nation savored its victory.

PART 3

THE AFTER *LIFE*

No, I do not consider it one of my best.

ALFRED EISENSTAEDT WITH JOHN LOENGARD, 1991
Thoughts about *V-J Day, 1945, Times Square*

14

NO ONE SEEMED TO NOTICE

*L*IFE published *V-J Day, 1945, Times Square* in its August 27, 1945, issue. The magazine did not put Eisenstaedt's photo on its cover and gave no indication that the issue addressed the end of World War II celebrations. Instead, *LIFE* editors chose a picture of Belita Jepson-Turner, a ballet swimmer submerged in a pool of water, to grace its cover. *V-J Day, 1945, Times Square* appeared on page 27. The caption read, "In The Middle Of Times Square A White-Clad Girl Clutches Her Purse And Skirt Aa An Uninhibited Sailor Plants His Lips Squarely On Hers." The photo took up the entire oversized page. You couldn't miss it. But no one seemed to notice.

In the weeks that followed, the closest any published letter to the editor came to mentioning the embraced couple appeared in *LIFE*'s September 17, 1945, issue with Douglas MacArthur, the "Commander of Japan," on the cover. Addressing the V-J Day story from two weeks prior, M. Susan Berry from Durham, North Carolina wrote, "Rah for *LIFE*! You now hold an unequaled record by publishing 42 kisses in one issue!" (In actuality, there were fifty three mugging couples.) One can safely assume that one of the fourty two kisses Ms. Berry referenced included *V-J Day, 1945, Times Square*.

By design, most of *LIFE*'s photos told a story. In the case of *V-J Day, 1945, Times Square*, *LIFE* published a mystery. *LIFE* editors printed too few words to crack the case. The publication that set out to show and inform fell short of its mark. While

LIFE readers could see an uninhibited sailor kissing a nurse dressed in white, they could not determine their identities. And neither could *LIFE.*

But how could that be? The kiss occurred in the world's most popular meeting place. Its occurrence marked Times Square's most cherished moment. An audience of more than twenty people gathered and gave eyewitness validation to the whole affair. Hundreds of other pedestrians moved about in the extended background. Two accomplished photographers took a total of five pictures of that kiss. One of those photographers was considered the world's premier photojournalist. The scene he photographed marked the closing act in history's most destructive conflict. The photo appeared in the nation's most popular photo journal. Over the next sixty-five years the photo was reprinted in periodicals and books, and it also appeared in documentaries and advertisements. However, owing to some peculiar formula, public viewing and familiarity made the pictured scene appear more mysterious.

In the coming years the sailor and nurse's anonymity generated many more questions. Did the sailor and nurse know each other? Were they kissing because the war ended? Was the kiss romantic? Did they date? Did they get married? Are they still together? Where are they now? How did they spend the rest of their lives? No one knew the answers to any of these questions.

The most prolific questions focused on the sailor and nurse's identities. Most onlookers felt that the photos showed far too few facial features to identify either kisser. It was almost as if the sailor and nurse had purposely hidden from the camera's lens. The two kissers might as well have been phantoms. To make matters worse, on that August 14, 1945, afternoon, the alleged paramours dispersed into the thickening crowd immediately after they parted. In their haste, neither took a memorable glance at the stranger with whom they had shared an intimate moment in the world's most public place. After shooting the scene, Eisenstaedt scampered away abruptly in search of

other happenings to photograph. He never asked for the participants' names and recorded no notes of the occurrence while
at the scene. No one did. Even the bystanders seemed sworn to
confidentiality. Seconds after the kiss, other V-J Day celebrants
traversed the cherished location, blissfully unaware of the earlier photographed occasion.

One day later, *LIFE* contacted Eisenstaedt to let him know
that he had shot an amazing photo the day before. Eisenstaedt
inquired as to what shot they meant.[1] He was not the only one
who had difficulty remembering the photographed scene. James
Sheridan, the tall, white-uniformed sailor in Eisenstaedt's second photo, barely recalled the particular occurrence when,
sixteen days later, his sister and mother recognized him in
Eisenstaedt's photograph.[2] While George and Rita remembered
the scene, they never once brought it up for thirty-five years.
Though future generations would consider the photographed
moment unforgettable, those most intimately involved with the
actual occurrence had minimized the kiss as soon as it expired.

Eisenstaedt's sailor and the nurse did not see the *LIFE* picture when it appeared in the magazine's August 27, 1945, issue
two weeks later. In 1946 the couple was afforded another opportunity to take notice of their shared moment, when *LIFE* republished the photo in their November 25, 1946, tenth-anniversary
issue. Again, the sailor and nurse did not see the photo and,
again, the photo journal did not reveal any names. But for this
printing, the caption called more attention to the nurse in a
"hammer lock" than the assertive sailor who arguably was more
responsible for the public display. Beside the title *The women
shared in victory and in fun*, *LIFE* included the following commentary: "This was the decade of the woman war worker, the
Army nurse and the WAC. But woman did not desert her role
as man's eternal companion in hours of gaiety. There was one
day (above) when no woman in America was safe from a man's
embrace. Nor, of course, was a man safe from woman."[3] While
it is doubtful that the nurse endangered the sailor at any point
during the photographed sequence, the lack of background

information allowed for the contemplation of almost any suggestion. Over the years, other sources suggested even less probable scenarios.

Even without knowing their photograph's main characters, *LIFE* continued to reprint *V-J Day, 1945, Times Square* in books, magazines, and other publications. And even as the popularity of the photo grew over the following years, the picture's two main characters remained unknown.

15

EISENSTAEDT NAMES THE NURSE

L IFE republished *V-J Day, 1945, Times Square* in 1966. Like earlier *LIFE* printings, Alfred Eisenstaedt's gem did not appear on the cover. Sophia Loren did. For this photo she was dressed in a black, see-through negligee. Eisenstaedt took that picture, too. On page 118 of the September 16, 1966, issue, *LIFE* editors spread out a full-page printing of the kissing sailor photo. The photograph helped promote Eisenstaedt's new book, *Witness to Our Time.* The caption over the photo referenced the kissing sailor photo as Eisenstaedt's most famous picture. Once again, the description did not include the sailor's or nurse's names, and it also claimed the picture was taken on V-J Day, September 2, 1945.[1] Though Eisenstaedt did not take any notes at the scene of the occurrence, in the picture's caption he recalled, "When I reached Times Square the kissing spree was in full swing. This sailor had kissed at least a dozen women when I saw him, but this nurse was the most attractive one he grabbed."

Though the reprinting in *LIFE* and the publication of *Witness to Our Time* focused more attention on the V-J Day kissing sailor photo, much of the hoopla surrounding the photo didn't occur until years after 1966. Nostalgia and the mystery surrounding the kissing sailor's identity caused a great deal of the later interest.[2] The nurse's identity was less of a fascination for the public. By 1980, most *knew* who she was.

In 1979 Alfred Eisenstaedt received a letter from Edith Shain, who claimed to be the nurse in his famous photo from the end of World War II. In her letter, Shain claimed she had recognized herself in the photo's first printing, but she did not share her story beyond a circle of close friends.[3] As she explained it, in the 1940s she felt her participation in the photograph lacked proper reserve. However, by the late 1970s she felt the times had changed sufficiently to permit a young lady's brief relaxation of inhibitions, especially given the moment in time she loosened them.[4] Shain explained that an article in the *Los Angeles Times* about Eisenstaedt and his famous photograph from the end of World War II prompted her to end her self-imposed silence.[5] With the changing times, Edith Shain let photographer Alfred Eisenstaedt—and presumably the world—know that she was the nurse kissing the sailor in his cherished photo. The letter she wrote to Eisenstaedt read as follows:

Dear Mr. Eisenstaedt,

Now that I'm 60—it's fun to admit that I'm the Nurse in your famous shot "of the amorous sailor celebrating V.E. Day by kissing a nurse on New York's Broadway." The article in the Los Angeles Times, which described your talents, stimulated the recall of the scene on Broadway. I had left Doctor's Hospital and wanted to be part of the celebration but the amorous sailor and subsequent soldier motivated a retreat into the next opening of the subway. I wish I could have stored that jubilation and amour for use P.R.N. Mr. Eisenstaedt, is it possible for me to obtain a print of that picture? I would be most appreciative. I regret not having met you on your last trip to Beverly Hills.

Perhaps next time: If not—I'll understand because "it's not only hard to catch him . . . it's hard to keep up with him." Have fun.

Fondly,
Edith Shain[6]

Interestingly, Shain identified herself as the nurse who got kissed on "V.E. Day" (V-E Day or Victory in Europe occurred on May 8, 1945), a date that also caused a lot of kissing in Times Square. But apparently Alfred Eisenstaedt knew that she confused the days. Upon reading her letter he became excited about meeting the long-lost nurse from his most famous photograph.

In 1980 Alfred Eisenstaedt visited Edith Shain. According to Shain, "He looked at my legs and said I was the one."[7] At some point after looking at Shain's legs, Eisenstaedt inscribed one of his books to Shain: "The one and only nurse photographed on August 15, 1945 at Times Square, New York City. With Love, Eisie."[8] Shain's discovery excited Eisenstaedt. In the coming years, Eisenstaedt kept in touch with Shain and even visited with her in New York.[9]

Edith Shain's commentaries about *her* V-J Day picture were published widely. But for the longest time, she had kept her knowledge of the photo to herself. She never secured a copy of the magazine as a keepsake.[10] Over the years Shain saw the picture numerous times, as *LIFE* and other publications reprinted Eisenstaedt's handiwork.[11] Every reprinting offered general captions that spoke more to the larger occasion than the specific incident. Shain knew the precise details, or at least more than all the published captions she read. However, not until more than twenty years of reading the photo's generic and vague descriptions did she decide to inform friends about her role.[12] The story she told fascinated them.[13]

According to Shain, on August 14, 1945, she worked at the Doctor's Hospital as a part-time nurse. Upon hearing a radio broadcast that announced the Japanese surrender, she felt an immediate sense of relief.[14] For one, the announcement signified an end to the horrors of war for numerous soldiers and sailors. On a more personal note, the announcement "saved" her from joining the Nurse Corps.[15] Relief soon gave way to elation. Shortly after the broadcast, the twenty-seven-year-old nurse left the hospital with a female friend and headed to where "New Yorkers go . . . when there's a celebration, and that's Times Square."[16] And apparently everyone, including many from outside the city, agreed with Shain's thoughts on an appropriate meeting place. Upon arriving in Times Square, she recalled, "the street was just wild with people. It was exuberant. They were dashing around and hugging and kissing and we walked in on that."[17]

Shain remembered becoming an integral part of *that*. Just a few skips away from the subway a sailor grabbed her.[18] While normally such an incident would be the cause of angst and alarm, on this day, at that moment, many allowed, even welcomed, the intrusion. Besides the occasion's gaiety and the sailor's assertiveness, another factor precipitating the happening might be, well, Edith. At this time in her life, Edith Shain recalled, "everyone was kissing me."[19] But this kiss compared favorably to the others. Shain acknowledged this "was a good kiss . . . that went on for a long time. . . . I closed my eyes, I didn't resist."[20] In another rendition of this story she offered a softer, more romantic version: "It was like a dance step, the way he laid me over in his arms. . . . I just got lost in the moment."[21] According to Shain, if it were not for her girlfriend she would have danced longer.[22] Instead, she left the scene immediately, never bothering to ask the sailor's name or take notice of his appearance. As she later explained, "When he grabbed me, I didn't see him, and when he kissed me, I didn't see him because I closed my eyes. And then I turned around and walked the other way . . ."[23]

Two weeks after Eisenstaedt snapped *V-J Day, 1945, Times Square*, Shain said she saw her own image on page twenty-seven of *LIFE*. The longer Edith stared at the full-page picture, the clearer her two-week-old memories came into focus. Though the picture's angle concealed most of her face from the camera's viewfinder, the vantage provided enough clearance to support a credible claim to the nurse's identity. To make her case, Shain took careful inventory of the photographed evidence. She recalled the shoes: white, wide, and high-heeled. That morning she put on stockings, white and lined. Her slip, again white, showed beyond her white dress' hemline.[24] And there was that sailor, assertive and victorious. She recollected herself, too; surprised, supportive, safe and sound.[25]

Owing to Eisenstaedt and *LIFE*, when Shain came forward with her story in 1979, almost everyone accepted her claim that she was, indeed, the kissed nurse in the famous photograph. From that point forward, captions that continued to call attention to the sailor's anonymity often referenced Shain as the photographed partner. Over the years, Shain's invitations to celebrations, commemorations, and coronations solidified her stature among backward-leaning nurse claimants.

Beginning in 1980, Shain toured the nation as if she were the queen of Times Square. She delivered speeches and partook in reenactments of the V-J Day Times Square kiss. Publications and television programs featured her story. Well-known figures and national organizations ordained her version of events. Celebrities posed for pictures with Shain. In 2007, President George W. Bush presented Shain with a proclamation recognizing her as a symbol of world peace.[26] Shain was treated as a national treasure.

Most kissing sailor claimants pursued Shain as if they were Muslim and she was Mecca. They wanted her confirmation of *their* kiss. Like the original sailor, the aging campaigners employed a youthful vigor that approached the same reckless abandon exercised when, according to them, they overtook a nurse on the day World War II ended. The latter-day pursuit paid dividends, too. Gaining Shain's blessings of their role in the famous scene, in effect, sanctified their claim with the public.

When Edith Shain died on June 20, 2010, her obituary ran as a major article in newspapers across the country, including the *Los Angeles Times*, the *Wall Street Journal*, and the *New York Times*. A *Washington Post* headline read, "Anonymously world-famous after WWII photo, she didn't kiss and tell." Though articles from the Atlantic to the Pacific mentioned that Shain's claim as the nurse in Eisenstaedt's photo remained a point of contention, the underlying message was clear—the nurse in the famous V-J Day photograph had died. The articles praised the nurse who "let" an assertive sailor kiss her at the end of World War II because "he fought for his country."[27] Edith Shain's passing was covered on national television programs, including the *Today Show* and *NBC Nightly News* with Brian Williams. Shortly after her death, Life.com released a statement that declared, "Shain's claim is the one that, over the years, has held up best and has been widely accepted and most often celebrated."[28]

While the nation mourned a precious part of *V-J Day, 1945, Times Square*, George Mendonsa did not receive a single inquiry from the media. However, Carl Muscarello, another kissing sailor candidate, received enough calls to make his "phone ring off the hook." He added, "They thought I died."[29] The comments Muscarello offered media outlets about Shain reinforced her part, as well as his own, in the picture that will forever epitomize the end of World War II.

To this day, almost everyone accepts and celebrates Edith Shain as the nurse who was kissed on V-J Day, 1945, in Times Square. After all, even Alfred Eisenstaedt said she was the one.

16

LIFE'S INVITATION

In August 1980, *LIFE* magazine organized a V-J Day reunion. Philip B. Kunhardt Jr., *LIFE*'s managing editor, thought it would be fun[1] to unite the nurse and sailor from the photo journal's most cherished image, thirty-five years after Eisenstaedt captured the renowned kiss. Kunhardt had the nurse. He needed the sailor. His invitation read as follows:

> Usually the actors in such fleeting real-life pageants remain anonymous. For 34 years Eisie had no idea who either participant was. But recently the nurse stepped forward and identified herself. You will meet her in our Camera at Work section in this issue—as well as some of the other war-weary people Eisenstaedt photographed that August day 35 years ago this month.
>
> Now, if the sailor can recognize himself, would he please step forward?[2]

He did. So did many others. More guests arrived than *LIFE* anticipated. To make matters worse, most overstayed their welcome. Some never left. While clearly a number of respondents had no business coming forward, *LIFE* should have anticipated the party crashers.

On V-J Day, August 14, 1945, friends kissed friends, husbands kissed wives, and sailors kissed nurses. Arguably, more people kissed on that day than on any other in history. Owing to sheer volume, distinguishing a photographed V-J Day kiss in San Francisco, California, from another in Minneapolis, Minnesota, or Times Square, New York, requires familiarity with each picture's surrounding geographic landmarks. The *LIFE* issue that focused on V-J Day celebrations caught enough kissing couples in the act for Dorothy Burkhart to write a letter to the editor suggesting the magazine change its name to "Love."[3]

Other magazines and newspapers also shared images of V-J Day couples with their readership. A few of those publications selected pictures snapped in Times Square, and for good reason. On August 14, 1945, probably more people kissed at that crossroads than at any other place in the world. In that specific section of New York, tens of thousands of revelers in the early afternoon swelled to well over a million partygoers by night. V-J Day pictures and films of Times Square show that just about everyone replicated a facsimile of Eisenstaedt's couple, or at least it seemed so. By the end of the day, no kiss stood out for acknowledgement—well, except for that one particular picture, of that one explicit kiss, performed by that specific couple whose color contrast, body configurations, and tangible passion forever expressed the relief and elation that World War II was over.

Interestingly, and perhaps predictably, more male suitors petitioned *LIFE* for the sailor's part in Eisenstaedt's iconic photograph than did female candidates for the nurse's role. One reason for the gender imbalance might be that *LIFE* invited only sailors to come forward. And, of course, that made sense. The magazine already recognized Edith Shain as the nurse. Another reason for the discrepancy in male and female applicant numbers could be feminine modesty, and sailors' lack thereof. After all, social norms suggest he gets to be a hell of a guy. She may get tagged with something a bit less flattering. But with all these contributing factors in place, the biggest reason accounting for the respondent gender gap might be the historical circumstance in August 1945. During that summer, many American servicemen enjoyed leave as the military made preparations for an invasion of Japan. This arrangement most certainly upped significantly the number of sailors in Times Square on August 14. Relatively speaking, caregivers were in short supply.

While circumstances and conditions determined one gender coming forward in greater numbers than the other, the situation did not affect the degree of insistence expressed by male and female applicants. In this arena, no gender gap exists. Responding sailor and nurse candidates *knew* they had a part in the famous photo. And they said so repeatedly and vehemently.

The sheer number of kissers increased the odds that a sailor or nurse might see themselves in the famed photo. But what details does the photo really hold? *V-J Day, 1945, Times Square* reveals little in the way of distinguishing facial features. The photographer's vantage point and the pictured couple's pose work together to conceal what might otherwise be telling traits. The viewer cannot determine a nose's exact length, an eye's precise shape, or the curvature of lips. Further, the sequence of pictures limits the view to the duration of the entanglement. No snapshots exist before or after the encounter. With no interviews, follow-ups, or written notes of the event, there is little with which to base identification.

Incongruously, the lack of available details about *V-J Day, 1945, Times Square* does not preclude people from consideration, but rather encourages persons of almost every physical composition to draw themselves into the picture. What is distinguishable in the picture—a tall, Caucasian sailor in a dark uniform with no indication of rank kissing a shorter nurse dressed in white with her hair tied up—resembles a host of sailors and nurses. If a sailor wore a formal blue uniform, ran through Times Square on V-J Day, 1945, and kissed a woman in a white dress, he can legitimately claim a part in one of the nation's most celebrated and revered photographs. The prospect of a leading role in the iconographic photo could seduce an aging sailor's or nurse's memory to revisit what did, or did not, take place on that August 14, 1945, afternoon. They might deduce: "I was in Times Square when World War II ended. I wore my Navy uniform (or nurse uniform) that day. I kissed a lot of WACs, teachers, secretaries, and nurses—or sailors. It was a hell of a time. I remember the occurrence as if it were just yesterday." But, of course, the photo was not taken yesterday. Well over a half-century has passed. Both photographers—Alfred Eisenstaedt and Victor Jorgensen—are dead. Only murky memories, contentious claims, and a processed role of film remain.

With limited substantiated evidence, but many eager applicants in waiting, *LIFE*'s 1980 invitation opened the floodgates. Former sailors from various geographic points rushed forward spouting their cases. The outpouring of candidates created a crowded pool of testimonies to wade through. In this teeming sea of competing and often conflicting "evidence," the sailors' and nurses' splashing made for a slippery deck, and one where *LIFE* officials needed to sort out authentic versions from red herrings. And for a time the magazine executives tried to do that.[4] However, after reading and listening to persistent petitioners' claims for several weeks, *LIFE* could not tell for sure which petitioner was the real kissing sailor. They determined that the mystery of who kissed whom would have to persist.

But even with an acknowledging nod to the choppy waters, the magazine performed their lifeguard duties miserably. Abruptly, *LIFE* turned away from the chaos and controversy they had put in motion. The trusted photo journal held no concluding ceremony and provided no closure. Instead, they threw their hands up, as if raising a white flag to an enemy that did not exist. Rather than investigating competing claims thoroughly and determining whose story and evidence deserved another hearing, they left the public drowning in competing testimonies. The magazine simply left matters floating.

This "ending" caused a problem. What was to be done with the sailors and home front nurses who had come forward in good faith? *LIFE* acted decisively on this front. In essence, they called everyone out of the pool. However, the sailors and nurses refused to leave. *LIFE* management then drained the water, leaving would-be competitive swimmers to sweat it out in a cement basin beneath the burning sun of public curiosity. Perhaps *LIFE* expected the swimmers to dry up and blow away. If that was the plan, *LIFE* sorely underestimated their fighting spirit. The

World War II sailors and home front civilians had persevered through the financial miseries of the Great Depression and survived the most destructive war the world had ever known. If need be, they had the stamina to prevail in a prolonged battle with a *magazine*. Unbeknownst to *LIFE*, the contest they sponsored had just begun.

17

I'M THE REAL KISSING SAILOR

Philip B. Kunhardt's reaction to the surge of kissing sailor claimants resembled a beachgoer trying to catch a wave much bigger than anticipated. Realizing the enormity of the task before him, *LIFE*'s managing editor probably decided from the outset to sidestep the cresting sea of testimonies. Perhaps he hoped the formation would crash under its own weight and get dragged back to the ocean's depths. Whatever his reasoning, the initially promising invitation turned into a sad spectacle where proud sailors waded out to sea in hopes of an affirmative call-out. *LIFE* proved practically mute.

The kissing sailor candidates proved to be anything but speechless or shy. Of course, some of the sailors' testimonies read more convincingly than others. Truman E. Sjerven of Wyoming, Minnesota, may win the prize for the least-persuasive written claim in 1980: "I was in New York on V-J Day. I was assigned to the *Valencia*. We were waiting for our ship to be completed to ship out. Every time I see that picture I tell everyone that's me. I remember grabbing the nurse and kissing her. I thought many times of writing to tell you. Now that she has come forward, you probably will receive many letters from sailors saying they are the ones. I don't have any proof, but I know it's me. There's no doubt in my mind."[1] While confident, Sjerven's assertions suffered from lack of evidence.

Other former sailors augmented their stories with interesting twists, explanations, résumé-like inclusions, and even con-

97

fessions. However, most of these petitions also lacked convincing verifications. Consider the offerings of A. C. Johnson of Staten Island, New York, to *LIFE* magazine:

> The day after V-J Day, being a young, inquisitive, red-blooded sailor, I headed up to Times Square. I had been there only a short while when my friend and myself were talking to two young, what we thought to be, student nurses. One thing led to another and I embraced the attractive young nurse who had been on duty V-J Day when Times Square came alive. I recall a photographer taking pictures and it was at that point, after the kiss, I blushed. I remember the grand-mother-type lady in the back-ground. I also remember distinctly that for some reason I did not want to touch the girl's head.
>
> When the next issue of *LIFE* came out, I saw the picture and was sure it was me. However, having just become engaged and feeling discretion was the better part of valor, I did not mention it to my fiancée. But as time went on my reluctance to tell my story of "my Times Square kiss" diminished. Wouldn't any young or old sailor, soldier, aviator, or Marine have done the same thing? I am now a gray-haired grandfather and vice-president of an international insurance brokerage firm who still feels that the best 15 years of my life were between 35 and 40.[2]

Whether or not the red-blooded sailor blushed, did not want to touch the girl's head, noticed a grandmother-type lady in the background, or recalls a photographer taking pictures, that he arrived in Times Square the day *after* V-J Day precludes him from consideration as the sailor in *V-J Day, 1945, Times Square*.

Some claimants added entertaining considerations but offered little in the way of sway-factor. Thomas Huff of Lake City, Florida, was stationed at Floyd Bennett Field in Brooklyn, New York. Speaking of the famous photographed incident, Huff said, "At the time I had a cold and I remember the nurse telling me after I kissed her, 'Maybe I'll have to give you a shot for that.'" Huff added, "I always wore my hat like that."[3]

Some of the sailors who came forward would tower over the nurse in Eisenstaedt's photo. In a letter to *LIFE*'s editor, Fred

Streck indicated that he stood at six feet, five inches. He added that he normally rolled up his sleeves and that he was "amorous."[4] He could have added "assertive" to his self-description.

Like Streck, other claimants referenced their height, as well, but in a more southerly direction. James Kearney, a refrigerator mechanic at Harvard University, allowed that while he stood only five feet, eight inches, on "that day I felt ten feet tall!"[5] A particularly comical offering in LIFE magazine involved a short, confessing sailor and his rather candid wife: "When Wallace C. Fowler confessed to his wife that he was the exuberant sailor, she retorted that that sailor appeared to be, well, taller. 'Consequently,' says the five-foot-seven Fowler, 55 of Tampa, Fla., 'I perished the thought.' But the blissful memory lingered. Fowler hit upon an explanation for the apparent discrepancy: 'I realized that the angle of the camera could give a taller impression.'"[6] Presumably a *much* taller impression.

Some 1980 LIFE petitioners referenced physical characteristics in their letters. Clarence "Bud" Harding called attention to his hairline, which came to a distinctive-enough point at the temple to separate him from other pursuers of the kissing sailor title.[7] Jack Russell, a fifty-four-year-old psychologist in Whittier, California, referenced his "unusual left-handed kissing clutch."[8] Other sailors writing to LIFE added explanations for their behavior. Donald Bonsack of Germantown, New York, wrote, "I lived with this for so long, I guess I can take it. I had a rate on my right arm but I had lost it for insubordination—which I won't go into. I was a hell raiser then."[9] Another former sailor, Bill Swicegood, included information for betting men. "Looks exactly like I looked—the hands, the body, everything."[10] The odds are on his side, too. Swicegood, a fifty-five-year-old Kansas City, Missouri, artist in 1980 explained, "I must have kissed a thousand women that day in Times Square." Many sailors boast similar exaggerated totals of that August 14 day of willing women and eased inhibitions.

Apparently Marvin Kingsbury of Round Lake Beach, Illinois, a school custodian, did not run into Bill Swicegood kissing a "thousand women." Kingsbury offered of his ardent behavior, "I was the only one on the street who did anything like that just then."[11] While that seems unlikely, he added that he encouraged his three friends: "The first girls we come to, grab 'em and kiss 'em." In a picture Kingsbury sent to *LIFE* to demonstrate his technique, he grips a woman in a bear hug. While the pictured grasp he sent to *LIFE* differs from that photographed by Eisenstaedt on August 14, 1945, early on Kingsbury gained a lion's share of recognition.

Not every person claiming to be the sailor or nurse in Eisenstaedt's *V-J Day, 1945, Times Square* responded to *LIFE*'s invitation in August 1980. Some of the most celebrated, persistent, and well-supported suitors gained considerable notoriety years later. But whether they came forward in 1980, 1988, or 1995, they all had two things in common: their claim's punch line, followed by *LIFE*'s disregard. The rest of this chapter offers the consideration they sought.

BLESSED WAS HE

George Byron Koch, pastor of the Church of the Resurrection in West Chicago, Illinois, bestowed forgiveness and maybe sanctity to Jim Reynolds' claim as the kissing sailor. Koch did not keep Reynolds' digressions secret—far from it. He sent a letter about the matter to the *Wall Street Journal*, which published the offering on August 14, 1986. Reynolds' confession makes for interesting consideration.

According to Pastor Koch, Mary Ann Reynolds, Jim Reynolds' newlywed wife, recognized *her* Jim in Alfred Eisenstaedt's photo when it first appeared in the August 27, 1945, issue of *LIFE*. As she peered at the full-page picture of Jim with his arms wrapped around another woman, she wondered how that could be possible. She and Jim married prior to V-J Day, 1945. Further, *her* Jim insisted that the sailor could not be him, as he was in San Jose, California, on V-J Day. While she (and Jim's mother) wanted to believe him, undeniably Jim resembled the sailor in Eisenstaedt's picture.

In truth, Jim Reynolds did celebrate V-J Day in California. However, that geographic reference does not necessarily clear him of a part in Eisenstaedt's photo. Reynolds celebrated New York's V-E Day (Victory in Europe, May 8, 1945) when New Yorkers and the rest of the world welcomed news of the Allies' victory in World War II's European theater. Pastor Koch (and others over the years) claimed that the evidence suggesting Eisenstaedt snapped his famous picture on V-E Day is right in the photo. According to informants, the formal, blue, Navy uniforms worn by most sailors in the photo were standard dress in May, but not in August. Pastor Koch charged that *LIFE* conveniently pulled the picture from their files of V-E Day and used the photo for their August 27, 1945, segment entitled *Victory Celebrations*. Pastor Koch explained his thinking in this excerpt from the *Wall Street Journal* article:

> On May 8, Signalman 2nd Class James Reynolds had just landed from England after release from the hospital. In Times Square a photographer named Eisenstaedt asked him to pose with a young woman in a nurse's uniform. Jim demurred; he was engaged to Mary Ann, and it wouldn't be right. The photographer persisted, promised to keep him anonymous, even to hide his signalman's crossed flags. Would he please help out? Shy and very reluctant, but always ready to help out, he agreed. Eisenstaedt posed the two of them carefully, even positioning their hands, the angle of their bodies, the position of their lips, the clutching of the purse and skirt.[12]

Koch's story caused quite a stir with the public and fascinated the media. Reynolds made the rounds on *Good Morning America*, *Fox in the Morning*, and many other television and radio programs.[13] His story was also carried in many newspapers. The signalman's concealed crossed flags, the wearing of formal blues in August, and the dramatic pose of the sailor and nurse cast serious doubt on the photograph's reported anonymity, timing, and captured spontaneity. To this day, Jim Reynolds' story of the kissing sailor and *LIFE*'s deceptive practices continues to fascinate curious *V-J Day, 1945, Times Square* viewers.

FLASHES WERE GOING OFF EVERYWHERE

As a model and an actor, Ken McNeel knows well how to strike an attention-getting pose. Perhaps he saved his best form for Times Square on the day World War II ended. Of that day, he insists he is the Coast Guard seaman in *V-J Day, 1945, Times Square*. McNeel's explanations and proof convince many of his claim as *the* kissing sailor.

Just ask Chris Palmer. He is so taken by Ken McNeel's version of events that he created a website to promote the telling. The address, http://www.kissingsailor.com, reveals the site's purpose. The information contained at the website makes a convincing case for Ken McNeel's part in V-J *Day, 1945, Times Square*.

One of the site's links directs the web-surfer to another, somewhat-related endeavor—selling authentic *LIFE* magazines. Palmer first learned of Ken McNeel during a discussion with a woman who placed an order from *Chris' Old Life Magazines*. He found the claim credible enough to pursue the lead. After several interviews with McNeel and an in-depth analysis of both Alfred Eisenstaedt's and Lt. Victor Jorgensen's photos, Palmer concluded that Ken McNeel is the real kissing sailor.

Ken McNeel was stationed on Ellis Island on August 14, 1945. Hearing the news that World War II had ended, he ventured to Times Square to celebrate. Prior to entering 7th Avenue, McNeel rolled up his uniform sleeves to conceal the Coast Guard insignia on his cuffs. He wanted everyone to think he was in the Navy. He felt that association gave him a higher ranking in the eyes of the general public. This point holds more importance than one might initially think. Eisenstaedt's sailor has no Navy chevron on his right shoulder. The omission requires an explanation. McNeel's accounting possesses credibility and comes across as self-effacing.

With friend Buddy Andrew (situated to his right in the kissing sailor photo), Ken McNeel made his way through Times Square among throngs of people who gathered to celebrate the news of Japan's surrender to the United States. McNeel entered

Times Square not to pursue peace, but rather revelry and home-front women—nurses included.

At some point during the celebration, Alfred Eisenstaedt, a "short guy" with a camera, said to Ken, "Young man, go over and grab the first girl out of the subway and I will make you famous." Years later, Ken recounted: "Two nurses were coming up out of the subway hand-in-hand laughing. I grabbed the first one who was quite unaware and said, 'Let's kiss.' The nurse replied 'OH!' She didn't know me and was astounded. . . . Her legs were crossed and her arms were at her side. Flashes were going off everywhere from all of the cameras. I just closed my eyes and got such a grip! . . . Later I talked to her and she said, 'I just sort of laid back and surrendered.'"[14]

McNeel's commentary sets him apart from other popular claimants in several significant ways. First, McNeel remembers more than one photographer taking pictures of him as he kissed a nurse in Times Square on August 14, 1945. His claim is verifiable. *LIFE* magazine's Alfred Eisenstaedt and Navy lieutenant Victor Jorgenson both shot pictures of the embrace. Interestingly, most other kissing sailor claimants have no recollection of any photographers. Another claimant insists there was only one photographer. Only McNeel suggests the presence of more than one person taking pictures.

Second, McNeel is the only claimant who speaks to a camera's flashes during the event. His reporting makes for noteworthy consideration. The two photographers took a total of five pictures. Therefore, a potential exists for at least five flashes of light within several seconds. Such an occurrence emanating from two locations would make for a startling spectacle that would account for McNeel's unique claim that "flashes were going off everywhere." Further, these flashes help explain why so many direct their attention to the photographed couple. A camera's flash draws attention.

Third, McNeel speaks to the photographer's specific directions prior to taking the picture. One can appreciate the considerable staging necessary to create such an eye-popping pose.

Such preparations help explain the picture's wonderful symmetry. Further, no one crosses in front of the scene's director, who also serves as one of the cameramen. This is notable, particularly when one considers all the movement recorded in the background of Eisenstaedt's four photos.

Fourth, rather than rushing off after the kiss, McNeel spoke with the nurse. This behavior is in keeping with what one might expect immediately after terminating a passionate embrace and kiss. Though McNeel established no long-term contact with the woman he held, they at least acknowledged one another. It is difficult to believe, as some claimants suggest, that the two engrossed individuals did not at least look to one another after finishing the interchange. McNeel's version of events plays realistically.

According to McNeel, shortly after the encounter, the nurse and her girlfriend departed. McNeel did not think about the incident again until Buddy Andrew pointed out the picture to him, at which time he realized, "That's me!" When McNeel later heard of *LIFE's* search for the kissing sailor, he held back his claim. His "unacceptable" behavior in that photo ran counter to the teachings of a church he belonged to at the time.[15] McNeel's unease accounts for his late entry as the kissing sailor.

While the exposure of McNeel's actions in Times Square on August 14, 1945, embarrassed the Coast Guard seaman, the same cannot be said of his immediate pursuits thereafter. In 1946 McNeel accepted a modeling assignment for a *True Magazine* piece about sex in a car. As Chris Palmer argued, McNeel's *True Magazine* shoot showcases a compelling likeness between him and *LIFE* magazine's kissing sailor. Their head shape appears the same, their cheeks pucker in similar fashion, their cheekbones form high just below the eye sockets, and the curvature of their hairlines follows the same path. The cross-referencing of kissing sailor pictures from Eisenstaedt and Jorgenson to the civilian picture of Ken McNeel approximately one year later suggests identicalness.

Ken McNeel's physical evidence and related details firmly anchor his claim to a part in Alfred Eisenstaedt's and Lt. Victor Jorgensen's pictures from Times Square on V-J Day, 1945. McNeel looks like the kissing sailor. His story accounts for many aspects of the famous V-J Day photo that other candidates' recollections do not. Even at the cost of marginalizing himself, McNeel provides a realistic, persuasive, and endearing story of the kissing sailor.

17-1. This photograph of Ken McNeel, taken approximately one year after *V-J Day, 1945, Times Square*, suggests a strong likeness to the kissing sailor in Eisenstaedt's famous photograph.

EVEN EDITH SHAIN THINKS SO

Many herald Carl Muscarello's claim to the kissing sailor. Evidence supporting his connection to *V-J Day, 1945, Times Square* persuades skeptics. In addition, his claim earned the approval of Edith Shain, the recognized nurse in Eisenstaedt's photo, and the most sought-after personal endorsement. Further, his story resonates well with the public.

Born to Sicilian parents on a kitchen table in Brooklyn, New York, Carl Muscarello joined the Navy shortly after his eighteenth birthday. On that day his father handed him ten dollars and a pint of whiskey and told him to take care of himself.[16] Heeding his father's advice proved relatively easy. Carl never shipped out to battle. He would not set foot on the USS *Orion*, a *Fulton*-class submarine tender, until October 1945.[17]

On August 14, 1945, Muscarello worked with a ship repair unit on Staten Island. Even though he was far removed from harm's way, the Japanese surrender provided him with cause for celebration. Unlike many other sailors who heard the news an ocean's distance from home, Carl was a short walk and a subway fare away from his boyhood stomping grounds.

With the announcement of Japan's surrender, Muscarello and other workers were granted a seventy-two-hour leave. He left the base with friend Eddie Leiskie and set out for Manhattan to pay tribute to the American victory.[18] While Carl normally had a self-imposed two-drink limit, that August day did not lend itself to moderation. How could it? His uniform inspired generous offerings from appreciative civilians. After downing several times his drink limit, Carl continued toward Times Square where the celebration grew exponentially.

When Muscarello arrived in Times Square, it seemed to him everyone was kissing. As he ran excitedly down 7th Avenue he took the opportunity to join in, grabbing and kissing several women. One of those women, he recalled, wore a nurse's white uniform. She had little choice but to acquiesce to the tall, dark, blue-uniformed Navy man during her nation's triumphant moment. Of that encounter Muscarello remembers, "I saw Edith and she looked very appealing, so I went to her and planted a hug and a kiss."[19] In another interview, he clarified, "I made sure I did not grope her or take any liberties I wouldn't want anybody to take with my sisters."[20] In keeping with the physicality of his introduction, he exchanged no words with the nurse. Carl knew a photographer had followed him around during his escapades in Times Square, and he was aware that "someone" had taken a picture of his encounter with a nurse.[21] Immediately following the kiss, Muscarello felt "breathless."[22]

According to Muscarello's telling, after the kiss he boarded a subway home to his parents' Brooklyn residence. Soon, Muscarello's exhilarating experience changed. While walking with Leiskie through his old stomping grounds, Muscarello noticed that the blue service star in the window of a friend's house had been replaced with a gold one. The switch communicated a change from active military duty to death resulting from the war. His childhood friend, Joe Toscano, had fought and died on the beaches at Normandy. While Muscarello had feared the loss of his friend months earlier, the gold star in the Toscano's front window confirmed his worry. In total, six boyhood friends from his old Brooklyn neighborhood never made it home from World War II. While on that August 14, 1945, evening Americans across the country continued to rejoice in the war's victorious conclusion, for Muscarello news of Toscano's death overwhelmed him. His V-J Day celebration ended abruptly.

While Carl never forgot that August, 14, 1945, walk through his childhood neighborhood, if his mother had not flipped through a *LIFE* magazine at a doctor's office two weeks later, one wonders if Carl would ever have recognized himself in Eisenstaedt's photo. But his mother, Maria Grazia Attenillo Muscarello, spotted her son, the kissing sailor, on page 27 of that August 27, 1945, magazine. According to Carl, she noticed his birthmark on the back of the kissing sailor's right hand.[23] Staining the back of his hand, the discoloration present at birth and once mistaken as dirt by a grammar school teacher serves as a key component to Muscarello's claim as the kissing sailor.

Upon determining the sailor in *LIFE*'s photograph to be her son, Maria had serious concerns. When Carl called his mother from Panama in February 1946 (he had not spoken with his mother since shortly after V-J Day), Maria communicated those worries. With the *LIFE* magazine picture vividly clear in her mind, she scolded, "Don't you know you shouldn't be kissing strange women? You'll get a disease." Carl tried to assure his mother the lady he kissed was a nurse. She responded, "They're the worst kind, always around sick people."[24] Detecting the seriousness of his mother's tone, he assured her that he would be more careful in the future.

From 1946 to 1995 Carl shared the news of his part in Eisenstaedt's picture only with family and some close friends. He did not come forward when *LIFE* magazine invited all suitors to do so in 1980 because he was working in South America for American Express and did not know of the publication's inquiry into the matter.[25] Not until 1988 did Carl contact *LIFE* regarding his claim. Another former sailor's lawsuit against *LIFE* for their use of his person for profit in the kissing sailor photo caused him to do so. According to Muscarello, upon receiving his letter, the photo journal responded that fifty others had come forward making the same claim. However, something about Muscarello's case must have caught the publication's attention. They inquired as to how Muscarello could be so sure he was in Eisenstaedt's picture. Muscarello wrote back and explained several factors that supported his conclusion and said that he would come to New York at his own expense to discuss the matter. He stressed that he sought no money or notoriety and only wanted the truth to be known. *LIFE* never responded.[26]

In 1995 Muscarello finally came forward publicly to state his role in *LIFE*'s most popular photo. During that same year, Edith Shain, contacted by a lawyer friend of Muscarello's, called Carl to discuss the matter. She had never recognized any claimant as the former sailor who kissed her on August 14, 1945. Later in 1995, Carl visited Shain at her home in California. During that meeting she asked Carl several questions about his claimed participation in the famous kiss. Shain tried to get Muscarello to commit to a version of the story she knew to be false. She asked him why he never called her after she gave him her number. She asked why he had not returned her calls. She wanted Carl to recall what he said to her after they kissed. Carl responded to Edith's questions succinctly and confidently. He told Shain he never got her number and that she had never called him. Further, he explained, they said nothing to one another before or after the kiss. Muscarello's responses to Shain were far different than other campaigning sailors' comments. For years they had sought Shain's endorsement as the sailor that kissed her on August 14, 1945, in Times Square. When Carl finished answering her questions, Shain reacted excitedly. She jumped around the room. Realizing that she had finally met the sailor who kissed her all those years ago, she exclaimed, "You're the one!"[27] Considering her status among all claimants, nurses and sailors alike, Shain's 1995 determination provides powerfully persuasive evidence of Carl Muscarello's claim to the kissing sailor's identity.

Further bolstering Muscarello's standing among other would-be kissing sailors are Alfred Eisenstaedt's remembrances of the V-J Day kiss. Over the years the *LIFE* photographer reported his August 14, 1945, memories of an assertive sailor running in Times Square, kissing many women of all sizes, shapes, and ages. Suddenly at his back, Eisenstaedt noticed the sailor grab something white.[28] When he spun around, he saw the sailor he had tracked embracing and kissing a nurse. Eisenstaedt fired off four pictures. Even though Eisenstaedt and Muscarello never spoke to one another about the happening, their telling of the event is virtually identical. No other sailor can make that claim.

Owing to his story's credibility and palpability, many media outlets (the *Today Show*, *Good Morning America*, and *The Late, Late, Show* with Tom Snyder) pursued Muscarello, eager to hear the behind-the-scenes details from the sailor in the best position to enlighten them.[29] Part of the reason so many sources support Muscarello's claim to be the kissing sailor springs from his delivery, which adds persuasiveness to convincing proof. He is respectful, humble, and gentleman-like. He appears often at charitable and civic events, usually dressed in Navy dress blues or a suit and tie. At these functions, Muscarello gains disciples to his version of events, that he was the sailor kissing Edith Shain in Times Square at the end of World War II. Carl has an ability to confirm believers' faith or convert doubters and detractors into followers and fans. A letter from an impressed schoolteacher, Eugene C. Cunningham of Plantation, Florida, provides evidence of Muscarello's charm and articulateness:

> Carl spent a good 30 minutes talking about this photo, and how he managed to end up in this photo. "If you were in uniform that day, you were gonna get kissed by a hundred girls!" to the laughter of everyone. "Mr. Muscarello," I asked, "did you ever know anyone who was killed in World War II?" Carl stood still for about a minute, turning red, with tears welling up in his eyes, while my entire class . . . sat in utter silence, some of them also with tears in their eyes. "Gene," Carl responded, "all my friends I knew growing up were killed, every one!" Then he gave his response, with

great effort, choking and sobbing as he answered. "All my buddies from Brooklyn, all the guys that hung out on the stoops and lied about girlfriends they didn't have, all my friends, ALL of them, were killed!" and listed a long line of very Italian names, one after another, and where they were killed: "so-and-so, killed in the Bulge, and so-and-so killed at Iwo Jima" and on and on.

As Carl named these friends, he walked around my classroom, pointing to students, saying, "so-and-so, killed in Germany, so you don't have to speak German . . . so-and-so killed at such and such island in the Pacific, so you don't have to speak Japanese . . . and so-and-so, killed so you can come to this Catholic school and worship as you wish."[30]

In the remainder of the letter Mr. Cunningham continues to extol Muscarello's virtues. "And of course Carl stayed and signed more than 60 photos, all personalized, and all paid for from his own pocket." Cunningham believes many of his Cuban students "became Americans that day." At the very least, owing in part to Muscarello's demeanor, dress, and delivery, they certainly became believers of Muscarello's part in the *V-J Day, 1945, Times Square* kiss.

Muscarello's presentation of amassed evidence sways people to his version of events. His birthmark, his memory's alignment with Eisenstaedt's recollections, and the recognition conferred by Edith Shain supply the most convincing fortifications for the former sailor's part in the *V-J Day, 1945, Times Square* photograph. To this day, Carl Muscarello continues to be considered seriously as the kissing sailor in one of history's most beloved photographs.

HE NEVER LIES

Glenn McDuffie is the most seriously considered kissing sailor candidate. Newspapers print stories about him. Television programs feature him. The Houston Astros introduced him to an enthusiastic crowd as the real kissing sailor. Well-credentialed sources earnestly back his story of that famous kiss. At speaking engagements, his audiences find him endearing. How could they not? He presents his case colorfully, comically, and credibly. Of all the kissing sailor petitioners, he draws the most national attention.

Born and raised in Kannapolis, North Carolina, Glenn McDuffie served as a Navy gunner's mate from 1943 to 1946. McDuffie was only fifteen years old when he enlisted in 1943. To get past Navy personnel screeners, he convinced a friend to forge his parents' signatures and get the paperwork notarized.[31] Working on cargo ships during the war, he and his crew delivered magnesium ore to the United States from Cuba, and later in 1944 they transported five-hundred pound bombs, small arms, and mustard gas. As the war approached its end, in July 1945, McDuffie served on shore duty. In August he was granted a short leave and visited with his mother in Kannapolis. On August 14 he set out to Brooklyn, New York. He wanted to meet up with Ardith Bloomfield, a red-headed girlfriend he had met earlier.[32]

On his way to Brooklyn, McDuffie stopped off at Manhattan's 42nd Street subway stop. As he climbed up the stairs to Times Square a female passerby said to him, "Sailor, I'm so happy for you." McDuffie inquired as to the reason for her animated expression and good wishes. The woman replied, "The war's over and you can go home."[33] Upon hearing the news, Glenn first thought of his brother, Willie Durant McDuffie, who had been captured and forced into a Japanese prisoner-of-war camp after the infamous Bataan Death March.[34] Overtaken by the thought of a family reunion, Glenn McDuffie ran into the street jumping and hollering. Fewer than fifty feet from the subway stairwell, a nurse beckoned him with open arms. Caught up in the excitement, he rushed over to the welcoming nurse, "tipped her back," and "kissed that woman for as long as I thought I should."[35]

McDuffie's commentaries about the V-J Day kiss are numerous and humorous. A collection of his utterances could serve as a documentary narrative starring Eisenstaedt's *V-J Day, 1945, Times Square* photo. From interview to interview, his reporting of the photographed event offers interesting considerations. "It was a good kiss. It was a wet kiss. . . . Someone asked me if it was a tongue kiss. I said, 'No tongue, but it was a nice kiss.'"[36] "She had the biggest mouth I ever kissed."[37] "We never spoke a word. . . . Afterward, I just went on the subway across the street and went to Brooklyn."[38] McDuffie's tale resonates with a curious public.

And his story amounts to much more than a barrel of laughs. Illustrated proof provides powerful testimony corroborating his story. Lois Gibson, the esteemed forensic artist from Houston, Texas, completed a detailed investigation in 2006 and concluded, "Glenn McDuffie is the swabbie that kissed the nurse that celebrated the war was over."[39] She is positive "beyond a shadow of a doubt" of Glenn's part in Eisenstaedt's photo.[40]

People take Lois Gibson's assertions seriously. They should. She sports impressive credentials, high-profile accomplishments, and gains the attention of national media outlets. She teaches at Northwestern University and has authored *Forensic Art Essentials: A Manual for Law Enforcement Artists*, and *Faces of Evil* (with Deanie Mills). In 2005 the Guinness Book of World Records announced that Gibson assisted in identifying more suspects than any other forensic artist in history. In 2007 Gibson helped crack the widely publicized Baby Grace case. She has appeared on *Dateline NBC*, *The CBS Early Show*, and in Oprah's magazine, *O*.[41] Her forthright presentation style persuades listeners. Certainly, Glenn McDuffie would be hard-pressed to find a better spokesperson for his claim to be the kissing sailor.

Gibson's confident conclusions stem from a thorough study of Glen McDuffie, Alfred Eisenstaedt's four photographs, and Lt. Victor Jorgensen's single picture. Gibson took pictures of Glenn McDuffie replicating the kissing sailor pose with a pillow substituting for the nurse. She then measured body parts and markings, scaled them to the sailor's hat in the kissing sailor photo, and made comparisons. Gibson found so many similarities that she is "positive" McDuffie and the kissing sailor are the same person. She stresses, "I don't say this lightly. . . . What I do is usually a matter of life and death, so I don't mess around when I identify someone."[42]

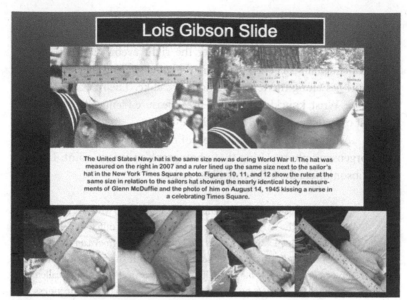

17-2. (*Permission granted by Lois Gibson*)

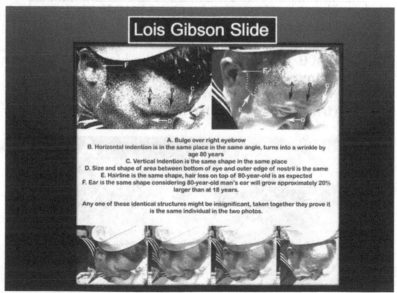

17-3. (*Permission granted by Lois Gibson*)

Gibson shoots out the likenesses between the kissing sailor and McDuffie with machine-gun velocity. McDuffie and the kissing sailor have a bulge over the right eyebrow. Their eye shapes are similar. Their noses are the same size and shape. Their hairlines along the temple regions are alike. Their ears are the same. Wrist, knuckle, and hand sizes measure identically. The hit list of matches can overpower the reviewer.

Another piece of Gibson's proof can be viewed in Lt. Victor Jorgensen's photo. Using that photograph's vantage point, Lois Gibson offers the following observation:

> The sailor shows a groove on the left side of his skull which runs diagonally from the hairline climbing down toward the outer, upper edge of the eyebrow. That sailor does *not have that same groove on the right side of his skull*. I have never seen anyone with this kind of groove on one side *and not the other*. Those grooves on the skull are called "keeling" like the keel on a boat, there are many variances of deepness and placement of these keelings on various individual's skulls. I saw

The sailor from the August 14, 1945 photo has a diagonal ridge on his skull, A, that originates from a midpoint of his eyebrow at B. Glenn McDuffie has the identical bony ridge on his skull that originates at the same location of his eyebrow and travels up his skull at an identical angle.

17-4. (*Permission granted by Lois Gibson*)

this same trait on Glenn. In an effort to be certain, I asked him if I could feel the groove on his left side and the smooth area on his right side. Sure enough, even though it is not so easy to see with the age spots, it is very easy, unmistakable to FEEL the groove on the left, and the LACK of the groove on the right.[43]

Like many of Gibson's conclusions, not only does her point about "keelings" confirm McDuffie's part in the famous photo, she uses the findings to exclude other claimants from further consideration as the kissing sailor. Lois Gibson's study in support of McDuffie's claims commands respect. When presented in rapid-fire motion, the barrage of evidence and confirmations delivers a most convincing case. McDuffie remains the most seriously considered candidate for the notoriety he and other former sailors seek.

■　■　■　■

All the renditions of that August 14, 1945, afternoon kiss in Times Square, New York, touch a nerve and translate credibly. Maybe the picture does originate from V-E Day instead of V-J Day. Perhaps Glenn McDuffie did kiss a nurse with the largest mouth he ever encountered. Conceivably Carl Muscarello did have a few drinks too many and grabbed a nurse dressed in white. Possibly Ken McNeel did follow a photographer's directions and strike a pose for the ages. At some level, one wants to believe them all. And for the time being, it is most fitting to do just that.

18

FOR DISSEMINATION OF NEWS

From 1980 to 1987 George Mendonsa premised his claim as the kissing sailor on large hands, a likeness in appearance, and other interesting considerations. While George accumulated little evidence to support his assertion during those years, his certainty only increased. Others doubted his story. They needed more proof—a lot more.

In 1987 George hit a gusher. More proof sprung forth than would have been needed to convict him of a crime. While his newly supported case might persuade a judge and jury, he had to convince *LIFE*. That was not going to happen. *LIFE* made sure of it.

This evidence resulted from a lawsuit George Mendonsa brought against Time, Inc. In 1987 George learned of an ad running in *LIFE* charging $1,600 for *his* picture—signed by Alfred Eisenstaedt. Incensed by what George viewed as the latest slight from the national photo journal, he contacted a childhood friend who practiced law. His lawyer friend charged $900 to start legal action against *LIFE* for the use of George's likeness for the magazine's profit. The firm agreed to take the case, thinking it would bring favorable publicity to their Newport-based law firm. In George Mendosa v. Time Incorporated, the complainant sought compensatory damages and injunctive relief for "appropriation of likeness" for profit by Time, Inc. under Rhode Island general laws.[1] That is, Mendonsa alleged that Time, Inc. had used a picture of him in various publications and in a limited edition autographed print for their profit without seeking George's consent. With the law firm fulfilling the role of the USS *The Sullivans*, the former U.S. Navy petty officer first class again set out to do battle against a formidable opponent.

As George readied himself for the suit, lawyers for Time, Inc., entered a motion to dismiss the case on the grounds that New York courts had "consistently emphasized that activities involving the dissemination of news or information concerning matters of public interest are privileged and do not fall within the purposes of trade . . . despite the fact that they are carried on for profit." The New York courts had decided earlier in Gautier v. Pro-Football, Inc., that the use of a name or picture in a newspaper, magazine, or newsreel is not a use for "purposes of trade" within the meaning of the Civil Rights law.[2] Time, Inc., presented an interesting, clever, and problematic argument. Rather than arguing that George Mendonsa is not the kissing sailor, Time, Inc., sidestepped a core issue and argued another, far-off—but related—topic. In essence, they contended that once a product qualified as news, the labeling insulates its future use from financial liabilities incurred from other profit-seeking ventures. According to their reasoning, news, regardless of its future handling or use, always remains news. If upheld in court, the lesson would be to classify any picture one might wish to employ later for profit by first securing the label "news." Otherwise, be prepared to deal with the liabilities associated with most other profit-seeking publishing efforts.

The reasoning of Time, Inc., and the verdict of the New York Court still required adjudication in the Rhode Island Supreme Court. While that state court did accept *LIFE*'s August 27, 1945, publication of the kissing sailor photo as falling under the interpretation of the New York Court, they could not conclude their numerous future employments of the same photo had "significance" as news. Moreover, Time, Inc.'s recent attempt to sell the photograph in *LIFE* with Eisenstaedt's autograph for $1,600 clearly had a commercial purpose apart from the dissemination of news. The court further argued, "Whether these more recent uses functioned primarily as a means of commercial exploitation or served some other protected public interest is a matter that will have to be decided after a full development of the facts. At this stage, viewing the allegations in the light most favorable to the nonmoving party, it appears that plaintiff has adequately alleged that his picture was used for 'purposes of trade' within the meaning of Section 9-1-28. Consequently, Mendonsa has stated a cause of action under that statute."[3] Time, Inc., failed to have the suit dismissed. George Mendonsa had a case.

Though the courts were poised to hear the arguments, the case never went to trial. After Time, Inc.'s initial attempt to have the case dismissed failed, George's lawyer friend's partner took over the case. The partner's resolve soon waned. He advised George that even if he won the case, Time, Inc., would likely appeal and the proceedings could be extended for years. Extensions meant money—lots of money. George asked how much capital the firm wanted in order to take the case. The firm specified no monetary amount. George then made several offers to the Newport law practice. Wanting the recognition far more than any payout, George asked, "How about if we sue for two or three million dollars and you keep 90 percent?" His friend's partner said the firm would not take the case on a contingency basis. George upped his offer. "Would you take the case for $25,000?" The partner said, "No." George said, "How about $50,000?" Again, the firm responded, "No." George explained that he needed to know what they wanted or he would have to drop the case. Time, Inc., might have unlimited funds, but George and his wife, Rita, did not. When the law firm could not determine an approximate final cost, George had little choice but to drop the lawsuit. The settlement did not state if George was the kissing sailor. There was no exchange of money between Time, Inc., and George, and Mendonsa acknowledged that Time possessed a copyright to the V-J Day kissing sailor photo and could use the photo as they wished.[4]

While George did not share his thoughts about his friend's law firm, Anthony Bucolo, another childhood friend, proved more vocal concerning the firm's handling of George's case. Anthony grew up on the docks of Newport in the late 1940s. During those years Anthony looked up to George, twenty years his senior. Anthony described George as hard-working, honest, fair, and talkative. He did not repeat these descriptors when discussing the law firm's handling of George's case against Time, Inc. "I think George got screwed by them. He won't say it. But I will." According to Bucolo, once the firm determined that there would be a long, drawn-out case with no assured payoff, their interest could only be aligned with an amount George, a fisherman, could pay toward the case preparation fees. Time, Inc., had much deeper pockets than George and therefore could figuratively and financially run him out of Times Square. The Newport law firm wanted no part of such a retreat—at least not without a guaranteed, lucrative, and timely payout.

Though George did not lose the lawsuit he brought against Time, Inc., the undertaking did him more harm than good. For one, he garnered an unfair reputation for being motivated by money. He wanted only to be recognized. The principle was important, not the payout. Additionally, many people erroneously concluded he either lost the suit or did not have a case in the first place. Neither is correct. George Mendonsa had a case and a cause. He still does.

PART 4

THE CASE FOR GEORGE AND GRETA

But how do you know for really sure?

SIMONE VERRIA, AGE 12
Asked of her father, Summer 2008

19

THE FORENSICS

As *LIFE* would likely agree, one encounters many obstacles when trying to determine the kissers' identities in *V-J Day, 1945, Times Square*. Elaborate stories, conflicting evidence, and clever claims create a maze of pathways and dead ends. However, despite *LIFE's* inferences to the contrary, the sixty-five-year trail to who kissed whom in Alfred Eisenstaedt's *V-J Day, 1945, Times Square* remains well marked. Experts in the fields of photography, facial recognition, and forensic anthropology serve as competent guides capable of marching through terrain that prevents other parties from naming the actual kissing sailor in Alfred Eisenstaedt's and Victor Jorgensen's V-J Day, 1945, photos. When the findings from invested groups are employed in tandem, they light the way to the kissing sailor almost as brightly as a Times Square neon sign.

Many undervalue the most readily available means for determining the kissing sailor's identity: eyesight. Most of the persuasive considerations for determining the kissing sailor's identity appear in plain view. Even the novice onlooker can make reasonable assertions about resemblances and dissimilarities between the pictured kissing sailor and the numerous claimants who have come forward over the past thirty-plus years. But just in case one does not trust their own acumen, qualified experts in several fields have made critical contributions to determining the participants in Eisenstaedt's most famous photograph.

The historical record is helpful in placing *V-J Day, 1945, Times Square* within a larger and accurate context. The photo was one of four photographs shot by Alfred Eisenstaedt. Another photograph was shot by Lieutenant Jorgensen. These other photos, in conjunction with newspaper accounts, radio recordings, newsreels, witness testimonies, and many photographs of Times Square on August 14, 1945, provide a broader view of the kiss. When one examines all the kissing sailor claimants' remembrances against geographic references and factual historical information, some accounts hold up well. Others do not.

Recent advances in technology provide tremendous help in rendering positive identifications. The same equipment and skill that can help locate an abducted child years later also can aid researchers in identifying an adult couple from almost seventy years ago. Scientists who utilize the latest facial recognition technology applied their well-honed techniques to confirm the kissing sailor's identity.

Some of the most persuasive findings about the famous kissing couple emanate from forensic anthropologists. Their examination of bony structures and other physical characteristics are admissible in courts—and for good reason. Their evaluations rely on measurable evidence from the human body. Isolated from the persuasiveness of candidates' stories and likable personalities, one of the nation's premier physical anthropologists agreed to study the matter of the kissing sailor's identity. He did so without the benefit of the photographic, technological, and historical findings that preceded his undertaking. After a three-month study, his conclusions paralleled the other disciplines' findings.

Photographic analysis experts may provide the most important evidence for determining the identity of the kissing sailor and nurse. Their educated eyes can ascertain what photos actually show, as well as what they do not confirm. A verifiable inventory of photographic clues informs every other discipline's work. One of the nation's most highly regarded photo analysis experts studied all four of Eisenstaedt's V-J Day kissing sailor

photos, and Lt. Victor Jorgensen's one photograph. His report
might be the most persuasive evidence linking one of the claimants to the kissing sailor's identity.

When all the evidence—observable, historic, technological,
physical, and photographic—converges, the complete collection leads to a most enlightening conclusion. The revelation is
as eye-opening as it is verifiable and inescapable. After countless
hours of study over a three-decade time span, a dream team of
highly qualified scientists, a forensic anthropologist, and a photographic expert proved what *LIFE* could not—or would not.
George Mendonsa is the kissing sailor. He kissed Greta Zimmer.

20

YOU WANT TO BELIEVE
THEM ALL

Despite their differences, the sailors and nurses who seek a part in the famous V J Day kiss have more in common than they may realize. All deserve their nation's gratitude for honorable service in defense of their country, whether at war or on the home front. Further, and sadly, for the most part *LIFE* ignored each of their claims to a role in Eisenstaedt's photo. Endeavoring to prove their version of events, the claimants expended energy, time, and money. Some sacrificed dignity while others avoided a milieu that they judged took more than it offered. With the passing years, the former sailors, nurses, and one dental assistant lost a step or two. The celebrated kiss, which they insisted they played a part in, moved further into the past. Soon they no longer could keep pace with the chase. They have been done a great dishonor.

This chapter does not set out to humiliate further the claimants who seek a part in Eisenstaedt's famous photograph. But undoubtedly the arguments put forth in the following sections will not be well received by most of the petitioners still alive. Overturning the convictions and beliefs of veterans from Tom Brokaw's "Greatest Generation" cannot be undertaken lightly. To tell a man who would have died at sea in service to his country that he doesn't get to be the kissing sailor feels unpatriotic, or worse. In many ways *all* the candidates for the kissing sailor deserve the distinction they seek. Very possibly each of them kissed a nurse in much the way they describe. It would be most just if a picture of their moment surfaced and that image epitomized the instance in the same way Eisenstaedt's *V-J Day, 1945, Times Square* did for the nation and another sailor and a woman dressed in white. But, unfortunately, a collection of such images does not appear to be on the horizon. So, as veterans and caregivers adamantly and passionately hold to their remembrances of a kiss from long ago, the mounting evidence leaves no reasonable choice but to support and defend one sailor's and one woman's claims against arguments that seek to award the recognition to others. The assuredness of those findings does little to ease the discomfort that is part of this task.

THE BLESSED

Pastor Koch's intercession raised Jim Reynolds' claim to the kissing sailor's part above other petitioners, at least for the short term. In Koch's conspiracy-oriented version of *V-J Day, 1945, Times Square* he asked the public to pardon a young fiancé's premarital indiscretion and to condemn *LIFE*'s willingness to conceal the transgression. Admittedly, it makes for an enticing story.

Despite the initial reception of Koch's August 1986 *Wall Street Journal* article, shortly afterward his version of events got stuffed back into the active imagination box from which it sprang. Daniel Okrent, the then–managing editor of *LIFE* magazine, lashed out at the *Wall Street Journal* in a letter to the editor the *Journal* published on August 20, 1986, less than a week after Koch's assertions first made news. In that letter, Okrent made reference to Pastor Koch's commentary on the sailors' blue uniforms, *LIFE*'s supposed V-E Day photo substitution, and Eisenstaedt's alleged posing of the kissing sailor and nurse. Okrent countered with the following:

> Each claim is ludicrous. First Eisenstaedt did not shoot any assignments from May 1 until June 20, according to the official assignments sheets in the Life archives. Moreover, the archive "set book" and the photo lab stamps show that the image was logged in,

developed and printed in August. In addition, V-J Day pictures taken by other photographers on both coasts show sailors dressed in blue and in white. One such picture taken on V-J Day by Navy photographer Victor Jorgenson, who was clearly standing next to Eisenstaedt, shows the same couple from a slightly different angle.

In fact, the day after your article appeared, Life's Director of Photography David Friend contacted Mr. Reynolds at his home in West Chicago, Ill., something the Journal didn't have the inclination or courtesy to do. "I couldn't say this is definitely me," said the 75-year-old Reynolds. "I've never claimed it is absolutely me. I've always hedged a little bit. In my mind, I always thought it was me." Reynolds remembers the photographer as having been "not a small man. He would pass for average height." Alfred Eisenstaedt is 5 feet 4 inches tall. . . . Finally, the suggestion that Alfred Eisenstaedt— certainly the most celebrated photojournalist of this century— would in any way produce a fraudulent picture is preposterous. A simple phone call to check your writer's sources could have spared this insult to Life and this embarrassment to the Journal.[1]

In addition to the above retort, the *Wall Street Journal* printed a reprimand in a letter from Edith Shain, the most celebrated candidate for the nurse in Eisenstaedt's photo. Shain said, "The editorial-page piece was entirely untrue." To that declaration she added her touted credentials: "The fact that I am the girl in the photo is indisputable. I can prove it with letters from Eisenstaedt himself."[2]

Despite the corrections that Okrent and Shain put forth, Pastor Koch's rendition still makes the rounds in internet articles, blogs, and various other communications as "evidence" of *LIFE*'s deceitful ploy. Juicy and scandalous tales always give truthful accounts a run for their money, at least during a sprint. However, in the long run, thankfully, Reynolds' version ceases to be taken seriously by most informed sources.

FLASH MAN

In some ways Ken McNeel's version of events actually sounds more believable than what truly did transpire in Times Square on August 14, 1945. His story comes across as logical and reasonable.

However, when one contrasts Coast Guard seaman McNeel's recollections with other observable considerations, his case unravels.
The discrepancies between his claims and what can be proven as
true reveal fatal flaws in his claim to be the kissing sailor.

McNeel recollected of his V-J Day kiss that "flashes were
going off everywhere from all the cameras."[3] While the claim
comes across as reasonable at first, further exploration of *V-J
Day, 1945, Times Square* does not support the use of flash photography. Eisenstaedt preferred to work almost exclusively with
natural light because his subjects appeared less encumbered
when they were little aware of his presence. As a result, most
of Eisenstaedt's published photos resonate with a spontaneous,
real-life feel. Dirck Halstead, editor and publisher of *The Digital
Journalist* and senior fellow at the Center for American History,
University of Texas, offers: "Eisenstaedt was very proud of the
fact the he never used flash, only natural light. He only shot with a
Leica, generally a 35mm lens. Certainly he did not use flash in the
Times Square photographs."[4] This leaves "flashes . . . going off
everywhere" as presumably applying to Lt. Victor Jorgensen's
camera, which recorded only one photo of the famous kiss.
Jorgensen's photo does not appear to have employed a flash
either. When McNeel was asked specifically about his remembrance of flashes during the photographed Times Square kiss,
he backed off a bit from his earlier conviction: "Well, maybe
there weren't five flashes. Hmm. I'm not really sure."[5] While
"flashes . . . going off everywhere" would add more glitz and
glamour to the moment, the weight of evidence suggests the use
of no artificial lighting during the outdoor afternoon shooting
of *V-J Day, 1945, Times Square*.

In yet another alleged departure from Eisenstaedt's well-
established and successful practices, McNeel said that Eisenstaedt
staged *V-J Day, 1945, Times Square*. According to McNeel,
Eisenstaedt offered to make McNeel "famous" if he grabbed
the first girl out of the subway. This version of events is highly
improbable because it is completely inconsistent with Alfred
Eisenstaedt's established practice. Eisenstaedt did not need or

want his subjects posed. He wanted to capture a moment, not stage it. Even when his subject knew they were being photographed, Eisenstaedt encouraged them to go about their business and leave the shooting to him.[6] The results of this approach continue to speak for themselves. When one examines the other three photos Eisenstaedt took of that occurrence, the abruptness of the encounter between the sailor and nurse comes across clearly. In the first photo the nurse braces herself in reaction to the surprise visitor. Her left arm cranks upward in a feeble and awkward attempt to thwart the intruder. In the last photo she again appears to be using her left arm to move the kissing sailor away from her. As she does so, a surrounding cast moves about, providing little evidence of a prearranged setting in the middle of a crowded Times Square. The photograph's spontaneity continues to contribute to the image's enormous popularity.

In order to make Ken McNeel "famous," it stands to reason that Eisenstaedt would record the sailor's name. However, Eisenstaedt took no notes. And McNeel, who kissed the girl to become "famous," among other possible motivations, did not try to cash in on Eisenstaedt's alleged promise until years later. Further, Eisenstaedt never made mention of the promise or any prearranging of subjects—quite to the contrary. Therefore, in order for McNeel's story to hold up, one has to either believe that Eisenstaedt lied about the circumstances leading up to the famous photograph or accept that he forgot entirely about his directions to McNeel and the nurse prior to the kiss. Neither scenario is probable. Eisenstaedt had no motivation to lie about any preparations leading up to the photo. The already well-known photographer did not need this picture to safeguard his position at *LIFE*. Further, when *LIFE* editors referenced the picture the next day, Eisenstaedt had to inquire as to what photo they meant. Eisenstaedt's query suggests that he had not toiled much to create the scene twenty-four hours earlier. A study of Eisenstaedt's four photos, a review of his established practices, and consideration of surrounding circumstances suggest that no posing of the sailor and the woman dressed in white in *V-J Day, 1945, Times Square* took place.

The recollections from the photo's two most popular nurse candidates also compromise McNeel's contentions. According to McNeel, he grabbed the nurse and said, "Let's kiss." Astonished, the nurse replied, "OH!" Continuing, McNeel added, "Later I talked to her and she said, 'I just sort of laid back and surrendered.'"[7] While Shain and Zimmer (Friedman) do remember succumbing to the event's momentum, neither recalls any conversation with their pursuer before, during, or after this event. Both women adamantly express this point.

McNeel's version of events does not line up well to known geographic landmarks. According to McNeel, he "grabbed" one of two nurses when they came out of the subway. The picture took place at 44th and Broadway, a full block away from the nearest subway station. Unless after suggesting, "Let's kiss," he then swung the nurse over his shoulder and carried her 150 feet as some kind of V-J Day kiss foreplay, McNeel's explanation of events is not possible.

The V-J Day kiss Eisenstaedt photographed took shape spontaneously. Eisenstaedt did not lie or forget about directing the kissing sailor. The sailor and nurse did not discuss matters before or after the kiss. Camera flashes did not light the afternoon scene. Someone other than Seaman Ken McNeel kissed the woman in *V-J Day, 1945, Times Square*.

THE NICE GUY

During the research for *The Kissing Sailor*, Carl Muscarello left several messages on one of the authors' answering machine. Occasionally Britney Verria heard his voice. She referred to him as the "the nicest kissing sailor." When it became clear that Muscarello was not the sailor in Eisenstaedt's *V-J Day, 1945, Times Square*, Britney would sometimes inquire, "Are you sure he's not the real one?" When the evidence was shared with her she would invariably interrupt with something along the lines of, "Well, maybe you'll change your mind."

Her wishes make for an important consideration of Muscarello's claim. People genuinely like Carl Muscarello. His amiable rapport with virtually everyone he meets promotes his kissing sailor candidacy well. He comports himself humbly, pleasantly, and expresses great respect for all concerned. Further, his story contains all the essential elements of a made-for-TV movie: patriotism, youthful and reckless abandon, and somber reflections on those who died before August 14, 1945, arrived. Amassed evidence also supports his claim. A birthmark, similar recollections to those of photographer Eisenstaedt, as well as Edith Shain's recognition, supply the most convincing fortifications for the former sailor's part in the *V-J Day, 1945, Times Square* photograph. However, as is the case with most kissing sailor and nurse claimants' assertions, Muscarello's proof wanes when critically examined. After close study, Muscarello's case is supported by little more than his magnetic persona.

Muscarello references a birthmark on the back of his hand as his chief physical link to the kissing sailor. And sure enough, the photographed kissing sailor's right hand appears darkened. As such, one initially accepts Muscarello's claim at face value. However, when one learns the exact location of Muscarello's reported birthmark, determining the same mark on the kissing sailor proves difficult, if not impossible. Muscarello's birthmark is located between his first and second set of knuckles. One cannot observe the same location on the kissing sailor's right hand because of the way the kissing sailor grasps the nurse. The back of his fingers are in shadow owing to their positioning to the sun. In Lieutenant Jorgensen's photo, one can't see below the knuckles because the nurse's left arm blocks the view. Therefore, while one cannot rule out the existence of a birthmark between the kissing sailor's knuckles, neither can one prove the existence of Muscarello's reported birthmark in that same area. Further complicating the identification of the claimed mark on the kissing sailor, no photos from Muscarello's youth remain that might clearly evidence his birthmark.[8] Also, the birthmark no longer stands out to provide for as clear a viewing as it once did.[9] In the end, Muscarello's assertion regarding the birthmark is unverifiable.

20-1. There does appear to be a darkened area around Carl Muscarello's right knuckles. However, determining the same "birthmark" on Eisenstaedt's kissing sailor is not possible because the knuckles are shaded in all four of his photographs of the famous V-J Day kiss. The right knuckles are not visible in Lieutenant Jorgensen's photograph. (*Permission granted by Carl Muscarello*)

Undeniably, Muscarello's remembrances line up well with Eisenstaedt's version of the event. Muscarello remembers rushing through Times Square, hugging and kissing women. Eisenstaedt recalled, "There was a Navy man running, grabbing anybody, you know, kissing. . . . He grabbed something white. And I stood there, and they kissed. And I snapped five times."[10] However, certain considerations diminish the impact of Eisenstaedt's and Muscarello's recollections matching up. Muscarello did not come forward with his claim until 1995. At that point Eisenstaedt's reporting had circulated widely. The power of suggestion from Eisenstaedt's published recollections could have informed or influenced Muscarello's memory. Also, as will be shown later, Eisenstaedt's recollections do not stand completely beyond reproach. Both these considerations impede the believability of Muscarello's part in *V-J Day, 1945, Times Square*.

In addition to the potential concern over the timing of Muscarello's story, Muscarello's recollections are not as unique as some reports suggest. At least one other candidate's version of events prefaced the kiss with no exchange of words, no meaningful glances, no exchanged phone numbers, and no communications after the kiss. While this consideration does not deflate Muscarello's contention entirely, its introduction does diminish the uniqueness and therefore the potency of his story's similarity to the two most popular nurse candidates' statements.

Compromising his case further, if Edith Shain's earlier declaration of Muscarello's participation holds as much clout as he (and others) suggests, her later withdrawal of that recognition comes as quite a blow to his standing among other candidates. While Shain did appear with Muscarello in several in-person events and on several television programs (such as the *Today Show*), and indicated that they partnered for a brief moment in Eisenstaedt's picture, she later changed her view, offering: "There was nothing to indicate he was the sailor. He just repeated all the things that I had said."[11] Shain implies that Muscarello boned up on Eisenstaedt's earlier reporting, as well as statements she had made (both well documented by 1995), and then wrote himself into the script. And Shain came just short of saying this when she offered of Muscarello's claimed participation, he was "knowledgeable and pretended to be innocent."[12] Regardless of the reasoning for her revised view, Shain's change of heart bewildered and angered Muscarello. It should. For many, her endorsement served as Muscarello's cornerstone argument.

But even if Shain did not change her mind regarding Muscarello's participation in the V-J Day photograph, her endorsement does not serve Muscarello as well as some think. Carl Muscarello stands at over five feet, eleven inces tall. In 1945, by her own account Shain measured four feet, ten inches. (Some sources suggest four feet, nine inches.) At either height, Muscarello dwarfs her.[13] (See page 187 for a photo of Muscarello and Shain standing beside one another.) Even accounting for Edith Shain's osteoporosis, the pairing does not come close to that of the kissing sailor and nurse in Eisenstaedt's *V-J Day, 1945, Times Square* photograph. One of them would have to be discounted. Considering it is Muscarello who seeks Shain's acknowledgement, then it follows that he would have to admit that someone else is the kissing sailor.

After evaluating each part of Carl Muscarello's overall claim, his net case rests on nothing more than a birthmark that cannot be seen on the kissing sailor, a former nurse who changed her mind, compelling personal testimony, and a likable personality. In the final analysis, Muscarello has no verifiable proof to challenge the mounting evidence that supports another candidate.

Shortly after evidence proved George Mendonsa to be the kissing sailor, Carl Muscarello communicated his disagreement, nicely. A week later he sent a large, personally signed poster of Eisenstaedt's print to Britney Verria and her two sisters, Chelsea and Simone. He signed it "To the Verrias, Carl Muscarello." They know he is not *the* kissing sailor. They kept the poster.

SWINGING AND SWEARING

Glenn McDuffie comes across as a sweet and humble old man who served his country during the big war, and then kissed a nurse in Times Square. However, when one challenges his version of events from August 14, 1945, he undergoes an abrupt metamorphosis. He makes no attempt to hide the transformation. He hollers that his competitors are "idiots," "liars," "pretenders," and "glory seekers." He would like to "kick all their asses." A meeting between McDuffie and other claimants would make for an interesting television special—though McDuffie's exploits would suit a Jerry Springer show better than a *Meet the Press* segment.

Glenn McDuffie's prominent standing among other kissing sailor candidates persists for numerous reasons. For one, McDuffie sounds like many people's image of a stereotypical sailor from that era. McDuffie speaks loudly. He swears. He talks brashly. He threatens to fight his competitors. One can believe he carried out the bold maneuver captured by Eisenstaedt's camera.

In addition to his attention-getting style, a persuasive ally promotes his case. Lois Gibson, a nationally renowned forensic artist, wholeheartedly backs the North Carolinian sailor's longstanding claim. As reviewed earlier, Gibson's flurry of terminology, declarations, and prepared slides in support of McDuffie's assertions convinces curious inquirers and, if needed, rebukes competitors. Her definitive statements employ words such as "absolute," "perfect match," "identical," and other terminology that demonstrates an assuredness beyond reproach. Her credentialed drawing of lines in forthright fashion all over pictures of an eighty-year-old Glenn McDuffie and Alfred Eisenstaedt's 1945 kissing sailor photograph provides an intimidating air of certainty. Rather than challenge Gibson's confidently expressed contentions, most nod and accept her findings. It is difficult to find a source that takes on her conclusions.

Lois Gibson shares her findings generously. She is energetic, invested, and comes across as the genuine article. However, her flurry of evidence lacks a knockout blow. Like a boxer who comes out of the corner too aggressively, her argument punches out in the early rounds. Under the strain of counterarguments, her once seemingly formidable barrage of points loses its sting. When questioned, she becomes exasperated. The more one learns of her arguments, the less convincing they are.

Surprisingly, one can gain some confidence questioning Gibson's conclusions by surfing her website. On her homepage

(LoisGibson.com) Gibson links to a slide show she prepared on President John Kennedy's assassination. Utilizing similar approaches and techniques to ascertain that Glenn McDuffie kissed a nurse in 1945, she reports that the three tramps found in a railway car behind Dealey Plaza in Dallas, Texas, shortly after President Kennedy's murder are Charles Frederick Rogers, Charles Harrelson, and Chauncey Holt. In 1991 at a Kennedy Assassination Symposium, a confident Gibson said she'd "bet the farm" on her identification of the three tramps.[14] However, in order for Gibson's wager to pay out, one must refute the Dallas Police files (released in 1989) that identify Harold Doyle, John Gedney, and Gus Abrams as the three tramps. Gerald Posner addressed these files in his landmark work on the Kennedy assassination, *Case Closed*. Posner wrote, "In February, 1992 researchers discovered that Dallas Police files released in 1989 showed the three tramps had indeed been booked on November 22, 1963. The records identified the suspects as Harold Doyle, Gus Abrams, and John Gedney. Two of the men, Gedney and Doyle, were still alive, and as it turned out were real tramps who had been to the local rescue mission the night before the assassination and were sleeping in the railway car when the police arrested them. The men had no connection to the events at Dealey, and the conspiracy press suddenly and quietly abandoned the issue."[15] While much of the conspiracy press quieted, Lois Gibson did not. Rather than hedging her bets, she continues to raise the wager. This may not be a wise gamble. Gibson's conclusions require a wholesale rejection of not only the police report that identified the blond tramp as John Gedney, but also the 1992 FBI report, produced from an interview with Gedney.

While doubting Gibson's conclusions in a field she demonstrates considerable expertise in is a lonesome endeavor, not everyone completely accepts the forensic artist's assertions. Consider Diane Sawyer's questioning on an August 14, 2007, episode of *Good Morning America*. While the program provided a friendly and receptive arena for both McDuffie and Gibson to present their case, the show's anchor pressed them both on certain aspects of their claim. At one juncture Sawyer pushed Gibson gingerly, "Let me ask about the nose because looking at it right here you would say one nose is a little different." Before Sawyer could continue her point about differences between McDuffie's and the kissing sailor's noses, Gibson interjected, "That's right. He's being pressed against the woman's face. And also your nose grows your entire life. Unfortunately your nose is made of cartilage. So of course being a fifty- or sixty-year distance there is going to be about 18 percent longer. But that's the only difference." Without waiting for Sawyer's reaction or rebuttal, Gibson continued on about McDuffie's nostrils, ear, and other measurements in comparison to those same reference points on the V-J Day kissing sailor. Gibson claimed, "He is so identical that it can't even be his twin because if it was an identical twin there would be mirror image's differences." Despite the potency with which Gibson delivers her statements, a picture of Glen McDuffie from the 1940s exposes a long and relatively slender nose. Whether or not McDuffie's nose grew 18 percent since the 1940s, one can clearly observe that around 1945 his nose extended well beyond the rest of his face. And though Gibson rightly points out that the 1945 kissing sailor pressed his nose into the nurse's cheek, making it difficult to determine an exact length and shape, the kissing sailor's nose appears more Roman than McDuffie's. So, as Diane Sawyer seemed to notice,

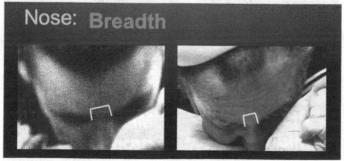

20-2. The bridge of Glenn McDuffie's nose appears narrower than the kissing sailor's in Lieutenant Jorgensen's photograph. (*Permission granted by Dr. Norman Sauer*)

McDuffie's nose does not appear to match that of the sailor in Eisenstaedt's Times Square photo.

McDuffie's nose is not the only physical contrast that compromises his claim to a part in Eisenstaedt's famous photograph. A comparison of his hairline in 1945 to that of the kissing sailor also works against his contention. Lois Gibson disagrees. She argues that a consideration of McDuffie's hairline actually supports *her* sailor's case. On the same *Good Morning America* show when she spoke of McDuffie's nose growing by 18 percent, Gibson pointed to an enlarged photo of the kissing sailor and McDuffie to suggest the following: "The hairline is the same right here. You lose hair on top. Okay, you're eighty years old. You lose hair on top but right here you have the same identical hairline." Upon initial consideration, Gibson seems to score a point. After all, the V-J Day sailor's hairline does appear to match the lower contour of McDuffie's hairline today. However, an examination of this hairline on other campaigning kissing sailors turns up matches as well. This scrutiny represents no breakthrough observation, although Gibson's remarks makes one think otherwise.

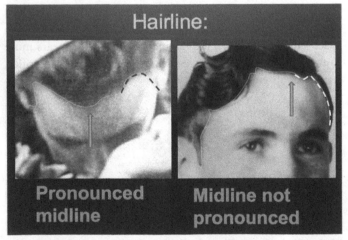

20-3. McDuffie's hairline does not follow the same path as the kissing sailor's in Lieutenant Jorgensen's photograph. (*Permission granted by Dr. Norman Sauer*)

While there are noteworthy comparisons between Glenn McDuffie and the kissing sailor's hair, they do not support Gibson's contention. For example, using the one picture that exists of McDuffie from the time period,[16] his forehead appears higher than that of the kissing sailor.

A tracing of both sailors' respective hairlines reveals that they retreat to different degrees and along dissimilar pathways. McDuffie's further receding hairline appears most apparent above and just to the right of his nose. McDuffie's and the kissing sailor's hairlines do not match.

In addition to physical features, other considerations damage McDuffie's claim to be the kissing sailor. For example, McDuffie spins an elaborate tale to explain the kissing sailor's stylish left-hand grip. According to McDuffie, he struck the pose to be polite. Upon hearing a photographer rush at him as he kissed the nurse, McDuffie recalled, "I bent my hand back so you could see the lady's face." In an interview the British Broadcasting Corporation (BBC) conducted with McDuffie, the sailor elaborated on the reasons he struck that pose:

> When I started kissing that woman nobody was taking my photograph. I heard somebody running from the Time building and they ran right up to us and stopped. I mean it sounded like a horse running. I thought somebody was going to run over us. And then I raised, opened up my eyes and it was Eisenstaedt taking pictures of us. So I started kissing her again . . . and trying to move my left hand out of the way so he could take the picture. And I kissed her longer than I thought I should.[17]

McDuffie repeats the general sequence in several other interviews. In one of those discussions McDuffie added, "I went over there and kissed her and saw a man running at us. I thought it was a jealous husband or boyfriend coming to poke me in the eyes. I looked up and saw he was taking the picture and I kissed her as long as it took to take it."[18] While McDuffie's "chivalrous act" impresses Lois Gibson, his rendition does not gibe with Eisenstaedt's repeated testimony or photographic evidence. For instance, according to McDuffie, Eisenstaedt moved toward him in a loud enough fashion ("like a horse running") to be heard above the competing sounds of Times Square's festive and crowded streets. That is not likely. Eisenstaedt makes no reference of running at the sailor and nurse. The *LIFE* photographer reported that he turned around and shot the pictures without taking a single step toward the sailor and nurse.[19] This would be consistent with his usual mode of operation. By design, Eisenstaedt carried out his practice stealthily. At five feet, four inches and 130 pounds, he would have to pound the pavement quickly and forcefully to be heard above Times Square's commotion.[20]

Other aspects of McDuffie's reported chivalry require questioning. In several interviews McDuffie said that he began kissing the girl, stopped when he saw a photographer taking pictures, and then moved his hand out of the way so the photographer could see her face. Again, evidence does not support his rendition of events. According to Eisenstaedt, he clicked his camera "the moment the sailor kissed the nurse."[21] Therefore, this instance would be the earliest point that McDuffie could have noticed the photographer. As such, in accordance with McDuffie's recollections, one would expect to see a different positioning of the hand in at least one of the last three photos. Instead, each of Eisenstaedt's four photos shows the left hand in the same position. Further, the four photos appear in continual succession, just as Eisenstaedt's quote suggests. The nurse remains bent backward with her right foot pointed downward. Also, the movement of the background crowd keeps pace with the rapid firing of pictures. So, considering Eisenstaedt clicked his first picture as soon as the sailor kissed the nurse, and that neither the reporting of Eisenstaedt nor the photographed sequence suggests a break in the action, one must conclude that McDuffie describes an event apart from the one photographed by Eisenstaedt.

Further challenging McDuffie's assertions of a broken photographed sequence in *V-J Day, 1945, Times Square*, the two most popularly quoted nurse candidates remember the event far differently than McDuffie. Nurse Edith Shain, whom McDuffie once claimed he was 99 percent sure he kissed,[22] does not recount the story with a break in the sequence. Neither does Greta Zimmer (Friedman), the dental assistant who claims to be the "nurse." Both Shain's and Friedman's reports are consistent with Eisenstaedt's remembrance. McDuffie continues to insist that all three remember the incident incorrectly—or that they lie.

The closer one scrutinizes McDuffie's version of events, the quicker his case unravels. For example, though McDuffie claims to have heard Eisenstaedt running at him, noticed him taking a picture, and reacted to the event by turning away his wrist, for some reason his amazing awareness of surrounding activities does not extend to Lt. Victor Jorgensen snapping at least one picture of the same happening. Though Jorgensen, positioned only a few feet to Eisenstaedt's right, clearly took a picture of the same event (a study of the background in Eisenstaedt's second picture and Jorgenson's one picture confirms this), McDuffie calls the messengers reporting this news liars. McDuffie holds that only Eisenstaedt took photos of him kissing the nurse that day. The suggestion is absurd.

Though McDuffie does not recall Jorgensen at the famous scene, he identifies the other two sailors in the photograph. According to McDuffie the sailor on the right in the white uniform is Bob Little from Buffalo, New York, who served with McDuffie on the SS *Alexander Lillington*, a cargo ship. Additionally, he claims the sailor in the dark Navy blues is Jack Holmes from Pittsburgh, Pennsylvania.[23] Glenn McDuffie is the only former sailor to name both sailors in the background of Eisenstaedt's photograph. This is impressive, but the veracity of these identifications does not stand up to scrutiny. For one, there are no other pictures of Little or Holmes for comparison. For that matter, although there is evidence that the two men did exist, efforts to find either of the two sailors come up short.[24] Furthermore, the sailor in the white uniform is likely James Sheridan. Unlike Little and Holmes, not only did he come forward to identify himself, but the photographic evidence strongly supports his claim.[25]

20-4/5. This photograph of James Sheridan (1945) shows a strong likeness to the sailor in the background of Alfred Eisenstaedt's second photograph. (*Permission granted by James Sheridan*)

Separate from Sheridan's claim, there are other factors that challenge Little's and Holmes' part in the famous V-J Day photo. First, Little's wearing of whites is peculiar because the Navy issued dungaree working uniforms (in addition to the dress blues) to sailors assigned to a ship.[26] (James Sheridan had been issued whites because he was part of an honor guard unit.)[27] This consideration suggests Little is not present in Eisenstaedt's photo.

Second, the odds that Little and Holmes arrived in the very spot of Eisenstaedt's famous photo independent of McDuffie's arrival to Times Square is, at best, a long shot. Even if McDuffie were to argue that he arrived in Times Square with Little and Holmes, the fact that they are walking in opposite directions is problematic. According to McDuffie, he entered Times Square via subway stairs and rushed less than fifty feet up 7th Avenue *from* the 42nd Street station to embrace a welcoming nurse. McDuffie's sailor-mates are moving *toward* the subway station.

Unless McDuffie argues that the other two sailors from his ship sped ahead of him and then reversed direction, their path of travel runs counter to what McDuffie's repeated telling would have one think. McDuffie's claim regarding Little and Holmes remains hard to accept.

If McDuffie references Little and Holmes erroneously, his guilt probably stems from mistaken identity rather than the falsifying of identities. Over the years McDuffie willingly took numerous lie detector tests to prove his part in the *V-J Day, 1945, Times Square* photo. All these tests report no deception in his claims. (No other candidate reports a single lie detector test result.) David Raney, a Houston polygraph expert, administered one of those tests.[28] McDuffie passed that test so convincingly that Raney hung a large poster of Eisenstaedt's photograph signed by Glenn McDuffie in the lobby of his workplace.[29] Further, upon viewing interview films of McDuffie, Houston Police Department detectives determined Glenn McDuffie's claims to be true.[30] Certainly, McDuffie does come across as sincere and passionate. Still, though McDuffie may be telling the "truth," criminal defense attorney F. Lee Bailey, the host of the show *Lie Detector* (where McDuffie took one of his ten polygraph tests), advised, "If you honestly believe something you won't flunk a polygraph."[31] The lie detector test proves that either McDuffie can beat the test or that he believes himself to be the kissing sailor. And of the two, one might be more inclined to believe the latter. His conviction over these years indicates that in his heart of hearts he truly does see himself in *V-J Day, 1945, Times Square*.

While one might be willing to allow that McDuffie could be wrong without actually lying, Gibson and McDuffie do not extend any benefit of doubt to *LIFE* magazine regarding the kissing sailor's chevron absent from the right shoulder. Military protocol calls for these rates to be sewn on the upper part of the sailor's uniform sleeve. Gibson thinks *LIFE* removed the chevron from the photograph to help conceal the sailor's identity.[32] She explains,

You can just make out a darker black triangular shaped area that obliterates whatever markings would have been on the sailor's uniform at that location. Any photographer from the old school can tell you how someone could do this in a dark room. You can even see where one corner of the triangle is a little outside the edge of the upper arm of the sailor's uniform. . . . I believe Eisenstaedt did this in his darkroom in the very beginning because he thought he could eliminate any problems for himself. I know it is hard to make it as a professional photographer. I know Eisenstaedt fled Germany ahead of the Nazi takeover. I do not believe he was in any way a German sympathizer. However, his being older, he did not care whether a heroic Navy man kissed the girl, he decided to let that sailor be "any man." That was the easy way out.[33]

While Gibson's contention raises an eyebrow, the technology required to pull off such a stunt did not exist in 1945.[34] And, this hoax would have had to be carried out on all four of Eisenstaedt's photos, as well as on Lieutenant Jorgenson's photo that also shows no rates on the kissing sailor's right sleeve. Further, Gibson does not explain why the same entity that erased the rates would invite the sailor to come forward in 1980. McDuffie's and Gibson's theory to deal with the missing chevron lacks persuasiveness and would fit better in a conspiracy-oriented novel.

The incompatibility of McDuffie's insistent recollections with actual geographic locations accelerates his case's demise. For example, McDuffie claims the sequence of events progressed as follows: "When I got off the subway I got to the top of the stairs and the lady up there said, 'Sailor, I'm so happy for you.' I asked her why and she told me the war was over and I could go home. I ran into the street jumping and hollering. . . . That nurse was out there and she turned around and put her arms out and that's when I kissed her."[35]

In another quote, McDuffie addressed events right after the kiss: "Afterward, I just went on a subway across the street and went to Brooklyn."[36] The reported sequence raises many doubts. If McDuffie is Eisenstaedt's kissing sailor, then he could not run into the nurse in Eisenstaedt's picture so soon after coming up the stairs from the subway. McDuffie said he encountered the nurse in Eisenstaedt's picture fifty feet or less from the stairs of the 42nd Street subway station, and that he caught a subway train across the street right afterward. Fifty feet from the top of the closest 42nd Street subway station exit would put McDuffie just across 43rd Street. The problem with this determination is that Eisenstaedt's four pictures took place one hundred feet farther north, just shy of 44th Street.

While it is only fair to allow for a slip of the tongue when retelling a story, McDuffie adamantly stands by his reporting of distances, locations, and sequences. When asked specifically how far he had traveled away from the subway station stairs before encountering the one nurse he kissed, McDuffie replied, "It couldn't've been no more than 50 feet." When given the opportunity to readdress the distance between the subway and where he encountered the nurse, he repeated emphatically, "Couldn't've of been 50 feet!"[37] If the kissing sailor's path of travel originated from the top of the subway station stairs, he would have to walk at least three times that distance before encountering the nurse. Also, if he entered Times Square from the nearest subway exit, then McDuffie would have had to turn around from the top of the stairway—and still travel 150 feet. He makes no reference to such a maneuver.

The positioning of the kissing sailor with respect to the nurse he kissed also damages McDuffie's case. Considering he states he ran out *from* the 42nd Street subway station *toward* the nurse who invited his approach with open arms, one would expect McDuffie's back to be facing Eisenstaedt. But the photo does not indicate that. Instead, the pictured sailor appears to have approached the nurse from 44th Street, not from the 42nd Street subway station as McDuffie recalls. While the nurse and the sailor could have changed their positions, the move would have been awkward for both parties. Further, Eisenstaedt's repeated commentary suggests no such maneuver. For that matter, no sailor or nurse candidate reports changing their position upon meeting their respective partner.

While McDuffie remains obstinate regarding his part in *V-J Day, 1945, Times Square*, that consistency does not carry over to all subtopics of the same subject. For example, in some instances McDuffie claims he kissed Edith Shain: "She's the one I kissed. . . . I'm the only one who really knows who the nurse is."[38] Adding more detail, he offers, "I know Edith Shain was the woman I kissed because she had the biggest mouth of anybody I ever kissed in my life—it went from ear to ear. I'll never forget it."[39] Over the years he attempted on numerous occasions to establish a connection with Shain, who rebuffed those offers. Such rejection might explain McDuffie's rethinking of whom he knew and would never forget he kissed in Times Square on August 14, 1945. Speaking of Shain's role in that famed embrace, McDuffie later said, "I know the woman I kissed. And she ain't it."[40] He further emphasizes this point: "She's been riding the train all these years, I just can't see it how everybody believes her. . . . She's been a smart ass about it all the time."[41] In another interview McDuffie professed that Shain earned her position atop the claimant hill by dating Eisenstaedt for a period of time back in the 1980s.[42] McDuffie's wavering on the identity of the nurse does not serve his case well.

In order to believe McDuffie's claim to be the kissing sailor, one has to struggle with many doubtful and disputable contentions. Dissimilarities with the kissing sailor's physical characteristics, a conspiracy mindset, inaccurate geographic references, and inconsistent testimony all combine to crush his claim's believability. In the final analysis, his supporting evidence weighs in light. Glenn McDuffie is not who he purports and believes himself to be.

21

MORE PLOT THAN PROOF

G eorge Mendonsa first learned of the *V-J Day, 1945, Times Square* photograph in August 1980. On that day he received an inquiring phone call from Francis Silvia, an old friend. Silvia asked, "Where the hell was you when the war ended?" His question confused George. Silvia knew well of George's whereabouts on that day. In a slightly aggravated tone, George answered, "I was in New York when it ended." Silvia shot back excitedly, "I know you was, because I got the picture. . . . I know it's you."[1] The picture Silvia "got" first appeared in every *LIFE* magazine across the country on August 27, 1945. The original printing celebrated the end of World War II. The 1980 reprinting had a different purpose.

Delivering an August 1980 *LIFE* magazine with the Muppets' Miss Piggy running for president on the cover, Silvia showed George his likeness on page seven. The caption read, "35 years ago a kiss celebrated the end of a long war." *LIFE* shared the nurse's identity and the letter that led to her discovery. Then, in an effort to complete the picture, the magazine's editor invited the sailor to come forward.

George did not need to read any further: "The minute I saw the picture I knew it was me. I looked at it. The first thing I noticed was the hands. I have very big hands from fishing all my life. And I said, 'Jeez, it *is* me.'"[2] But George needed to prove that.

In 1980 George still remembered kissing a nurse in Times Square on August 14, 1945, following word that the Japanese had surrendered. While the occasion had not been the subject of frequent reflections over the years, *LIFE*'s August 1980 issue gave him reason to revisit the instance. George recalled, "It was no big deal. It just kind of happened." It did. And Eisenstaedt's photo offered verification. That evidence drew admirers. Over the years they couldn't stop looking. Now, neither could George.

During his first viewing of the August 14, 1945, photograph, many of the sailor's features jumped out and caught his attention. In addition to a hand that looked like a baseball mitt, he took notice of the sailor's dark hairline, tall body frame, and his face's shape. As George continued to stare at the sailor's embrace, memories from that time and place surged forward. He recalled kissing a nurse in an emotional response to the moment at hand and holding her tightly in an "awkward headlock like grip." In addition to being against the norms of the era, prior to that pictured moment George had never attempted such a bold move on any unsuspecting female. George thought his reasons for the maneuver offered further proof of his part in the now-famous photo.

Standard operating procedures did not characterize August 14, 1945. On that day, several dynamics combined to cause a stark departure from George's normal conduct. One of the factors, the war's anticipated end, summoned a crowd to *where people meet*: Times Square. As that day progressed, kissing and hugging broke out right in the middle of the nation's heavily traversed crossroads. Especially by evening, a uniformed sailor entering the patriotic arena was practically assured his own version of *V-J Day, 1945, Times Square*.

Alcohol played a part in the revelry. The greater the quantity consumed, the more amorous and less reserved the drinker became. On that August 14 afternoon, George knocked back several drinks at Childs Restaurant, near 7th Avenue and 49th Street. No doubt, after a few celebratory libations, Times Square took on a different look. George had changed, too. Upon leaving Childs, his impulses outranked his inhibitions.

Upon further examination of Eisenstaedt's kissing sailor photo, George discovered another distinguishing consideration:

his attire. While the Navy uniform was known more for its convention than its distinctiveness, George noticed one aspect of his dress that stood out—his chevron, or lack thereof. George's chevron did not appear on the uniform's sleeve. He remembered why.

When George returned to Newport during his summer1945 leave, he had a new uniform made. He instructed the tailor to forgo attaching the rating badge. George knew the tailor would use a sewing machine to attach the chevron. That wouldn't do. George wanted to hand-sew the rate. He felt a herringbone stitch gave the uniform a more "classy appearance." Despite his intention to do just that, he was preoccupied with a new girlfriend and left the matter for another day.

On August 14, 1945, George entered Times Square with a lively spirit, but without an attached chevron. He did, however, take his rate with him in case a shore patrol officer stopped him. Not having rates on his person could lead to penalties, including detainment, a dock in pay, shortening of a future leave, or closer inspections in the future.[3] At the day's outset George carried the chevron in his uniform's left shirt pocket, but before embarking down Times Square, he transferred the stripes to his trousers' right inside pocket and stuffed his money into his shirt pocket for safer keeping. In 1980, George identified his stripes hanging from the kissing sailor's right side—an uncommon placement. As such, the rate's unusual location offers a key consideration for identification. Further, both Glenn McDuffie and Carl Muscarello, two other well-known sailor candidates, held lower rankings than George did, and therefore would not have the same number of chevrons dangling from the right side. The visible U.S. Navy petty officer first class rate (three chevrons) bolsters Mendonsa's case.

The aforementioned considerations aside, George's uncharacteristically forward behavior on V-J Day, 1945, requires another explanation, one with more pull than a military uniform and of greater control than alcohol. And an additional motivator did enter into the picture that day. It came in the form of a war memory. The sight of a nurse standing in the square summoned an earlier scene in the Pacific where nurses mended maimed sailors. The contrast between killing and curing overtook George. In the midst of war's hardening experiences, George developed a soft spot for nurses. On August 14, 1945, the announcement that signaled an end to all the injuring and killing of American sailors mixed with the sight of a pretty nurse in a crowded square, creating an irresistible circumstance for George Mendonsa. He recounted later, "I darn well know if that girl didn't have a nurse's outfit, I never would have done that." But she did wear a nurse uniform. And he did do that. And the picture proved it—or at least that's what he thought.

He figured wrong. For the next sixty-seven years the picture stood alone, wanting for an authoritative voice to explain the image's surrounding circumstances and larger story. George's and many others' reporting provided only biased versions.

Although the contentions of *The Sullivans'* former quartermaster make for remarkable reading, they fall short of the irrefutable proof needed to advance his case. George's inebriated state, World War II memories of nurses mending sailors, and the improperly positioned chevron make for entertaining possibilities. In addition, his delivery resonates with compelling emotion. (Rarely can he tell his war story about nurses caring for *Bunker Hill's* wounded sailors and not get choked up.) However, absolutely verifying his stories and points remains difficult, if not impossible. Lots of sailors flocked to Times Square on August 14, 1945. Also, there is no way to know if the kissing sailor consumed alcohol before making his way down the square. And certainly one could come up with a more mainstream explanation for his actions than memories of maternal care at sea. Further still, the referenced chevrons hanging from the sailor's inside pocket could be another article of clothing, belonging either to the sailor or nurse. One just cannot tell for sure. In the end, George's story does little to solve the mystery of who kissed whom in Times Square on V-J Day, 1945. While his contentions do not boomerang against his position, in the final analysis they provide more plot than proof.

22

CONSIDERATIONS

Consideration of other assertions made by George Mendonsa adds to the plot *and* the proof of his case. George claims that his tattoo can be detected on the kissing sailor's right arm. The suggestion makes for interesting contemplation, and an amazing find. Also, evidence that his then-girlfriend (and present-day wife) can be detected in the background of the *V-J Day, 1945, Times Square* photo offers a most persuasive possibility. Further, even a matter that initially seems to work against his case, Eisenstaedt's recorded remembrances of his famous photo, might actually provide support of George's part in *V-J Day, 1945, Times Square.* In the end, the questions surrounding a tattoo, George's girlfriend's part in the picture, and revisiting Eisenstaedt's testimonies about his famous photograph add considerably to George Mendonsa's claim to the kissing sailor's identity.

DOES THE KISSING SAILOR HAVE A TATTOO?

A prominent mark appears on the kissing sailor's right forearm, most clearly in the fourth of Eisenstaedt's 1945 V-J Day photos. Interestingly, despite the marking's high visibility, other than George Mendonsa, no kissing sailor candidate ever made anything of its existence. George sees this inscription as critical proof backing his claim regarding the kissing sailor's identity. He is correct, but for different reasons than he espouses.

According to George Mendonsa, the tattoo on the kissing sailor's arm is one he reluctantly had inscribed in 1940 when he and several of his friends celebrated their entry into the Maritime Service. (The Maritime Service was established in 1936 to train young men for possible future service in the Merchant Marine.) George's friends had large, colorful drawings tattooed on their arms. After being goaded by his friends, George acquiesced and had his right forearm inscribed with his initials, "G.M." The tattoo, located a few inches below his elbow, remains on his arm to this day. While only a few inches in length, when he wears short sleeves the lettering stands out prominently.

George Mendonsa thinks that his tattoo from 1940 appears on the kissing sailor's right arm. And upon initial consideration, he seems to make a valid observation. Just above the kissing sailor's darker patch of hair, a legible *M* stands out. Less clear, but also evident on the kissing sailor's right arm, to the right of the *M,* one can discern a thin marking that could be a *C* or a poorly written *G.* The marking's location appears remarkably close to the *G.M.* tattoo located on George Mendonsa's right forearm. If the two are indeed the same, such a find would go a long way to making an ironclad case.

As it turns out, George Mendonsa's insistence regarding the existence of his tattoo on the kissing sailor's right forearm drills a dry well. Some scrutiny and measuring indicates the two reference points cannot be the same marking. The tattoo on George's arm is located approximately three inches too high for a perfect match with the kissing sailor's similar marking. Even after factoring in the angle from which the viewer sees the mark, these two locations do not coincide.

In addition to the two markings' different locations, the lettering in Mendonsa's tattoo evidences better penmanship than does the lettering on the kissing sailor's arm. Though the letters are shaped similarly, they cannot be perfectly overlaid. The kissing sailor's *G* is hard to make out and may even resemble a *C* more so than a *G.* Unlike George Mendonsa's tattooed *M,* the kissing sailor's *M* collapses and turns inward on the letter's left side. Claiming a match between Mendonsa's tattoo and the kissing sailor's marking is just not a realistic conclusion.

But all this still leaves one to account for the kissing sailor's visible M and less discernable G on George Mendonsa. How could the kissing sailor's two letters appear so similar and exist in such close proximity to George's tattoo, and yet not be the same markings, arguably on the same person? John Hopf's 1987 photograph of George Mendonsa's arm helps answer that question.[1]

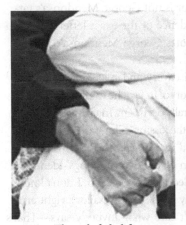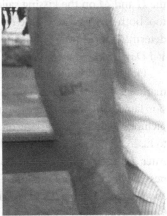

22-1/2. Though faded from more than forty years of exposure to the elements, the kissing sailor's "G M" appears in a 1987 photograph of George Mendonsa's right arm, just above a thick patch of hair. (Left photo courtesy of Bobbi Baker Burrows at *Time-LIFE*. Right photo permission granted by George Mendonsa.

Hopf took this photograph to demonstrate the darker patch of hair on Mendonsa's arm for use by Richard Benson in his report on the kissing sailor's identity. (The findings of the Benson study are discussed in chapter 23.) That same picture also exposes a surface marking just above the patch of thicker, black hair. What the viewer actually sees on both the kissing sailor's and George Mendonsa's arm is not a tattoo but rather a naturally occurring skin marking. On Mendonsa's arm one can make out a faint and cockeyed C—or very lazy G—and a poorly constructed M.

The skin marking appears right where the darker patch of hair ends and just to the left of a vein that is visible in Hopf's 1987 photo, as well as Eisenstaedt's 1945 V-J Day kissing sailor photo. Admittedly, determining the marking in the 1987 photograph requires scrutiny (Hopf's photo was taken forty-two years after Eisenstaedt's *V-J Day, 1945, Times Square,* during which time the marking's pigment likely faded), but undeniably the *G* and the *M* do appear on George's right arm exactly in the same location as the matching shapes on the kissing sailor's right arm. So, while the *G* and *M* on the kissing sailor is not George Mendonsa's tattoo, both arms show visible evidence of the exact lettering. The determination powerfully supports George Mendonsa's part in *V-J Day, 1945, Times Square.*

One might think that the discovery and matching up of the markings would excite George. Not so. In fact, he found the conclusion faulty. When shown the naturally occurring markings in Hopf's picture and the same marking on the kissing sailor's arm, he pointed to Eisenstaedt's picture and asked, "Yeah? Well, where is my tattoo?" After a more detailed explanation of the two markings' identicalness, he became more resolute. George insisted: "Oh, I don't know about that." Looking more closely at the kissing sailor's right arm George concluded, "Well, I don't care what anybody says—That's my tattoo." And that is what he believed to his dying day.

EISENSTAEDT DIDN'T BELIEVE GEORGE

The mounting evidence supporting George Mendonsa's claim to the kissing sailor did not convince everyone of his part in *V-J Day, 1945, Times Square.* Predictably, Carl Muscarello, Glenn McDuffie, and other claimants r emained adamant regarding their version of events. The fact that *LIFE* did not experience a change of heart may be disappointing, but considering all the factors in play, it is far from shocking.

But one individual's continued opposition to George Mendonsa's claims remains most baffling—Alfred Eisenstaedt. The famous photographer's remembrances and opinions of *V-J Day, 1945, Times Square* do not support Mendonsa's claims. If

George Mendonsa is indeed the kissing sailor, then one has to reconcile the differences in Alfred Eisenstaedt's memory of the event with George Mendonsa's recollections.

In 1992 John Loengard, *LIFE*'s highly respected photographer and picture editor, interviewed Eisenstaedt for a book entitled *LIFE Photographers and What They Saw*. In addition, Loengard interviewed other giants in the photography world, including Gordon Parks, Nina Leen, and George Silk. Loengard recorded the photographers' memories of their most widely recognized photographs, many of which enjoyed a long life via reproductions. The photographers spoke to aspects of their classic photos that extended well beyond the pictures' borders. They indicated what they thought before and after the shot, how they came upon the pictured scene or happening, and speculated why a photograph proved appealing to audiences. The photographers' comments breathed life into the still frames.

Appropriately, the first chapter of Loengard's book focused on the Father of Photojournalism, Alfred Eisenstaedt. A good part of that chapter discussed the *V-J Day, 1945, Times Square* photograph. Eisenstaedt's recollection of events highlights the differences between his recollection of the day's events and those of George Mendonsa:

> Four or five different photographers got assignments to go to different places in New York to photograph the celebration, and I was assigned to Times Square. There were thousands of people milling around, in side streets and everywhere. Everybody was kissing each other, civilians, Marines, people, soldiers and so on. And there was also a Navy man running, grabbing anybody, you know, kissing. I ran ahead of him because I had Leica cameras around my neck, focused from 10 feet to infinity. You had only to shoot; you don't have to fumble around. I ran ahead and looked back all the time. I didn't even know what was going on, until he grabbed something in white. And I stood there, and they kissed. And I snapped five times. A reporter was with me, but we were separated. I turned the film in at 8 p.m. at Life magazine. Next day they told me, What a great picture! I said, "Which picture?" I forgot already. Had no idea.[2]

Eisenstaedt's and Mendonsa's remembrances contrast starkly. While Eisenstaedt remembers *the* sailor, Mendonsa has no memory of a photographer tracking him or taking his picture four times. Further, and more important, Mendonsa claims he did not grab, kiss, or otherwise make meaningful contact with anyone else before coming upon Greta Zimmer. Reviewing the two dissimilar accounts, a reader might reasonably determine that the two men describe separate events in the general proximity on the same day.

Eisenstaedt's extended commentary becomes even more damaging to Mendonsa's claim. When Loengard inquired, "You never got the sailor's name?" Eisenstaedt, in an unmistakable reference to George Mendonsa, added the following: "Never, no. I remember only it was a mistake when *LIFE* published the story on the nurse and said, 'Will the real sailor now come forward?' I think 80 sailors came forward. One man even attempted to sue *LIFE*, but it was rejected in court. That man still says he is the sailor and the woman he married was the woman in the picture. It's not true."[3]

An initial reading of Eisenstaedt's 1992 recorded memories would appear to refute George Mendonsa's version of events. However, a careful and more nuanced analysis of Eisenstaedt's statements provides some insight as to how the *LIFE* photographer may well have recalled the order of events incorrectly.

Alfred Eisenstaedt recalls a chaotic scene in Times Square on August 14, 1945. People scattered about—"thousands," "everywhere," "milling around," and "kissing." In this sea of chaos, with emotions churning, Eisenstaedt ran ahead of a sailor who he remembered kissed many women. As the *LIFE* photographer hustled forward, he tried to keep track of the darting sailor by looking back over his shoulder. Keeping tabs on that particular serviceman among "Marines," "soldiers," and numerous other sailors proved dizzying. Eisenstaedt stated that he "didn't even know what was going on."

It is completely conceivable that in a frenzied Time Square a rushing photographer could, for a moment, become disoriented and mistake one running sailor grabbing "something in white" for another sailor moving through the same crowded streets. The possibility of making a mistaken identity becomes even more probable when one considers that, in order to maintain an unencumbered path through a shifting crowd, Eisenstaedt would have had to continually take his eyes off the sailor he was tracking, if for no other reason than to avoid crashing into someone or being trampled by one of the thousands of emotionally charged revelers who towered over his small frame.

The specifics of what Alfred Eisenstaedt saw, or did not see, might well become fuzzy, hazy, or just plain wrong when, after spinning around and rapidly firing off four pictures (he *remembers* he snapped five times), he rushed off to photograph other subjects and scenes. In his haste, he did not take down either the sailor's or the nurse's names. As such, his recollection of what really occurred in Times Square on V-J Day is almost entirely dependent on his reconstruction of events after they occurred. Eisenstaedt's recorded remembrances of his famous photo date from two or more decades after he shot *V-J Day, 1945, Times Square.*

And beyond the scene's quick and haphazard development, there is reason to question Eisenstaedt's memory of the event. It is entirely plausible that Eisenstaedt recalled incorrectly the precise details of events that less than twenty-four hours later he had "forgot already" and of which he "had no idea." He could very well have confused the run-up to the photo he referenced afterward as "which picture?"

Interestingly, the photo Eisenstaedt took just prior to the V-J day kissing sailor picture sequence was just south of 42nd Street. Therefore, he probably had to travel approximately three hundred or more feet north before spotting a sailor running through the maze of people. Because the sailor would have been traveling south, Eisenstaedt would have had to change his direction abruptly and travel south, too. While this scenario is not impossible, Eisenstaedt never mentioned that he had to change direction. Additionally, though he said, "Everybody was kissing each other, civilians, Marines, people, soldiers and so on," no one in the background of any of his four pictures is kissing. Further, even though Lieutenant Jorgensen's photograph shows a different background, no one else is kissing in that photo, either. Instead, the people in the background of Eisenstaedt's and Jorgensen's photos seem amused and even surprised by the kissing sailor and nurse, as if they are viewing an action that is completely out of the ordinary.

While most certainly other people kissed in Times Square around the same time frame, most of the widespread kissing occurred closer to seven o'clock when President Truman announced the official surrender of the Japanese, followed closely by the *New York Times* zipper's scrolling message: *** OFFICIAL*** TRUMAN ANNOUNCES JAPANESE SURRENDER. Several recollections of Times Square during that August 14, 1945, afternoon and early evening do suggest a scene of building excitement and the arrival of expectant victory celebrants, but they do not report the kiss-in festival that occurred throughout the crossroads later that evening. On August 15, 1945, the *New York Times* reported that most people in Times Square "harnessed" their emotions dur-ing the prior day *until* seven at night.[4] Most photographs and film footage of V-J Day kissing couples were taken in a packed Times Square. The area's population swelled throughout the day to approximately 500,000 by seven o'clock and increased four-fold by ten.[5] Alfred Eisenstaedt could well be confusing the kissing sailor sequence with a scene closer to seven, when "everybody was kissing" became more the norm.

In addition to doubting George Mendonsa's declared participation in the August 14, 1945, photo, Eisenstaedt was also skeptical about other related matters concerning the Rhode Island fisherman. In an inescapable reference to George Mendonsa, Eisenstaedt referred to a rejected legal case that "one man" tried to bring against *LIFE* over his part in the photo.[6] (More accurately, the case was brought against Time, Inc.) However, Eisenstaedt's understanding of the case he refers to is completely inaccurate and, in reality, has the facts reversed.

In truth, the courts rejected a motion by Time, Inc., to have George Mendonsa's case thrown out. The same court determined that George Mendonsa had a case. In another disparaging comment about George, Eisenstaedt asserted that George Mendonsa erroneously claimed to have married the woman in the 1945 V-J Day picture.[7] His comment insinuates a reference to the nurse. In actuality, the woman George identifies as his future wife is barely visible over his right shoulder in the celebrated picture. And he did marry her. (This issue is examined in considerable depth later in the chapter.) Eisenstaedt's doubts about Mendonsa's part in his most famous photo likely stem from misinformation, misunderstanding, or inaccurate recall.

An examination of the differences between Eisenstaedt's and Mendonsa's precise recollections of the events of August 14, 1945—some not brought forward until almost a half-century after the chaotic event—must be put in the context of those of other claimants to the title of kissing sailor, whose remembrances do not line up well with Eisenstaedt, either. Here it becomes a matter of degree, not kind. In other words, is it easier to reconcile the discrepancies between Eisenstaedt's and Mendonsa's recollections of that day, or between Eisenstaedt's and other sailor-claimants? The overwhelming weight of evidence strongly suggests Mendonsa's case is more compelling. Other kissing sailors' differences with Eisenstaedt's recollections are difficult to accept.

Two of the more widely touted kissing sailor candidates are Ken McNeel and Glenn McDuffie. Clearly (and often dramatically), their accounts of the events of August 14, 1945, do not square with Eisenstaedt's expressed memories of the same event, either. However, to accept McNeel's or McDuffie's accounts of events requires that one completely deny what the photographs clearly show. For instance, McNeel suggests Eisenstaedt posed the sailor and nurse before taking the picture. McDuffie states that Eisenstaedt ran at him after he began kissing the nurse. To believe either account of events from V-J Day, 1945, one must believe also that Eisenstaedt lied about the circumstances surrounding the photograph, and that the photographed V-J Day kissing sequence was doctored to conceal the series of events professed by McNeel and McDuffie. Further, *LIFE* would have to have been an accomplice to the deception and fabrication of these photographs. Such damning verdicts are clearly farfetched.

While conspiratorial plots—like doctoring pictures—might entertain readers, the sensational tales offered by McDuffie and McNeel are more fiction than fact. Reconciling Eisenstaedt's and Mendonsa's versions of events requires only reasonable explanations, revisiting known conditions, and logical analysis. To reconcile McDuffie's or McNeel's versions of events with Eisenstaedt's remembrances demands selective use of evidence, a blanket rejection and disparagement of Eisenstaedt's testimony, and turning a blind eye toward the photographic and historical records. Though it is challenging to completely reconcile Alfred Eisenstaedt's recorded commentary with George Mendonsa's (and others') memories of what happened on August 14, 1945, a careful consideration of the scene in Times Square during that afternoon might help eliminate the discrepancies between the two otherwise reliable sources.

Eisenstaedt's reputation as a world-class photographer is a matter of record and his title as The Father of Photojournalism is unchallenged. However, he was not a detective. Had Eisenstaedt recorded his recollections at the scene, or even a short time afterward, his reporting might be different than what he stated decades later. Fortunately, his Leica's images captured the precise details of the event and these, more than hazy recollections or outlandish claims, strongly favor the Rhode Island fisherman's part in *V-J Day, 1945, Times Square*.

THE WOMAN BEHIND HER MAN

In 1980 George focused all his attention on the sailor in Alfred Eisenstaedt's *V-J Day, 1945, Times Square*. Rita, George's wife of almost thirty-five years, widened his view. Well, at least she tried. When Rita looked at Eisenstaedt's famous photograph she noticed a woman whose eyes and forehead appear over the kissing sailor's right shoulder. While pointing to that woman, Rita said to George, "I was there with you on that day. I think this person is me." George didn't think so. He gave Rita's observation little consideration. He should have known better.

In 1987 George secured Eisenstaedt's three other photos of the V-J Day kissing sequence. What Rita tried to point out seven years earlier came into better view. In the first of Eisenstaedt's four V-J Day photos, the woman over the sailor's right shoulder is fully visible—though a bit out of focus. Still, one can discern the woman's body frame, hairstyle, face shape, and facial features. The woman appears with her right arm at her side and a broad and attractive smile across her face. As most other people in the photograph are in motion (as is clear when examining Eisenstaedt's other photos from the same occurrence), the woman over George's right shoulder remains in the same proximity during all four photos. She appears to be taking in a scene she is somehow connected to. Only the three women to the sailor's left hold more stationary positions in all four pictures.

With the above in mind, Richard Benson's (Yale University Dean of Arts and recognized photo expert) photographic analysis warrants serious consideration. Benson studied the woman over the kissing sailor's right shoulder and pictures of George's girlfriend, Rita Petry, from 1945. Addressing the first photo in the V-J Day kissing sequence, Benson offered; "The woman . . . behind the sailor, though not in focus, clearly has considerable physical resemblance to a photograph of Mrs. Mendonsa taken at approximately the same time as Eisenstaedt's photographs. This similarity even extends to the woman's hairdo. This leads me to believe that the same woman is depicted in both photographs."[8] Professor Benson makes an important point. The resemblance between the identified woman and Rita Petry in 1945 is striking.

Bolstering this assertion, Rita swore under oath in an affidavit that she was present during George and Greta's famous kiss and embrace. Further, no other claimant for either the sailor or nurse has any connection to the woman over the kissing sailor's right shoulder. Even Lois Gibson, the famed forensic artist who contends vehemently that Glenn McDuffie is the kissing sailor, admits that the woman over the kissing sailor's right shoulder could be Rita Petry. However, she clarifies that George might be the man behind the kissing sailor.

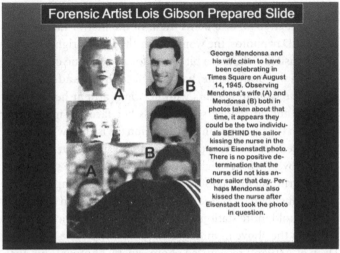

22-3. (*Permission granted by Lois Gibson*)

While Gibson's assertion is not outlandish, at least not initially, the argument relies only on assumptions that support her suggestion and does not consider other points that negate her contention. First, in order for the scenario she suggests to be true, Edith Shain, whom Gibson continually references as the nurse, had to have had a serious lapse in memory or be lying outright. Shain contends that only one person kissed her on V-J Day in Times Square. (Shortly after the kiss photographed by Eisenstaedt, a soldier tried to kiss her.) Greta Zimmer, a dental assistant who claims to be the nurse in the picture, insists that only one sailor kissed her while she made her way through Times Square. So, unless someone other than Edith or Greta participated in the famous kiss, and willingly let sailors line up to take their turn, then the scenario Gibson suggests is likely fictional.

Second, though the man over the sailor's right shoulder in *V-J Day, 1945, Times Square* could resemble George Mendonsa, suggesting that George and the man over the sailor's shoulder are the same person asks too much of the compromised view. One can only see the man's eyebrow, forehead, and crop of hair. Determining his identity is even more challenging than identifying the kissing sailor. Gibson's suggestion depends on too limited a view.

Third, the man in question is not wearing a sailor's cap. Every viewable sailor in the photograph wears his cap properly. While it could be argued that George did not wear his cap or perhaps even the rest of his uniform on August 14, 1945, that runs counter to what he and Rita report and violates Navy regulations. Further, sailors always wear their Navy uniforms with pride, and perhaps never more so than on this day. No convincing reason exists for George not to wear his sailor's cap on August 14, 1945.

Fourth, the right arm and hand of the man Gibson references over the kissing sailor's right shoulder appears in Lt. Victor Jorgensen's photo. He took that picture at the same moment as Eisenstaedt's second shot, though from a different angle. Lieutenant Jorgensen's vantage point provides a better view of the man behind the kissing sailor's right shoulder. In Jorgensen's picture the hands of the man behind the kissing sailor appear to be very small. Because George's hands are enormous, the man behind the kissing sailor cannot be Mendonsa.

Fifth, the man behind the kissing sailor in Eisenstaedt's second photo is likely a man more visually apparent in the first photograph of the kissing sequence. In that photograph a man with his back to the camera walks along the right side of the kissing sailor. He looks to his right in the location behind the kissing sailor. He appears to be motioning in the direction he is looking. This man wears a black or dark-blue pinstriped suit, has small hands, and styles his dark hair like the man over the sailor's shoulder in the second and third photos referenced by Gibson. (He is probably still behind the kissing sailor in the

22-4/5/6. The civilian walking to the kissing sailor's right in Eisenstaedt's first photograph also appears in the background of the second kissing sailor photograph. That man's right hand (visibly smaller than George's hands) is visible in Jorgensen's photograph (third photo above), taken at the precise moment as Eisenstaedt's second photograph. (Top photos permission granted by Bobbi Baker Burrows at *Time-LIFE*. Bottom photo courtesy of the U.S. National Archives.)

fourth picture, but the more erect, tall frame of the kissing sailor hides the shorter man to his back. George Mendonsa stands at six feet, two inches.) Additionally, in the first picture the walking man's right arm sleeve extends to the same length on the hand of the man behind the sailor as in Jorgensen's photograph. These observations suggest that both subjects are the same individual.

Emphasizing the above point, the man to the left in Eisenstaedt's first photo likely pursued a path of travel that put him right behind the kissing sailor in time for *V-J Day, 1945, Times Square*. After appearing in the first of Eisenstaedt's four pictures, the man from the first picture does not appear anywhere else in Eisenstaedt's subsequent photos or Jorgensen's single photo.

Therefore, a thorough consideration of Lois Gibson's suggestion reinforces an argument contrary to the one she extends. As Gibson allows, the woman over George's shoulder in three out of the four pictures appears to be Rita Petry. However, the man to the back of the kissing sailor in Eisenstaedt's second photo appears to be the civilian to the right of the kissing sailor from Eisenstaedt's first photo. The overwhelming weight of evidence strongly suggests the kissing sailor must be George Mendonsa.

The identification of Rita Petry behind the kissing sailor, the marking on George's and the kissing sailor's arm, and an explanation for Eisenstaedt's recollections of the kiss he photographed in 1945 support George Mendonsa's claim well. But unfortunately not everyone was convinced by this evidence. To convince them of George's part in *V-J Day, 1945, Times Square*, one would have to produce a mountain of evidence.

23

A MOUNTAIN OF EVIDENCE

In April 1987 George Mendonsa took his first step in amassing a mountain of evidence to link him to the kissing sailor. While George did not know that he had embarked on a long and difficult climb, two decades later he would stand atop that mountain of evidence supporting his part in *V-J Day, 1945, Times Square*.

On that 1987 spring morning, Francis Silvia, who originally recognized George as the sailor in *V-J Day, 1945, Times Square*, contacted his old friend with a news update. This phone message sounded more frantic than the call he had placed approximately seven years earlier. "You're for sale!" he blurted into the phone receiver that spring morning. Francis had come across a *LIFE* ad selling a framed *V-J Day, 1945, Times Square* with Alfred Eisenstaedt's signature. The advertisement offered the photo for $1,600, considerably more expensive than other autographed pictures on the same page. When he saw this advertisement, George became enraged. He felt exploited. The same company that had brushed aside his claims continued to profit from his likeness.

After looking at—and stewing about—the advertised photo with Eisenstaedt's signature, George contacted *LIFE* and inquired as to the price of the same photo with the sailor's signature. The magazine's respondent told George that *LIFE* could not identify the sailor. George raised his voice and declared, "I'm the sailor!" as if *LIFE* would then just acquiesce to the Rhode Island fisherman's declarations. If only the mystery could be resolved so simply. It could not.

Infuriated by what he perceived as *LIFE*'s audacity, George Mendonsa brought a lawsuit against Time, Inc., over the improper use of *his* picture for their profit.[1] Via a court order, George secured the four photos Eisenstaedt shot of the sailor kissing the nurse on August 14, 1945. At the time, most people in the general public had not viewed these photos.

THE BENSON REPORT

To determine if Eisenstaedt's other photographs of the V-J Day sequence provided more proof of George's claim to the kissing sailor, his lawyer sought the expertise of Richard Mead Atwater Benson. Richard Benson is a nationally recognized photography expert, a master printer, a professor of photography at Yale University, and Yale's Dean of the School of Art from 1996 to 2006. He has extensively researched photomechanical reproduction and published three books, including the highly acclaimed, *The Printed Picture*, which offers an extensive history of image reproduction. In 1987 Benson studied Alfred Eisenstaedt's four photographs of a sailor kissing a nurse on August 14, 1945, to see if they contained evidence supporting George Mendonsa's claim to the kissing sailor.

Benson scrutinized Eisenstaedt's four V-J Day photographs, and subsequently examined George Mendonsa. Benson also reviewed photographs of George Mendonsa produced by John Hopf, a professional Newport photographer hired by George's lawyer. After a meticulous two-week study of all the photos and George Mendonsa, Richard Benson concluded, "Based on a reasonable degree of certainty, George Mendonsa is the sailor in Mr. Eisenstaedt's famous photograph."[2] The Benson Report provides convincing proof, based on a number of factors, that George Mendonsa is the kissing sailor.

Benson's study gave considerable attention to the kissing sailor's right arm. In Eisenstaedt's photographs the sailor's right side is more visible than his left side. Benson determined: "George

Mendonsa has a well-defined patch of dark hair on his right arm which is evident in all four of Eisenstaedt's photographs but most clearly in photograph No. 1 taken by Eisenstaedt. The patch of dark hair exists today and I have had the occasion to personally observe it and it appears in photograph No. 5 taken recently by photographer John Hopf."[3] Despite the patch of dark hair's stark appearance on the kissing sailor's right arm, surprisingly no other claimant has ever referenced the area for the purpose of making their claim.

Just as observable as the dark patch of hair on the right arm is a shading difference between the sailor's right hand and forearm. Benson noted of this subject, "The hands of the sailor in the Eisenstaedt photographs are heavily sunburned, while the arms are not. This is a characteristic of the working fishermen that distinguishes George to this day."[4] During his three-week leave prior to visiting Times Square, George fished with his "old man" almost every day. Referencing George's activities during July and August of 1945, Benson concluded, "This is a reasonable explanation as to the hands being dark and the arms light or white."[5] Like the dark patch of hair on the kissing sailor's arm, no other candidate references the kissing sailor's dark hand for identification purposes.

In his report Benson calls attention to the kissing sailor's hands, especially the back of his right hand, which is fully visible in all four of Eisenstaedt's pictures. After examining the picture and George Mendonsa, Benson found: "The hands in the photographs are huge and there is not much question that George's hands are immense in a similar way."[6] Though Benson's observation of the kissing sailor's hand size addresses one of the most obvious physical characteristics found in *V-J Day, 1945, Times Square*, other than Lois Gibson, no other source makes mention of the kissing sailor's hand size.[7]

Continuing the focus on the sailor's hands, Benson added the following two observations in his report: "The pattern of veins shown in the Eisenstaedt photographs on the back of the sailor's right hand is the same as those shown in a recent John

23-1/2. Like the kissing sailor's hand, George Mendonsa's hand is abnormally large. (*Permission granted by Bill Powers*)

Hopf photograph of George Mendonsa's right hand." Benson further notes, "The sailor's right thumb in Eisenstaedt's photos bends in a certain way at the second joint that is a distinct characteristic. I have seen this characteristic in George Mendonsa and it is shown in photograph No. 8."[8]

Considering that the right hand and arm are among the most highly visible physical characteristics available for inspection in the famed picture, the evidence presented in the Benson Report is compelling and of critical importance in identifying the kissing sailor. In laymen's terms, the right hand is dark, huge, and has distinct surface markings, identified both in Eisenstaedt's 1945 photographs of the kissing sailor and John Hopf's 1987 photographs of George Mendonsa. As convincing as those comparisons are, there is even more compelling evidence from the Benson Report to consider. Much more.

In addition to the kissing sailor's right hand and arm, in his report Benson focused attention on other important distinguishing characteristics. Studying the sailor's right eyebrow, Benson noted, "Mr. Mendonsa presently has what appears to be the long-lasting evidence of a scar within the area of his right eyebrow. A separate photograph of the subject Mendonsa taken during the time of his World War II Navy service . . . demonstrates what appears to be a scar in the same area and the No. 4 photograph taken by Mr. Eisenstaedt also shows a strongly similar mark."[9] Benson does not reference other photographs for this purpose because Eisenstaedt's fourth photo offers the best view of the right eyebrow area.

While Benson's focus on the right side stems from the juxtaposition of the 1945 kissing sailor and the photographer, Benson's examination of the kissing sailor's left side reveals an extraordinary discovery. Most other claimants' commentary about the sailor's left side speculates on why the left wrist contorts up and away from the nurse's face. Such remarks rely on unverifiable explanations or questionable story lines. Benson's finding regarding the left arm requires no elaborate explanation and is visible to the untrained eye. Benson noticed that when the kissing sailor twisted his left arm away from the woman's neck and chest, he exposed his lower forearm to Eisenstaedt's camera. Though this observation may seem, at first, insignificant, closer study confirms an extraordinarily distinguishing feature. As Professor Benson explains:

> I discovered . . . an unusual bump that appears on the inside left arm several inches below the wrist of the sailor which had not been pointed out to me prior to my examining of the photographs. Immediately thereafter, I arranged to personally examine the same location on George Mendonsa's left arm and a virtually identical bump is there at exactly the same location. This small bump, lump or subcutaneous growth, probably called a wen in medical terminology, appears very clearly in the present day photograph taken of Mr. Mendonsa's arm by photographer John Hopf of Newport, R.I.[10]

Benson's report goes on to share the significance of this finding. "It is impossible for me to believe that George Mendonsa and the sailor in the photograph could share this uncommon physical oddity and not be one and the same person." George had never taken any notice of the "wen" and did not think to look

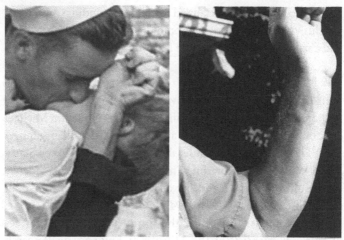

23-3/4. After determining there was raised tissue on Eisenstaedt's kissing sailor's left forearm, in 1987 Professor Richard Benson found the same bump in the exact location on George's left forearm. (*Permission granted by George Mendonsa*)

for it in the photograph. That Benson discovered the identical markings in Eisenstaedt's fourth photo and on George's left arm independent of any prodding from George or his lawyer makes this discovery all the more important to proving the identity of the kissing sailor beyond a reasonable doubt. No other sailor-claimant has ever come forward to present a distinguishing feature even remotely matching what Benson found in the photograph and on George Mendonsa's arm. The "wen" remains plainly visible on George's left arm to this day.

Professor Richard Benson's observations of physical markings, aberrations, and raised tissues provide conclusive and seemingly irrefutable proof that George Mendonsa is the kissing sailor in Alfred Eisenstaedt's famous photograph. The evidence Benson provides is compelling, clearly identifiable, and in most cases unique to George Mendonsa.

One might think the Benson Report would terminate any further debate concerning the kissing sailor's identity. Sadly, for a host of reasons, it did not. Other experts and authorities either ignored

Benson's contribution or claimed to trump his findings with more conclusive evidence. The new opinions gained media attention and a national following. George Mendonsa had to fight on.

THE MERL EVIDENCE

Fourteen years after Yale University photo expert Professor Richard Benson pinned Mendonsa as the kissing sailor, Michael Cardin, Katherine McMahon, and Jerry O'Donnell organized *The VJ Day Sailor Project* under the auspices of the United States Naval War College Museum. They hoped to produce evidence that could prove once and for all who the kissing sailor is in Alfred Eisenstaedt's *V-J Day, 1945, Times Square*.

To accomplish this goal, the group secured the services of research scientists at the Mitsubishi Engineering Research Laboratories (MERL) in Cambridge, Massachusetts. *The VJ Day Sailor Project* organizers selected George as the subject for this investigative mission because they considered his claims to the kissing sailor's identity the most credible among all the kissing sailor claimants.[11]

The MERL team members who brought their expertise to *The VJ Day Sailor Project* were experts in the fields of computer graphics and computer vision technology.[12] The MERL scientists had published widely on the latest technology's use, including a report entitled *A Bilinear Illumination Model for Robust Face Recognition*, which was presented at the International Conference on Computer Vision in Beijing, China. Led by Baback Moghadam, PhD, and Hanspeter Pfister, PhD, the MERL scientists employed cutting-edge technology that had been awarded honors by the U.S. Defense Advanced Research Project Agency (DARPA) in an official face-recognition competition.[13] Cutting-edge vision technology in the hands of world-renowned vision technology experts created an identity-seeking "dream team."

The MERL scientists produced a report entitled *3D Facial Modeling & Synthesis of the Sailor in Alfred Eisenstaedt's "VJ-Day Kiss" Photo*. Their report's findings mirrored Richard Benson's conclusions, but derived from a completely different set of determinants. Rather than relying on the power of informed observation and photo analysis· expertise, the MERL scientists used 3D face-recognition digital scanning technology to establish whether the contour of George's "de-aged" face matched the contour of the kissing sailor's face in *V-J Day, 1945, Times Square*. Typically the technology was used for biometrics research, security and surveillance applications, or by law enforcement agencies to age missing children from still photos for identification years after a child's abduction. In the summer of 2004 that technology was employed for the benefit of correcting the historical record.

The first step in creating a 3D shape of George's face required Mendonsa to sit inside MERL's custom-made face spanning dome. Surrounded by 16 high-resolution color cameras and 150 computer-controlled, white LED lights, the MERL scientists collected more than 4,000 digital images of George's face within one minute. Those pictures were then processed to obtain very high-resolution shape and reflectance models. In addition, the team scanned George's face to obtain a registered 3D model and skin texture. After some digital editing to remove sensor noise and other scanning artifacts, the 2004 George 3D face was then "de-aged" by "projecting George's 3D face shape onto progressively refined subspaces of increasing dimensionality (N "eigen-modes") and selecting the one which required the fewest number of bases."[14] The reverse-aged 3D shape for the younger George was then fitted to a 1940s photograph of George. The scientists then used George's face texture from the input photograph to create a textured 3D face model of George. After accounting for George's pose (via an optimization algorithm) and Times Square's illumination environment (via a global linear illumination subspace model for Lambertian objects), the "mask" was then superimposed onto the kissing sailor in *V-J Day, 1945, Times Square* using computer graphic image rendering. The "de-aged" 2004 George model overlay blended well with the 1945 image. The MERL scientists' report provides "compelling evidence" that George Mendonsa is the kissing sailor.[15]

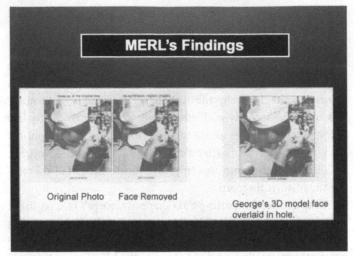

23-5. The slide from the Mitsubishi Electric Research Laboratory shows George's facial mask superimposed onto the kissing sailor's face. (*Permission granted by Baback Moghaddam, PhD, and Hanspeter Pfister, PhD*)

Despite the persuasiveness of MERL's findings, some remained less than convinced by the reporting. For instance, famed forensic artist Lois Gibson sees little significance in MERL's report. When asked about the scientists' findings on *Good Morning America* in 2007, Gibson reiterated other factors she felt supported Glenn McDuffie's claim to the kissing sailor. Rather than address the reliability of MERL's advanced technology, Gibson replied that Mendonsa had "more of a square head." Her comment does nothing to refute the evidence produced by the MERL scientists.

Referring to MERL's findings, Jerry O'Donnell, a retired Navy captain and leader of *The VJ Day Sailor Project* said, "If this evidence were presented in a trial, it would have to lead to a conviction."[16] While publicly the MERL scientists were reluctant to be drawn into any legal haggling over their conclusions, the Mitsubishi (which includes MERL) news brochure *CONNECTions* ran a story entitled "60 year old mystery solved— MERL IDs 'Kissing Sailor' of WWII." In the article Mitsubishi

Electric referenced the MERL scientists' evidence that identified George Mendonsa as the kissing sailor as "compelling."[17]

By the sixtieth anniversary of *V-J Day, 1945, Times Square*, one of the nation's leading photo experts as well as a team of world-renowned technological identification scientists had conclusively proven the kissing sailor's identity. While that body of work was impressive, the most persuasive confirmation of George Mendonsa's contention still lay four years in the future.

TRUMP CARD: THE SAUER TEAM'S FINDINGS

Of the four most prominent "kissing sailor contenders," Glenn McDuffie is the most vocal and widely acknowledged. The reason for his popular standing can be captured in two words: Lois Gibson. Lois Gibson's opinion on the identity of the kissing sailor benefited McDuffie handsomely, and for good reason. The renowned forensic artist is credentialed and confident. Soon after she came out in support of McDuffie's claim to the kissing sailor, her arguments gained a faithful following from the press. Many in the public accepted Gibson's opinions as if they were beyond reproach. As far as they were concerned, the search for the kissing sailor was over. It wasn't.

Converting Gibson's flock to disciples of George Mendonsa presented a significant challenge. While the evidence supporting George Mendonsa's case was substantial, Gibson's and McDuffie's disciples thought those findings originated from sources inferior to Gibson's proven forensic identification qualifications. In their opinion, photograph analyzers and technology gurus were no match for the facial recognition expert who had helped convict more lawbreakers than any other forensic artist in history. Converting her followers required divine intervention—or something just as compelling.

In the absence of a godly source, the conversion called for an earthly authority with greater forensic qualifications than Lois Gibson. That authority had to be well trained in identifying bony structures, able to detect similarities and differences between individuals, and, most challenging, had to determine their findings from black-and-white photos. The investigation required a forensic physical anthropologist of the greatest skill. The quest to find such an expert was extraordinarily difficult. College anthropology department heads provided well-meaning but vague direction. Inquiries to university professors typically wrapped up with similar refrains:

"What you need is a physical anthropologist."

"Great. Who can I speak with?"

"Ah, for what you're doing, working off pictures to determine an identity, we are not going to be much help. Hmm. That's a tough one."

It was tough. Few forensic anthropologists worked off photos—especially sixty-five-year-old black-and-white prints. When college professors familiar with this discipline did return e-mail requests for assistance, they often suggested a person who might be able to help. Those suggestions all led to dead ends. However, there was one exception.

Several sources suggested Dr. Norman Sauer as *the* physical anthropologist for determining physical identifications from photographs. His accomplishments and a long list of published articles substantiated accolades from colleagues across the country. Dr. Norman Sauer practices forensic anthropology at Michigan State University. He ranks among the top in his field. In 2007 the American Academy of Forensic Science awarded Dr. Sauer the T. Dale Steward Award for Outstanding Contributions in the Field of Physical Anthropology. In September 2008 Dr. Sauer agreed to conduct a study of the kissing sailor's identity, assisted by his graduate students, Amy Michael, Jamie Minns, and Megan Moreau. He indicated that the challenge interested him and his students. They understood that their work would make a contribution to history.

The Sauer team conducted their examination over a four-month period, starting in December 2008. They scrutinized photos of popular kissing sailor candidates and studied Alfred Eisenstaedt's four photographs and Lt. Victor Jorgensen's single photo from August 14, 1945. They cropped pictures, compared and contrasted facial features, and cross-referenced notes. They showed no interest in the story behind the photo and never inquired about the saga surrounding the conflicting claims regarding the kissing sailor's identity. Instead, they focused on hairline curvatures, widths and lengths of facial features, and bony structures. While they took note of similarities, differences commanded most of their attention. Different people can share likenesses. Discrepancies eliminate candidates from further consideration.

In April 2009 the Sauer team completed their study. They expressed great confidence in their findings and a willingness to share their determinations with the general public. Because their findings were heavily based on visual determinants, they produced a slide show to demonstrate their conclusions.

The Sauer team's findings are extraordinarily convincing. Their study provides substantial and persuasive evidence that proves George Mendonsa is the kissing sailor. The Sauer team found consistencies between George Mendonsa's cheekbones, nose bridge, nostrils, hairline, and ears and those of the kissing sailor in *V-J Day, 1945, Times Square*. But the Sauer team went further. They put aside those *consistencies* and went in search of *inconsistencies* between Mendonsa and the sailor in the photographs. After an exhaustive effort, they discovered no inconsistencies.

Interestingly, the Sauer team found Glenn McDuffie the earliest and easiest candidate to eliminate for further consideration. Inconsistencies between his features and the kissing sailor accumulated quickly. McDuffie's ear, hairline, nasal breadth, and cheekbone were determined to be inconsistent with those of the kissing sailor. In addition, the Sauer team found no dark spot on McDuffie's arm. After a few days of study, McDuffie's inconsistencies with the kissing sailor far outnumbered his consistencies.

The Sauer team's elimination of Ken McNeel from further consideration was not so easy. They found that Ken McNeel's hairline, cheekbone, and nose proved consistent with the kissing sailor. However, the team concluded that McNeel's eyebrows and ears were not consistent with the kissing sailor. Therefore,

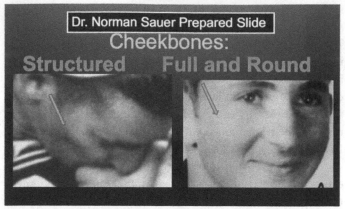

23-6. Glenn McDuffie's rounded cheekbone contrasts with the sculpted cheekbone of the kissing sailor. (*Permission granted by Dr. Norman Sauer*)

Sauer and his graduate students eliminated Ken McNeel as a viable candidate for the kissing sailor.

Unlike his competitors, George Mendonsa's consistencies with the kissing sailor were not marginalized by inconsistencies. One of Sauer's team's more visually apparent observations of Mendonsa and the kissing sailor focuses on the shape of the right cheekbone, clearly visible in both Eisenstaedt's and Jorgensen's photographs. Like Mendonsa's, the kissing sailor's cheekbone appears "sculpted." The cheek's skeletal contour is positioned high on the face with no excessive flesh. The trim face with slightly protruding cheekbone creates a sunken cavity above the jaw. This hollow becomes accented further when puckering the lips as one would do when kissing.

Other Sauer team findings present comparisons of the kissing sailor's nose to that of George Mendonsa. For this purpose, owing to the photographers' positions in reference to the kissing sailor, Lieutenant Jorgensen's picture proves more helpful than any of Eisenstaedt's four photos. The Sauer team determined that the nose of both Mendonsa and the kissing sailor sport the same breadth between the eyebrows. (Sauer focuses attention to this fact by drawing a yellow caret at the ridge of the nose

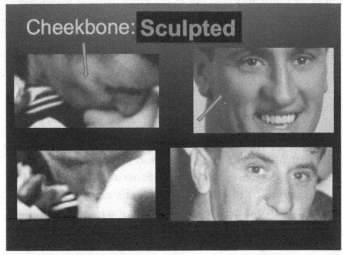

23-7. This Sauer team slide points out a sculpted cheekbone on both the kissing sailor and George Mendonsa. (*Permission granted by Dr. Norman Sauer*)

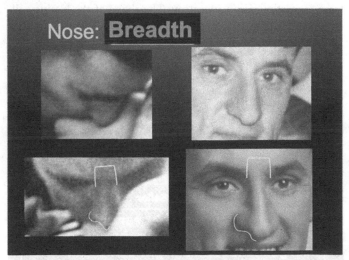

23-8. The kissing sailor and George Mendonsa have the same nose shape. (*Permission granted by Dr. Norman Sauer*)

between the eyes.) Additionally, Sauer observed that the kissing sailor's nostrils flared out in the same shape as Mendonsa's.

The Sauer team's examinations of the kissing sailor's eyebrow region also showed evidence that favored Mendonsa's claim. Employing Eisenstaedt's pictures, the Sauer team noticed that Mendonsa and the kissing sailor sport the same arch-shaped eyebrows. Their examination of three different pictures of George Mendonsa during the World War II era supported the same conclusion.

The kissing sailor's right ear garnered much of the Sauer team's attention, and for good reason. An ear's shape offers a litany of distinctive characteristics. Sauer and his graduate students determined that the kissing sailor's ear shape is consistent with that of George Mendonsa. The top right of the kissing sailor's ear runs north to a pointed peak. The top of that same ear seems narrow in relation to the lower lobe of the ear, which protrudes in a southeasterly direction. Also, though all of the kissing sailor photos offer only angular views of the right ear, another observation of the right ear not offered by the Sauer team is worthy of consideration. The shape of the kissing sailor's and Mendonsa's right ear canal entrance is similar to a

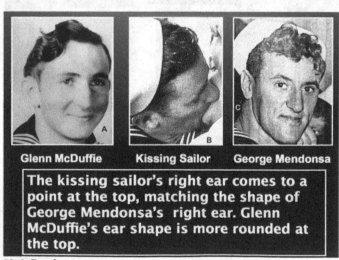

Glenn McDuffie   Kissing Sailor   George Mendonsa

The kissing sailor's right ear comes to a point at the top, matching the shape of George Mendonsa's right ear. Glenn McDuffie's ear shape is more rounded at the top.

23-9. Ear shapes

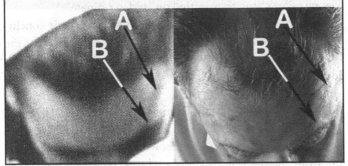

> The sailor from the August 14, 1945 photo has a diagonal ridge on his skull, A, that originates from a midpoint of his eyebrow at B. Glenn McDuffie has the identical bony ridge on his skull that originates at the same location of his eyebrow and travels up his skull at an identical angle.

23-10. (*Permission granted by Lois Gibson*)

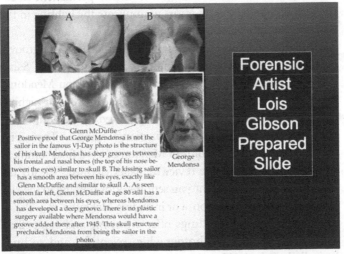

Glenn McDuffie

Positive proof that George Mendonsa is not the sailor in the famous VJ-Day photo is the structure of his skull. Mendonsa has deep grooves between his frontal and nasal bones (the top of his nose between the eyes) similar to skull B. The kissing sailor has a smooth area between his eyes, exactly like Glenn McDuffie and similar to skull A. As seen bottom far left, Glenn McDuffie at age 80 still has a smooth area between his eyes, whereas Mendonsa has developed a deep groove. There is no plastic surgery available where Mendonsa would have a groove added there after 1945. This skull structure precludes Mendonsa from being the sailor in the photo.

George Mendonsa

Forensic Artist Lois Gibson Prepared Slide

23-11. (*Permission granted by Lois Gibson*)

mushroom with the stem intact. All the previous ear comparisons—the pointed peak, protruding earlobe, and canal shape—
strongly support Mendonsa's claim to be the kissing sailor.

For each examined area—the cheekbone, the nose, the
hairline, and the ear—the University of Michigan researchers reached the same conclusion: consistent with Mendonsa.
Revisits, crosschecks, and repeated observations solidified their
determinations. Regarding the eyebrow and dark spot on the
kissing sailor's arm, they settled on "Indeterminate."[18]

Four months after the Sauer team produced their conclusions, Dr. Sauer agreed to review a Lois Gibson finding that she
asserted solidified Glenn McDuffie's claim to the kissing sailor's
identity and eliminated George Mendonsa from any further
consideration.

After reviewing Gibson's commentary and slides, Dr. Sauer
wrote of the diagonal ridge on McDuffie's head, "There is no
known structure on the skull that would form a ridge originat-
ing from the midpoint of 'his' eyebrow. Note that the 'ridge'
is unilateral. The apparent ridge is all about the light source
and reflection. It has nothing to do with a permanent structure. Note that there is an effort to duplicate the lighting in the
McDuffie and the kissing sailor images."[19]

Regarding Gibson's claim that "Mendonsa has deep grooves
between his frontal and nasal bones . . . similar to skull B," Sauer
counters, "In fact the furrows between the brows on Mendonsa
likely reflect the fact that brow ridges continue to grow throughout
life and any grooves are probably emphasized by the addition of
soft tissue in the area, also likely a function of aging. . . . There is no
such groove in earlier pictures of Mendonsa." As a final comment
about the Gibson slides he reviewed, Sauer clarified, "Clearly the
evidence in the Power Point you sent me adds nothing to the evidence for excluding Mendonsa or including McDuffie."[20]

The Sauer team's findings offer crowning and compelling
proof atop anecdotal, photographic, scientific, and techno-
logically based considerations that point directly—and only—
toward George Mendonsa as the kissing sailor. In addition to

providing convincing proof that George Mendonsa is the kissing sailor, the Sauer study gave equal consideration to other kissing sailor candidates. Their approach was different from other studies, for they did not try to prove any one candidate was the kissing sailor, but rather set out to determine which candidate, if any, matched up with the kissing sailor's appearance. Considering Dr. Sauer's standing in the forensic anthropology field, his study's open-minded approach, and the details of his findings, there is no question regarding the identity of the kissing sailor in Eisenstaedt's *V-J Day, 1945, Times Square.*

At the conclusion of the Sauer team's months-long study, Dr. Sauer reflected candidly on the accumulated evidence in support of George Mendonsa's contention: "You have quite a case. You could go to court with this." George preferred delivering the information to *LIFE.*

24

INDISPUTABLE?
THE CASE FOR GRETA

Edith Shain's part in *V-J Day, 1945, Times Square* seems to qualify as a gimme. From 1980 onward she captured the nation's eye and proved a most charming and outgoing icon. There were few other female candidates, and almost no sources supporting their cause. Virtually every magazine article discussing the nurse's identity supported Shain's part in Eisenstaedt's photo. The casual observer saw no reason to question her standing. But in the event their curiosity tempted them, Shain clarified that her part in the famed photo continues to be "indisputable."[1] Shain's assumed role in the famous photo stems from a letter she wrote to Alfred Eisenstaedt in the late 1970s. That one-page, handwritten note caught Eisenstaedt's attention, and maybe even stirred his imagination. He raced out to Los Angeles to meet Shain and soon thereafter named her *the* nurse in his iconic photograph. Eisenstaedt's recognition of Shain set in concrete her part in *LIFE*'s most popular photo.

In August 1980 *LIFE* strengthened Eisenstaedt's recognition of Shain by running a flattering feature article that amounted to a coronation of the long-lost nurse from the magazine's most famous photo. In this celebratory piece, *LIFE* announced, "His [Eisenstaedt's] most famous couple has long been nameless, but when the nurse recently wrote to him, a delighted Eisie visited her and took the pictures that follow."[2] Those pictures included a posed 1945 portrait of Edith in her nurse's uniform. Other pictures showed Edith with her family and one of her bunny-hopping with a kindergarten class she taught in 1980. On the same page Eisenstaedt referenced Shain as a "vivacious, lovely woman."

Including Eisenstaedt's glowing commentary of Shain did not exactly roll out a welcome mat for other candidates. Though *LIFE* did introduce claimants Greta (Zimmer) Friedman and Barbara Sokol to their readers in the magazine's October 1980 issue, the late arrivals never stood a chance. *LIFE* provided Shain a wider spread atop her two competitors who shared the bottom half of the page. Dethroning the crowned queen in white stockings proved almost impossible. Since neither challenger possessed a knockout punch, *LIFE*, in essence, consigned them both to audience members. With Eisenstaedt in her corner and *LIFE* refereeing matters, nobody could dispute Shain's claim, at least not for the foreseeable future.

Over the coming years, few hunted for the proof supporting Shain's claims. Those who gave chase found little evidence supporting her contention—and for good reason. Little exists. That reality might explain why Shain's reign as undisputed queen at *LIFE* lasted only two months. In October 1980 *LIFE* offered the following: "No fewer than 10 sailors, as well as two more nurses, have managed to recall to the last detail how it happened and how they happened to be in Times Square—persuading us that all their stories are true. But who is in the picture? And who kissed whom? Truth be told, only Eisie ever knew the answer. But since his notes and other negatives have vanished, he cannot make a final choice."[3] This statement falls short of a wholesale endorsement of Shain's assertion, not that it mattered. The echoes from *LIFE*'s original declaration would muffle Friedman's and Sokol's future challenges to Shain's standing.

Though most assumed Shain's claim to the kissed nurse in Eisenstaedt's photo rested on secure footing atop the claimant hill, over the coming years her standing as the nurse in *V-J Day, 1945, Times Square* eroded, slowly. In 1984 a German network came to the United States to interview Alfred Eisenstaedt about his life's work. Interestingly, the show's producers contacted Greta Friedman rather than Edith Shain (and George Mendonsa rather than other kissing sailor candidates) for the interview because their researchers determined that they had the most credible case. Though Eisenstaedt did not speak to the identity of the sailor and nurse in the documentary, *Bilder Die Geschichte Machten* (*Pictures That Make History*), directors spliced in Friedman's commentary amongst the photographer's memories of the famous photograph.

Pictures That Make History's referencing of Friedman for the documentary takes on greater significance when one considers the input of Bobbi Baker Burrows, Director of Photography at *LIFE Books*. Over her forty-year career at *LIFE*, Burrows edited some of the magazine's most memorable photographs, ones that captured events such as the Apollo Space Program and the Olympics. At *LIFE*, Burrows worked as Alfred Eisenstaedt's boss. Of that role she once remarked, "But secretly we both knew that I was his assistant."[4] As boss or assistant, Burrows knew "Eisie" well and spent many summers on Martha's Vineyard in his company. Burrows' recollection of conversations with Eisenstaedt severely undermines his early endorsement of Shain's part in his most famous photograph. On one occasion, speaking to Eisie about his selection of Shain as the nurse, Burrows asked, "Why did you ever endorse her as the one?" (Burrows never thought Shain was the nurse in *V-J Day, 1945, Times Square*.) Eisie responded, "I know, I know. It just kind of happened that way."[5] Eisenstaedt never settled on Shain's role in his famous photograph. Nor should he have.

Eisenstaedt's lack of conviction probably derives from plainly visible observations. If one bothers to compare the nurse in *V-J Day, 1945, Times Square* to the three primary claimants for her part, an important detail comes into clear view. Greta (Zimmer) Friedman resembles the nurse in Eisie's photo much more than does Edith Shain or Barbara Sokol. The most vulnerable aspect of Shain's claim to being the kissed nurse involves the couple's respective heights. If the backward-leaning nurse stood upright in her stocking feet, the top of her hairdo would meet the sailor's chin. An upright Edith Shain would not extend to the sailor's

24-1/2. Carl Muscarello towers over Edith Shain in a photograph taken in 2005. The couple's height discrepancy is far greater than that between the kissing sailor and the nurse in Alfred Eisenstaedt's famous photograph from 1945. (*All rights reserved from Getty Images, #10804623*)

collarbone. Edith Shain, by her own admission and the determination of any standardized measuring stick, is short. Whether she stands in at four feet nine inches"[6] or four feet ten inches,[7] Shain had this to say of her miniature frame: "I always wanted to be a nurse at that time, but the problem was I'm very small and I couldn't get into the hospitals [because] there was a height requirement then." Emphasizing this admission she added, "I remember one hospital where all of the nurses looked like the [Radio City] Rockettes, so I put my hair up to get height, but no one was fooled."[8] And just as Shain could not fool the staff at the hospital, she cannot convince an observant viewer that she is tall enough to be the nurse in *LIFE*'s most reproduced photo. A picture of Edith Shain and Carl Muscarello at a 2005 Times Square Alliance reenactment of *V-J Day, 1945, Times Square* underscores the enormous height discrepancy between Shain and Muscarello. Unless the kissing sailor stood on his tippy toes at approximately five feet six inches tall, Shain cannot possibly have participated in the original famed Times Square kiss.

Adding weight (and height!) to this crucial discrepancy in Shain's claims, all of the most popular kissing sailor claimants stand taller than Carl Muscarello. Glenn McDuffie claims to have stood at six feet in 1945. Ken McNeel and George Mendonsa measured six feet two inches in 1945. If matched with Edith Shain, all the most seriously considered kissing sailor candidates would be deemed freakishly tall. Even Muscarello, at five feet eleven inches, appears to be a giant beside Shain. Though all four candidates make strong cases for their part in the famed kiss, if one accepts Edith Shain's claim to the nurse's identity, then McDuffie's, McNeel's, Muscarello's, and Mendonsa's heights remove each of them from further consideration as the kissing sailor. Could the odds against such an unbelievable conclusion have motivated Shain to employ a cleverly deflective strategy concerning the sailor's identity?

Of course, a look at the photographed nurse's facial features would go a long way toward identifying her. Unfortunately, the sailor's positioning effectively blocks a meaningful viewing of the nurse's mouth, nose, eyes, and ears. Still, there are revealing characteristics that can be observed and that can assist in

24-3/4. Eisenstaedt's photographed nurse is not full bodied. This observation is more in keeping with Greta Friedman's physique than Edith Shain's body composition. (*All rights reserved from AP Images, #05081109005.*)

"Let me tell you," says Edith Shain, "the sun goes up, the sun goes down. It didn't change things. It wasn't a big deal." After all, a pretty girl gets more than one kiss, right? But for the record, Edith describes the situation. "It was a good kiss. It went on for a long time," she recalls. "I closed my eyes, I didn't resist. I think, sometimes, if I hadn't been with my girlfriend, I might have stayed."

Greta Friedman is understanding. "There's no doubt that Mrs. Shain was there and got kissed," she grants, "because every female was grabbed and kissed by men in uniform." But, says Greta, 56, of Frederick, Md, "a definitely is my shape. I used a comb in my hair. I had a purse like the one in the nurse's hand. I remember being kissed by a sailor, right on Broadway."

Just before it happened, Barbara Sokol recalls, she got "an icky, sloppy kiss" and was wiping her mouth with a handkerchief when up walked this gob who yelled, " 'Gotcha!' I said. 'No! No! No!' and when he bent me back I thought, 'My God, I'm gonna fall!' " Barbara, 56, a nurse in Derby, Conn., has kept the pictured moment preserved in a frame, "my one claim to fame."

24-5. In 1980 Edith Shain, Greta Freidman, and Barbara Sokol submitted photographs of themselves from 1945 to *LIFE*. Notice Friedman's hair (bottom left) is styled the same as the nurse in *V-J Day, 1945, Times Square*. (*Permission granted by Bobbi Baker Burrows at Time-Life*)

determining the nurse's identity. For example, the legs of the photographed woman in *V-J Day, 1945, Times Square* are long and thin, certainly not short and fleshy. Her frame is slender, not stout or full-bodied. She is not busty. These descriptors characterize Greta Zimmer in 1945 far more accurately than they describe Edith Shain during the same time frame. Edith appears far shorter, shapelier, and more endowed than the nurse in Eisenstaedt's photo. By contrast, Greta Zimmer's relatively tall frame (at five feet four, and, three-quarter inches she stood more than a half-foot taller than Shain) sports a trim build that distinguishes all aspects of her body. Zimmer matches the nurse in the *V-J Day, 1945, Times Square* photo far more than does Shain.

The female candidates' hairstyle and length also help narrow the field of would-be kissed nurses. In 1980 each claimant provided *LIFE* with a professionally posed shot from 1945. In those photos the candidates wore their nurse's or dental assistant's uniforms. One of the three portraits suggests a strong resemblance to Eisenstaedt's nurse.

Barbara Sokol's photo shows her hair parted from the top left side of her head, and brushed over to the right where she clips the wave into place. Her hair falls at the sides, completely covering her ears. Her long locks rest on her shoulders, hiding the back of her neck. In the picture Edith Shain provided *LIFE*, her hair stands up in front, creating a wave maybe five inches or higher. (She may have styled her hair this way to appear taller, which would be consistent with her commentary about trying to get hired at a hospital with a height requirement.) Her hair is pushed back at the sides, but covers the top half of her right ear. The back of her hair falls to shoulder length. Unlike Barbara and Edith, dental assistant Greta Zimmer's photo demonstrates a tightly drawn hairstyle, held together at the crest of her head by a hair comb. The hairstyle completely exposes the ear on the left side of her head. One cannot determine her hair's length because it is pinned together above her exposed hairline.

Collectively, these observations make for interesting and telling comparisons with the woman in the center of Eisenstaedt's V-J Day picture. Again, admittedly, the pose of the nurse and the angle from which the photographers took the picture presents less than a complete viewing, but one can make a comparison worthy of consideration. Noticeable similarities and differences clearly suggest a closer likeness between the kissed nurse and Greta Zimmer than to either Barbara Sokol or Edith Shain. In all five of Eisenstaedt's and Lieutenant Jorgensen's photographs, the nurse wears her hair tightly bound above the ears, not allowing her locks to extend beyond the neck hairline. The look compares very similarly, perhaps identically, to the picture taken of Greta Zimmer a month or so before August 14, 1945. The dental assistant's and nurse's hairstyles appear interchangeable. By contrast the *V-J Day, 1945, Times Square* nurse's hairdo differs from both Sokol's or Shain's styling taken during the same general time frame. The examination of hairstyles suggests that George Mendonsa kissed Greta Zimmer in *V-J Day, 1945, Times Square*.

While kissing sailor candidates direct significant attention to the photographed sailor's hands to prove their case, the nurse's hands receive little notice. Perhaps they should garner more. Those hands provide clues to the kissed woman's identity. Like other physical comparisons, a study of the nurse's hands reveals a likeness to Greta. Greta has long slim fingers that extend from slender, even bony, hands. The description applies equally well to the kissed woman in both photographers' V-J Day 1945 photos. In Jorgensen's photo, the nurse's clenched left hand exposes its skeletal structure. Of the same hand, Greta's future husband noticed the woman's fingers tucked tightly inward while the thumb extends outward. This feature is best seen in *V-J Day, 1945, Times Square*. Over the years he had noticed this same formation in Greta's hand whenever she became tense. Eisenstaedt's second photo also provides a good view of the kissed woman's long fingers as they clutch a small tapestry purse. (Greta reports that she carried that patterned hand purse with her to Times Square.) Interestingly, the other two nurse candidates never speak about their hands, despite the fact that the woman's hands have high visibility in *V-J Day, 1945, Times Square*.

In addition to physical comparisons, the three female candidates' renditions of the V-J Day kiss offer interesting considerations. While Edith Shain's and Greta Friedman's accounts are similar, Barbara Sokol's version differs greatly. Greta Friedman's remembrance comes across as the most believable.

Barbara Sokol's version of *V-J Day, 1945, Times Square* varies tremendously from photographer Alfred Eisenstaedt's memory of that day. In 1980 Sokol, fifty-six years old and working as a nurse in Derby, Connecticut, described the August 1945 kiss as "ucky" and "sloppy." She wrote that she had been wiping her mouth with a handkerchief (apparently a multicolored designer handkerchief) "when up walked this gob who yelled, 'gotcha!' I said, 'No! No! No!' and when he bent me back I thought, 'My God, I'm gonna fall.'"[9] In another interview she provided to *20/20* that same year, she explained the manner in which the sailor approached her: "He sort of had it hunched down and said 'you're for me.'" While Sokol describes what one might expect of a self-assured and assertive sailor, her story contrasts dramatically with every kissing sailor candidate's reported memories. These irreconcilable differences help explain why, beyond 1980, Sokol's candidacy drew little attention.

Edith Shain's memory of the 1945 photograph rarely evokes strong opposition. That is not surprising. In addition to introducing her story before any other candidates, her tale matched standard-bearer Alfred Eisenstaedt's earlier printed memory of the event. Further, Shain's story shared themes that draw universal praise rather than challenge. For instance, Shain said she let the sailor kiss her because he had fought for his country. In one interview she said the sailor swept her away as she gave over to his force. She remembers "he laid me over in his arms."[10] Shain described the resulting picture to the Associated Press as being about "hope, love, peace and tomorrow."[11] Her recollection of events evokes patriotism, romanticism, and optimism. All play well with a sentimental public.

In addition to playing her hand well, Edith Shain's recollections avoided specifics. For instance, Edith claimed she arrived in Times Square on August 14 with another nurse who does not appear in the picture. Even when pressed to offer her friend's name, she refused to do so. When asked pointed questions, she responded in noncommittal or vague terms. Replies along the lines of, *I didn't get a good look*, *We didn't talk*, and *It's difficult to say*, dominated her interview commentaries. She offered up nothing that could be easily taken to task. Instead, for over thirty years she remembered and relayed only the idealistic elements of the famous photographed kiss. Her comments drew admiration, acclaim, applause, and affirmation.

By contrast, Greta Friedman did not try to sell her story

with references to romance or patriotism. She arrived in Times Square alone, did not speak to or take a meaningful look at the sailor who kissed her. She had no idea that two photographers and a group of about twenty or so people had looked on when the sailor kissed her. According to Friedman, learning that the war had ended "was what mattered." The kiss with the sailor "happened fast," "wasn't a big deal," and "then it was just over." (Or so she thought.) She never describes the experience as anything even approaching "He laid me over in his arms." Her most lasting impression of the kissing sailor is, "He was very strong."[12]

Greta's telling lacks passion, ecstasy, and drama. While she begrudges no sailor for kissing a woman on V-J Day, 1945, unlike Shain, she doesn't salute them for their last action of the war. While Shain's story sells, Greta's remembrances get shelved. That is unfortunate. The fact that Greta makes little of the event and passes it off as insignificant becomes part of her story's credibility and appeal. Over twenty years passed before she first saw the photo in a book of Eisenstaedt's finest photos. Rather than making up a fantastic plot to further enhance her role in the photo, she minimizes the occurrence's importance. Her humble reflection of that photographed moment speaks to the haphazard nature of the kiss. Interestingly, the general sequence Greta recalls matches up well with George Mendonsa's recollections. Both shared their memories of the photo prior to hearing one another's memories of that day and moment. When combined with her physical characteristics, and those of the nurse in the famous photo, Greta's remembrance of events makes for a far more believable case than does Shain's story.

Alfred Eisenstaedt and Lt. Victor Jorgensen did not photograph Barbara Sokol or Edith Shain in any of their celebrated photos from Times Square on V-J Day, 1945. When one considers the height, build, hairstyle, and surrounding testimony of each female candidate, all indicators point decisively to Greta Zimmer (Friedman), not Edith Shain, as the dental assistant, not the nurse, whom the sailor kissed and Alfred Eisenstaedt immortalized. Consequently, the story Edith Shain considers "indisputable" is hardly plausible.

PART 5

WHAT HAPPENED
TO THE TRUTH?

*Today I can truly say that I met an icon . . . the Sailor
in the infamous picture of a sailor kissing a nurse on
August 14, 1945 in Times Square. The picture appeared
on the front page of LIFE magazine.*

TERRY LONGPRE
After meeting Carl Muscarello in 2009

25

THE CARNIVAL

*L*IFE's 1980 invitation to the kissing sailor, perhaps origi nally heartfelt, ultimately morphed into a humiliating affair. Former World War II sailors who accepted *LIFE*'s invite as a personal summons expected a crowning. Instead, *LIFE* hosted a carnival and tossed the expectant would-be kissing sailors onto a carousel. Movement substituted for progress. The passengers got nowhere. As the ride went round and round, an amusement park atmosphere took hold, complete with rigged games, questionable salesmanship, and smoke and mirrors. The carnival ran for years.

In 1992 Alfred Eisenstaedt referenced *LIFE*'s 1980 invitation to the sailors as a "mistake."[1] His conclusion probably reflected the chaos that followed when eighty sailors (according to Eisenstaedt) answered *LIFE*'s call. Undoubtedly calmer seas would have prevailed if *LIFE* never churned up the waters over the issue of their kissing sailor's identity.

But *LIFE*'s invitation did stir up the waters, and George Mendonsa, who fished daily on Rhode Island's Narragansett Bay, responded immediately. His letter arrived at *LIFE* with a wave of other persuasive statements from many former sailors who for years just *knew* they were *the* kissing sailor. *LIFE* filed George's response promptly with about a dozen other sailors. More sailors' claims followed later.

Rather than separate the most credible assertions from the farfetched, *LIFE* heaped all the sailors from different ships into the same hull. Although each sailor had provided personal and unique substantiations of their claim, *LIFE* followed with a blurb clearly intended to be generic and noncommittal:

> Thus it was that memories stirred old seafaring hearts across the land, moments of danger and tossing sea and those too-brief winsome moments ashore. Then, most vividly, that unforgettable day—August 15, 1945[2]—when any swabbie worth his bell-bottoms kissed any girl within reach. No fewer than 10 sailors as well as two more nurses have managed to recall the last detail how it happened and how they happened to be in Times Square—persuading us that all their stories are true. But who is in the picture? And who kissed whom? Truth be told, only Eisie ever knew the answer. But since his notes vanished, he cannot make a final choice. It leaves us to wonder if, in some almost supernatural way, through the magic of his photographic artistry he didn't manage to get a picture of all of them. To be continued.[3]

As it turned out, *LIFE's* promise of "to be continued" proved limited. And, of course, sailors knew well that Eisenstaedt photographed only one of them—not all of them—on August 14, 1945. Each sailor had accepted *LIFE's* August 1980 invitation as a sincere inquiry to determine the sailor's identity in the *V-J Day, 1945, Times Square* photo. Instead of resolving to do just that, *LIFE* left readers from across the country to decide for themselves who the kissing sailor might be. *LIFE* gave them little with which to make an informed decision. Their October 1980 issue offered only snippets from the sailors' original letters. George's printed excerpt was less persuasive than those selected for his rivals.

While the printed piece did not promote George's case very well, someone thought enough of his story to call him and request that Peter Kunhardt, son of *LIFE's* managing editor Philip Kunhardt, conduct an interview with him. When George agreed, the news show *20/20* sent a crew to Rhode Island to meet George at his house in Middletown, and at his second home, *Maria Mendonsa,* floating in Newport Harbor. Shortly afterward, *20/20* invited George to New York to meet Greta

Friedman (Greta Zimmer in 1945), one of three women claiming to be the other participant in Eisenstaedt's famous Times Square picture. In New York, George was instructed to get out of a limousine in Times Square and walk over to Greta, who stood at the approximate spot that the original kiss transpired thirty-five years earlier. The *20/20* handlers told George to walk over to Greta and reintroduce himself. At that point, they informed George, they would start filming.

The reenactment proved contrived and awkward. As George recalls, "I approached Greta, grabbed her hand and said something like, 'I'm finally glad to meet you after all these years.'" Then he kissed her "because that was what they expected me to do." Alfred Eisenstaedt witnessed the reunion. Again, he took pictures. For this shoot, he angled his camera to catch the marquee on the Times Building, which read, "It had to be you." While the message rang true, those in a position to validate the words did not heed the boldly lit statement.

George thought all the hoopla with *20/20* acknowledged his part in Eisenstaedt's most famous photograph. It did not. In actuality, the aired *20/20* piece did nothing to separate Mendonsa's claim from other would be V-J Day Time Square kissing sailors. In fact, editors gave other claimants more time during the fifteen-minute segment than they allotted George. *20/20*'s longest treatment of Mendonsa (there were only two brief clips about George) discussed the chevron he claimed to be hanging from his right pocket in the 1945 photo. In that piece George offered: "And the way I tucked it in my right hip pocket I'd say I must have had a quite a few drinks in me because it was luck I didn't tuck it away good—the way it should have been tucked away."

Hugh Downs dismissed any persuasive value that Mendonsa's segment might have had (and certainly little existed) by following up the clip with, "A more obvious clue is the hair." Downs transitioned to other sailors whose hairlines he compared to Eisenstaedt's kissing sailor. Mendonsa did not appear in the piece. The program implied that Mendonsa's hairline followed a different contour than that of Eisenstaedt's kissing sailor. But

Mendonsa's 1945 hairline traveled the exact path of the kissing sailor's. Unfortunately viewers remained ignorant of that fact. Removing Mendonsa further still from serious consideration, Downs ended the show in a noncommittal fashion: "Now there may be conscious imposters in this group, but I think several of these nurses and sailors really believe they were in that picture. Who do you think is the real one?"

For a viewer to make an informed decision they needed to hear more from the sailors and nurses. The *20/20* snippets reduced the determination to a guessing game. The last prospective kissing sailor to speak on the program went right along with the show's apparent resolved position: "So maybe we will never know, but maybe that is just as well. Keep these two people symbolic of a fantastic day when a long war ended." The real kissing sailor could never agree to that.

Alfred Eisenstaedt's exact thoughts regarding these developments remain unclear. He did attend festivities put on by *20/20* to celebrate (or at least observe) both George and Greta. Also, Greta Friedman remembers Eisenstaedt approaching her after the filming to say, "I'm sorry," in an apparent reference to all the attention lavished on Edith Shain. On that same day he took numerous pictures of George and Greta together. However, despite all the attention Eisenstaedt focused on this occasion, he never issued a public statement affirming George's or Greta's part in the famous kiss. Consequently, almost everyone continued to believe Edith Shain was the nurse Eisenstaedt photographed in *V-J Day, 1945, Times Square.*

From October 1980 onward *LIFE*'s communications were more in tone than Eisenstaedt's. *LIFE* expressed no interest in recognizing George or Greta in their iconic photograph. If fact, just the opposite seems true. Over the following years *LIFE* expended great effort disregarding Mendonsa's claim to be the 1945 V-J Day kissing sailor. Whether the new posture resulted from apathy, disdain, or incompetence, in the fall of 1980 the transformation came on abruptly, and upsettingly so, at least from George's vantage point.

But just in case George wasn't already clear as to *LIFE*'s thinking regarding his claim to the kissing sailor's identity, the magazine's executives clarified matters when he visited the Time-Life Building at Rockefeller Center in the early 1980s. George had hoped to speak with the magazine's editors and managers about his claim. At first, one *LIFE* employee led him to hope for a positive reception. On the elevator ride up to the *LIFE* offices, the female escort said to him, "I know you're the kissing sailor." Others in the Time-Life Building thought so, too. On George's way to the managing editor's office, another female employee noticed him and yelled across the room, "Look! Didn't I tell you about those earlobes? He's the guy. Look at his nose and his hairline. He's the one."[4]

While these affirmations lifted the old sailor's spirits, his soaring pride crash-landed in *LIFE*'s lobby soon afterward. *LIFE*'s top brass refused to meet with the former sailor. Instead, he talked with Ann Morrell, a *LIFE* magazine secretary. After Morrell informed George that there would be no discussion with *LIFE* executives, he raised his voice, declared that he had had enough, and turned to leave the premises. Morrell encouraged him to stay. She said several people in the Time-Life Building had gathered to greet him. When George met with the congregated group, they all expressed a fascination with the whole ordeal and an interest in his version of events. Someone asked him if he kissed Edith Shain on August 14, 1945. George blurted, "No. She's too short." *LIFE* employees' interest in George's rendering of events contrasted starkly with that of their employer's cold shoulder. However, their thinking never made it to press. Any lingering hope of recognition that might have survived within George after the *LIFE* office visit soon evaporated. *LIFE* never again invited George to a function associated with their famous photograph.

One indirect communication from *LIFE* did make its way to George in 1981. That communiqué, written by *20/20*'s Peter Kunhardt, imparted a more congenial tone than that conveyed earlier by the magazine's executives. In a handwritten letter,

Philip Kunhardt's son explained *LIFE*'s reasoning for not pursuing the story of the kissing sailor's identity any longer:

> I was finally able to have a good long talk with my father about the possibility of looking at new evidence in the VJ Day Sailor story. I showed him your photo and we were both impressed. But he says that LIFE is not going to go back and open up the story again. It's not a matter of a cover-up, or anything of that kind, but simply a matter of public interest. The story ran 2 x already and LIFE feels that's plenty. Needless to say, ABC doesn't plan to run it again either. If by chance they select the V-J Story to run as a re-run this summer, I'll let you know and maybe we can add some new information then.

Peter Kunhardt finished the handwritten letter by telling George he still planned on coming up to Newport to go out on the fishing boat with him—if that was "still OK." George made good on the promise.

LIFE would have done well to have Peter Kunhardt handle all their communications with George. They did not. In one brush-off, *LIFE*'s aggravation with George became clear. Once again, secretary Ann Morrell fulfilled the role as communications expert. In a typed letter dated January 15, 1987, Morrell lectured George:

> Dear George:
>
> Yes, I'm still here. I'm still hearing from a few sailors, and I'm sorry to report that our position remains the same. We cannot positively identify the sailor—or the nurse.
>
> Since a large part of 1986 was devoted to LIFE's 50th Anniversary and looking back, we are now concentrating on looking forward. Our managing editor is not interested in pursuing the subject further.
>
> As for your quote in YANKEE, "Some lawyer has probably scared them that I want royalties." George,

even if you were the sailor in the photograph, you would not be entitled to royalties. Royalties are not paid to subjects in news photos. The photograph belongs to Alfred Eisenstaedt, and he is the only one who gets paid when it is reproduced. So believe me there would be no reason to be afraid to identify the sailor if we could. But as I said before, at this point we are not interested. We've all had some fun with it. Why not just leave it at that.

Best wishes,
Ann Morrell

What Morrell termed as "fun" did not equate with George's experiences. Though *LIFE* wanted the matter ended, George was married to the cause. He took his vows most seriously.

Several factors might account for *LIFE*'s dramatic transformation from a search party looking for the kissing sailor to a retreating force firing rounds at George Mendonsa. Perhaps *LIFE* feared a potentially expensive payroll recipient. George assured *LIFE* that monetary considerations played no part in his quest. Maybe *LIFE* didn't trust the former sailor's word—especially after the 1987 lawsuit. And after all, a lucrative bonus check from the photo's royalties might go a long way to speeding up an aging fisherman's retirement from choppy waters, cutting winds, and tangled nets.

But money matters aside, George Mendonsa's version of events probably would have earned a more receptive reaction from *LIFE* if it were not for, well, George. Conceivably, Mendonsa's conviction on matters of recognition could be interpreted as shrill. Compare Edith Shain's polite and demure letter to gain Eisenstaedt's attention with George Mendonsa's assertive lobbying for recognition. As a sole petitioner, Shain gingerly requested acknowledgment. A "delighted" Eisenstaedt got to play the discoverer of his lost nurse. In stark contrast, Mendonsa had to be picked from a stampede of charging sailors. And Mendonsa, the bucking seahorse, could not accept anything short of absolute identification.

Executives at *LIFE* found George difficult to work with.[5] His expectations of the magazine were too great. He wanted things on his terms and made demands without a hint of humility. He came across as rough and rude. His phone messages were gruff and accusatory in tone. From *LIFE*'s standpoint, whether or not George was truly the kissing sailor, he was impossible to take. In a sense, George may have shot himself in the foot.

No matter what George did or should have done, and regardless of why *LIFE* abandoned the hunt for their kissing sailor, one thing remained certain: without the magazine's cooperation George could not gain the recognition he sought. As he already knew, but would be tutored forever more, *LIFE* had no limits of will or resources to combat the Rhode Island fisherman's every move.

Though *LIFE*'s rejection of George wore on him, the former sailor persisted in his efforts to gain recognition as the kissing sailor. Over the coming years George continued to try and make some sort of contact with the publication giant. He made any number of attempts to do this. But he received an equal number of rejections or snubs. Most of the time *LIFE* never responded to George's inquiries. One such appeal and rejection occurred in 1987. During that year *LIFE* published a special issue with the *V-J Day, 1945, Times Square* photo on the cover. *LIFE*'s special issue included a story on Vice President George Bush and Barbara Bush. The image of the couple and their grandchildren inspired George to send an autographed copy of the magazine to Barbara Bush and also to *LIFE*. George told both parties that they should save the offering because they would possess one of only two autographed copies by the sailor in the photo. George thought the two parties might talk and renew *LIFE*'s interest in determining the kissing sailor's identity. His judgment missed the mark on both accounts. There is no evidence that Barbara Bush talked to *LIFE*, but she did send George a cordial thank-you note. *LIFE* never even acknowledged receipt of George's letter and offering.

Over the years, George's efforts to gain recognition had long-distance company. While competitors for the kissing sailor rarely communicated directly, occasionally one candidate had to answer to another's successful invasion of his turf. Predictably, the resulting commentary came across as something short of supportive. When MERL's 2004 findings gained some attention in Florida where Carl Muscarello lived, the retired former New York detective commented, "My understanding is that the laboratory findings are not conclusive."[6] While arguably not conclusive, one would think that even Muscarello would have to allow for convincing. He did not.

Though Carl Muscarello and George Mendonsa never met, in 1995 they did exchange letters. George made the first contact. The publicity surrounding Muscarello's claims to the kissing sailor motivated him to do so. The one-page note fell far short of congratulatory. Mendonsa's correspondence to Muscarello read more like a résumé than the beginning of a dialogue between two former sailors. George dropped the names Peter Kunhardt and Professor Richard Benson and referenced all the evidence that *proved* he, not Muscarello, is the kissing sailor in *V-J Day, 1945, Times Square*.

Less than a month later, Muscarello wrote a letter in response. The wording flowed with vintage Muscarello politeness, congeniality, and reverence. Muscarello assured George, "I have the utmost respect for you as a fellow World War Two veteran." He continued in the letter with offerings like, "It has never been my intention at any time to begrudge you or anyone else for their belief that they are the sailor or nurse," and "I've been fortunate enough to be able to donate to charity any small amount of monies I have made from this event." Niceties aside, Muscarello also scored his counterpoints, no doubt designed to trump George's earlier brag sheet: "I believe like you and many others that I am the sailor in the photo. I base this belief on personal recollections and conversations I've had with Edith Shain. Ms. Shain was identified by Eisenstaedt and a subsequent Life magazine article to be the nurse in the photo and fifteen years later she identified me. There are things that happened that day that only Edith and I can know about."

Muscarello finished his letter in the same tone he began with: "I have been fortunate in that most of the happiness in my life has come from my children, their children, my family and friends and my belief in God. I hope that you've experienced the same happiness." Muscarello and Mendonsa never communicated directly with one another again.

From 1985 to 2005, as former sailors battled one another's claims for the kissing sailor title, Edith Shain had an easy time safeguarding her claim as Eisenstaedt's kissed nurse. Her competitors were in short supply, and lacked a substantial following. Further, her most formidable contender, Greta Friedman, did not seek the limelight. Friedman ranked so far behind the widely recognized front-runner that Shain rarely had to acknowledge her.

Even though evidence of Greta's part in *LIFE*'s most famous photograph exceeded that supporting Edith Shain, she never stood a chance of unseating the peppy former nurse. For one, Greta's campaign for the nurse's part in *V-J Day, 1945, Times Square* ran on a shoestring budget. The entire operation consisted of paper, envelopes, and postage stamps. Rather than releasing statements and making presentations, she employed a promotional strategy that focused solely on responding succinctly to queries. To satisfy inquiring reporters about her claimed part in the kissing sailor photo, Greta sent along a one-page, double-spaced, reproduced letter. Her response put forth limited proof, no visuals, and a passive tone. The offering did little to entice further interest. Most follow-up appeals for information met with Greta's reluctance to share any thoughts beyond that which she described in the earlier correspondence. Greta saw those who persisted in their appeals for further details as invaders of her privacy. On the few occasions she relented to pressure, she did so with considerable trepidation and in a guarded manner.

George Mendonsa once said of Greta's efforts to be recognized in the famous photo, "Well, Greta doesn't really care too much about all this." That is not entirely true. While not a publicity hound, when provoked, Greta speaks with adamant conviction of her part in Eisenstaedt's most well-known photo. Her backbone is steelier than Eisenstaedt's photo of a backward-leaning nurse might suggest.

Greta's tenacity rose to the surface when *LIFE* magazine first declared Edith Shain the nurse in the *V-J Day, 1945, Times Square* photograph. "I immediately protested it," she offered in a very self-assured, forthright, and slightly annoyed tone. Later, even when a source reported her part in the famous picture, she corrected details, specified matters, and otherwise set the record straight. In a letter written in 1991 she scolded Bryant Gumbel with the following reprimand: "During the last part of the VJ sailor-nurse 'reunion' on Times Square, George Mendonza [*sic*] and I were directed by you to pretend that we were meeting for the first time since 1945. I don't want to go along with that and misrepresent my experience. I never said that I had not seen George since 1945. As you know, we met again in 1980 for the 20/20 Show and in 1985 for the Today Show."[7]

When Gumbel later changed his mind on the identity of the kissing sailor and nurse, Greta shot off a letter that demonstrated her spine's tautness:

Dear Mr. Gumbel:

We were amazed when viewing the Today Show from Los Angeles on August 9 when you named Mrs. Edith Shane [*sic*] and Mr. Carl Muscarello as the kissing people in Alfred Eisenstaedt's VJ Day photograph.

Ten years ago Mr. George Mendonza [Mendonsa] and I were on the Today Show in person and were interviewed by you.

We are the actual people in the picture.

Mr. Mendonza had the photograph analyzed by an expert who concluded that the sailor is indeed Mr. Mendonza. In the background of the picture and over the sailor's shoulder is the woman who shortly thereafter became Mr. Mendonsa's wife.

I am enclosing a copy of page 72 from the October 1980 issue of Life magazine so that you can see that I was the only one with the same hairdo as in the VJ photo. I also remember the little purse which I am holding in my right hand.

I hope this settles the matter.

While Friedman wrote an additional two letters, Gumbel never replied to any of them. Indicative of Greta's modus operandi, she did not forward nor mention any of the letters during the interviews in preparation of this book. George Mendonsa passed along all four notes.

In one out-of-character instance during 2010, Greta Friedman inquired as to what "we" were going to do about all the attention being afforded Edith Shain after her passing. After a short discussion she agreed the we should let everything take its course, give everyone time to grieve over Edith's passing, and otherwise lay low for the time being. She never brought up the matter again.

Greta did not get drawn into *LIFE*'s carnival. And thankfully, during the carnival's thirty-two-year run there were other reprieves from the absurd. One respite originated from Guido Knopp, a highly respected history professor from Germany. In a documentary that considered all the evidence supporting George Mendonsa's candidacy as the kissing sailor, the professor was certain: "We have the right guy." Knopp did not suffer the loneliness of sole opinion. Patricia Redmond interviewed both Glenn McDuffie and George Mendonsa for the Library of Congress. She determined Mendonsa, not McDuffie, to be the kissing sailor. (She also believes Greta Freidman, not Edith Shain, is the embraced dental assistant.) Occasionally an expert opinion added emphasis to previous findings. In an interview with a television news show host, Dr. Richard Benson of Yale University augmented his 1987 report that affirmed George Mendonsa's claims: "I am just completely convinced. I haven't had any doubt about it since I've looked at the pictures. I really haven't had any doubt about it at all." To this, *The Crusaders'* narrator added, "Nor did we." Forensic anthropologist Dr. Norman Sauer and the material produced by MERL scientist Hanspeter Pfister, PhD, reinforced the other credentialed judgments. If only a mountain of qualified opinions and validated evidence could convince *LIFE* to recognize their kissing sailor. But then the carnival would be over.

During the years that *LIFE* sidestepped the issue of their kissing sailor's identity, different works explored the origins of other famous photos. James Bradley's *Flags of Our Fathers* was, arguably, the most noteworthy project of this sort. Published in 2000, his work about Joe Rosenthal's image of the Marines raising the flag at Iwo Jima quickly climbed the national bestseller list. Bradley confronted a carousel of opinions encircling photography's most reproduced image. While he did not have to concern himself with the flag raisers' identities (one of them— Dr. John Henry Bradley—is the author's father), Bradley did contend with readers' prior misconceptions. Some people *knew* that the photographer staged the whole scene. Others *thought* that the raising of the flag immediately followed a harrowing battle to take Mount Suribachi. Still others were *sure* the raising marked the end of the fight to take Iwo Jima. None of these accounts proved accurate. For the benefit of history, Bradley's scholarship shared the true story of those heroic men raising the flag at Iwo Jima.

During the same general time frame of Bradley's book, another image, that of a young Afghanistan woman from a June 1985 *National Geographic* cover, gained much attention. Like the kissing sailor, the Afghan girl remained nameless. However, unlike *LIFE*'s withdrawal from the effort to recognize their kissing sailor, *National Geographic* supported efforts to locate their Afghan girl seventeen years later. The undertaking presented challenges. Undaunted, photographer Steve McCurry traveled halfway around the world, employed interpreters, and utilized some of the world's most sophisticated technology to find the subject of his 1985 photo. The Afghan girl, Sharbat Gula, adorned the June 2002 *National Geographic* cover. The title read proudly, *FOUND, After 17 Years An Afghan Refugee's Story.* Writer Cathy Newman shared Gula's journey from childhood in a Pakistan refugee camp to motherhood in Afghanistan after the Soviet Union's withdrawal. The mystery ended. A curious public learned Gula's amazing story.

If executives at *LIFE* read Bradley's or Newman's treatments, they missed the authors' messages. A compassionate and responsible retrospective look at *LIFE*'s prized photograph did not follow suit. In the face of such disappointment, others continued to appeal to *LIFE*'s journalistic integrity, appreciation of history, and human compassion.

Around the time that Glenn McDuffie's claim to the kissing sailor's identity gained significant public attention, Jerry O'Donnell, a retired Navy captain and head of the *VJ Day Sailor Project*, organized a packet of updated evidence to support George Mendonsa's claim to the kissing sailor's identity. The proof included a review of Professor Benson's findings, the MERL laboratory scientists' procedures and conclusions, and recent photograph enhancements. O'Donnell sent the prepared packet to *LIFE* for their review and reply. His accompanying letter, cordial in tone, called attention to the urgency of the matter at hand. O'Donnell's letter concluded as follows: "I hope you will consider the request. I recognize that your identification of the sailor in the 1945 photo is a business decision that only your organization can make. I would be happy to answer any questions that you might pose or provide any additional information. . . . It would be very sad if this situation is not resolved during George's lifetime."

Once again, *LIFE* did not reply.

Capt. Jerry O'Donnell was not accustomed to being ignored. George Mendonsa was well schooled in such treatment. In fact, he could be considered an expert. *LIFE* had tutored him well. They continued to do so. And the carousel went round and round, faster and faster.

26

THE CIRCUS

At times the who kissed whom carnival turned into a circus. Some media outlets and function organizers played the claimant kissing sailors as a sad sideshow. The World War II veterans unwittingly cooperated with those who used their claim for their own benefit. Some kissing sailor candidates finger-pointed and swore at one another. During each undignified ordeal, one sailor's volume trumped another's reasoning. Misinformation reigned. While at times entertaining, the endeavor paraded the former sailors as a spectacle. People looked at them and listened to their spiels but did not know whom to believe. The sorry exposition continued. *LIFE* watched and let it all happen.

The circus employed almost every aspiring kissing sailor. Sometimes what thrust them into the center of the ring had little to do with the attention they sought. In 2006 an alarming incident propelled kissing sailor claimant Carl Muscarello into the news. Two burglars, seventeen and nineteen years old, entered Muscarello's home in Plantation, Florida, they found with the intent to harm anyone in their way. Muscarello's wife standing in her kitchen. One of the thugs stabbed her with a screwdriver. Shortly afterward the burglar took a golf club to her thirty-six-year-old son's head. As the seventeen-year-old accomplice fled, Carl Muscarello, a former New York police officer, came upon the ruckus and proceeded to put a chokehold on the remaining burglar.[1] The eighty-year-old Muscarello kept his grasp on the intruder as they crashed into several fixtures and walls, ulti-mately landing on the back patio. Muscarello explained, "I had him pinned down to the concrete by the pool floor when the police got here."[2] The ensuing headline in the *Miami Herald* read, "'Kissing Sailor' Sinks Invader." Muscarello made the most of the otherwise troubling occurrence. In a not-so-veiled ref-erence to his part in Eisenstaedt's photograph of the 1945 V-J Day kiss, Muscarello offered, "I often happen to be at a strange place at a strange time."[3] The story ran in several publications nationwide and appeared for months on the internet. During this time frame Muscarello's link to the kissing sailor enjoyed far more attention than Mendonsa's assertion or, for that matter, any other claimant's story.

Approximately a year after Muscarello's headline grab, Glenn McDuffie burst onto the kissing sailor scene. Propelled forward by forensic artist Lois Gibson, the "proof" she presented convinced many to believe McDuffie's claim to be the kissing sailor. Though *LIFE* continued to communicate its noncom-mittal mindset through short and snappy prepared statements, McDuffie's story created feverish activity among other media outlets. Arriving on the scene swinging and swearing, McDuffie put on too good a show to ignore. Cantankerous, sometimes controversial, and more often than not confrontational, this contentious kissing sailor candidate abruptly bumped every other petitioner one step down the kissing sailor claimant peck-ing order.

In his quest for recognition as the kissing sailor, McDuffie took no prisoners. Of *LIFE*, McDuffie claimed, "They stole my picture and they didn't tell nobody about me."[4] To Edith Shain he charged, "You didn't even know he (Eisenstaedt) took your picture until somebody told you!"[5] Of photographer Alfred Eisenstaedt, McDuffie charged, "That man's been lying about that picture ever since he took it."[6] And of an article of clothing (or rates) hanging from the kissing sailor's right side, McDuffie stressed, "There ain't nothing hanging from no pocket."[7] The North Carolinian former sailor never lost his World War II fighting spirit.

Though no television program ever ventured to interview all the sailor claimants together, Glenn McDuffie and George Mendonsa participated on the same radio program in 2007.[8] During the Johnny Brandmeier radio program on Chicago's WLUP 97.9, George experienced McDuffie's wrath via the arrangements of a less-than-forthcoming Chicago radio programmer. A spokesperson for the station had contacted George to see if he would call in his remembrances of the 1945 V-J Day Times Square kiss during Brandmeier's show. George accepted the invitation, welcoming the opportunity to reintroduce his version of the occurrence and the reasons he, not McDuffie, is the kissing sailor. The station did not inform Mendonsa that Glenn McDuffie would also take part in the conversation. (McDuffie was also unaware of Mendonsa's participation.) The ensuing combative dialogue between the two former sailors served the purposes of entertainment more than the dissemination of meaningful information. This may well have been the design and to the liking of the station's producers. Throughout the exchange, McDuffie fired off several personal attacks at George. The comments included, "You're a Goddamn liar," "You're a son of a bitch," "You sorry son of a bitch," and "Ugly bastard." McDuffie's most purposeful utterance (repeated numerous times throughout the program) questioned Mendonsa, "Why don't you take a polygraph?" By the show's end, neither sailor could be taken seriously. The station used the World War II veterans for audience appeal. Regrettably, ratings trumped respect. Undoubtedly, many listeners were part of the generation that had benefited generously from McDuffie's and Mendonsa's sacrifices.

A year later Glenn McDuffie appeared on a television show hosted by Johnny Brandmeier.[9] Neither the guest nor the host had mellowed over the passing year. Brandmeier loaded up the show's docket with telephone calls from George Mendonsa and Edith Shain. Once again McDuffie took shots at everyone. To Mendonsa, he said, "All you done is lied and ripped people off. . . . You don't have any proof you ugly son of a bitch. . . . You ought to die you lying bastard." He spoke in a similar demeaning tone to

Edith Shain: "How did he [Eisenstaedt] remember about you? You couldn't see nothing but your leg, hand and arm?" Brandmeier played up all exchanges, repeating McDuffie's charges, posing as the nurse while McDuffie demonstrated his hold on the nurse, and then leaving the set with his guest to get a drink at a bar. And the circus sideshow played on.

Though McDuffie frustrated Mendonsa, he was not George's biggest problem. *LIFE* continued to command that role. They had cemented that function in an earlier brush-off scene. In that particular occurrence, *LIFE*'s rejection of George lacked decorum. Their message came across as belligerent and belittling. When a television reporter approached *LIFE* for commentary about George's claim to be the V-J Day kissing sailor, the megapublishing firm held nothing back. *The Crusaders'* commentator shared with George, "They're not interested in you. They're not interested in the photo. They don't want to talk about it. And whatever you do, leave the photographer alone." While certainly *LIFE* continued to be interested in the photo, George, the subject of the magazine's most popular photograph, had become a nuisance to the multi-million-dollar magazine firm. They wanted no part of him.

The rejection hurt but did not deter George. For more than thirty years he continued his overtures to Time-Life. In fairness to *LIFE*, they probably couldn't hear him, unless he screamed really loudly from the street. *LIFE* barred George from entering the very building that hosts one of history's most popular photos, the one George helped make famous.

Over the ensuing years, spokesmen at *LIFE* claimed no interest in all matters involving the kissing sailor's identity. But that wasn't true. While *LIFE* bolted the front door shut to inquiries directing the kissing sailor's identity, they left the back door ajar. The magazine used this exit to aggressively challenge related kissing sailor matters that concerned them. Their actions reveal an interesting dichotomy.

When confronted with George's and many other claimants' questions, the publishing giant replied in a passive-aggressive tone. The responses vacillated between two prefabricated renditions; the helpless, *we cannot determine the identity* variety; or the more heartwarming version, *somehow Eisenstaedt managed to get all the kissing sailors in one picture*. However, when one claimant's story proved provocative enough, then the publishing giant that earlier ventured no opinion on the matter charged forward to thwart the claim. Suddenly, the publication that knew so little could access a stuffed treasure chest of archives, logs, time sheets, and contextual references. *LIFE* then heaved the barrage of proof to bury the former World War II sailor who dared to suggest that he might be the kissing sailor in Eisenstaedt's photo. Once they settled the matter before them with counterarguments, the magazine's spokesperson returned to the safe confines of their tall, glass building, making sure to close the door behind them. Once again, their modus operandi, *we just don't know*, returned.

LIFE also unleashed its more assertive side on entities who did not claim to be the kissing sailor, but who did have kissing sailor business to attend to. In at least one instance Time, Inc., forthrightly pursued an artist who wanted to honor World War II's triumphant end. Seward Johnson approached *LIFE* to sculpt a statue of Eisenstaedt's *V-J Day, 1945, Times Square*. When *LIFE* refused to grant permission, Johnson used the picture of the same event taken by Lt. Victor Jorgensen.[10] Duplicating Jorgensen's image does not infringe on copyright laws because it is filed in the National Archives and therefore is part of the public domain.

Johnson sculpted a piece that looked very much like Lieutenant Jorgensen's still frame, *Kissing the War Goodbye*. Of course, a likeness to Jorgensen's picture also means that there would be a strong resemblance to Eisenstaedt's *V-J Day, 1945, Times Square* photograph—for anyone who cared to make such an observation. Jeff Burak, *LIFE*'s business development manager, cared—a lot. He stated that Johnson needed the magazine's permission to create the sculpture because the creation was a "derivative" of Eisenstaedt's protected photograph.[11]

Burak argued that, unlike Eisenstaedt's four photographs, Jorgensen's singular photograph does not show the nurse's knees or pointed white-shoed foot. Johnson's sculpture treats these limbs because he presumed the nurse had both knees and feet. Time, Inc., showed little interest in Johnson's presumptions. The publishing giant concerned itself solely with guarding the by-then-deceased Eisenstaedt's famed photo, apparently for the image's continued dissemination as news.

While Johnson did not enjoy *LIFE*'s surge of attention, in some ways, George Mendonsa envied him. Unlike Johnson, from 1987 onward, George did not receive a communicative drop from *LIFE*. However, in August 2007 that drought almost ended. Barbara (Bobbi) Baker Burrows, director of photography at *LIFE Books*, contacted George Mendonsa by phone. Though she made it clear that her call did not speak for her employer of forty years, according to George, Burrows felt badly about the way *LIFE* had treated him over the years. She was bothered also by the latest publicity enjoyed by Glenn McDuffie. She conveyed interest in meeting George and learning more about his claims. Within the coming weeks George offered Burrows more than she had bargained for.

George wanted to tell Burrows everything, and often. He had questions, too. Why had *LIFE* treated him so harshly? Did they look over his proof? What did they think? Why hadn't *LIFE* treated him with the respect he deserved? He demanded answers. He didn't like waiting. He never did. Besides, he thought, thirty years was a long time to figure out who was in that picture. He thought *LIFE* should know by now. He wanted and needed their recognition. Maybe, George thought, Burrows could get him the credit he deserved. George kept calling her. She stopped answering the phone.

Bobbi Baker Burrows knows a lot about *LIFE*. She should. She worked there for most of her adult life. During her climb up the media ladder, she never lost her grounded sensibilities, pleasing disposition, and love of *the picture*. In keeping with her persona, her Time-Life office amounts to a modest cubicle void of any intimidating pretense. Time-Life books form piles on desktops. Classic *LIFE* pictures hang on the walls. She can tell visitors the story behind all of them, and about the photographers who took them. Of all those photographers, she knows most about Alfred Eisenstaedt.

Burrows worked closely with her friend Eisie. As his boss, assistant, friend, and admirer, she and her husband Russell Burrows (son of famous *LIFE* photographer Larry Burrows), knew Eisie well. Over the years Bobbi vacationed with the Father of Photojournalism on Martha's Vineyard. At work and at play, their conversations often focused on photography, including Eisie's most famous photo.

Bobbie Baker Burrows wanted to find out who kissed whom in her old friend's most popular photo. And after studying the picture for years, she thought she knew the identity of Eisie's kissing sailor. But she wanted to be sure.

Her employer was less concerned about recognizing their kissing sailor. If anyone ever doubted *LIFE*'s resolve to maintain the kissing sailor's anonymity, Time-Life Books editorial director, Robert Sullivan, removed all uncertainty. In 2007 a front-page *USA Today* Associated Press article quoted Sullivan, "The recent (claims) are 'CSI' type inquiries. We think that's great but we just can't know for sure on our end. We can't be in a position of anointing one or the other without hard proof." In the same article Sullivan indicated that the identities of the couple in the famous photo will officially remain a mystery.[12]

In 2009 Bobbi Baker Burrows came closer than any *LIFE* employee ever had to publicly ending the mystery over the sailor's identity. In a rare article on Greta Friedman's claim to the V-J Day nurse in Eisenstaedt's picture, *Frederick* magazine writer Guy Fletcher wrote, "Bobbi Baker Burrows, director of photography for Life Books, thinks she knows the identities, but she's not ready to say, at least not publicly." He then quoted Burrows: "I want to have it completely and well-thought-out before I issue a public statement."[13] While Burrows thought, Mendonsa continued to wait, and grow older.

Even without *LIFE*'s valuable participation in determining the sailor's and nurse's identities, one might think others' attention to the kissing sailor's identity would at least lead to better informed opinions. However, just the opposite seems to be more accurate. According to Marshall Berman, author of *On the Town*, Eisenstaedt's *V-J Day, 1945, Times Square* appeared on the cover of *LIFE*.[14] It did not. Another article claimed the *New York Daily News* published Lieutenant Jorgensen's *Kissing the War Goodbye* on August 15, 1945.[15] They did not. Many assume Eisenstaedt took his famous picture just after the official announcement of Japan's surrender. He did not. In actuality, Eisenstaedt snapped the picture hours before that radio broadcast.[16] When President Truman made his announcement just after 7:00 PM, the center of Times Square appeared packed with people. Far too much open space exists in the background of *V-J Day, 1945, Times Square* and *Kissing the War Goodbye* for the pictures to have been taken during the evening.

While some sources may unknowingly spread erroneous information about the kissing sailor photo, others profited from the dissemination of mistaken reporting. On Ebay one can purchase copies of *V-J Day, 1945, Times Square* with the "real kissing sailor's signature." Most often Glenn McDuffie or Carl Muscarello pens their name to those pictures. One can buy a valuable "piece of history," usually for $29.95. One ad on Ebay in 2008 read:

> The nurse was identified as Edith Shane [Shain] and the sailor because of his job with the New York City Police Department was kept as secret till the 50th anniversary when Carl and Edith were re-united by Life magazine. A lot of old sailors claim to be the sailor but the proof is the birthmark that shows up in the original photo on his right arm. That birthmark is still there and not on the pretenders. Here is your chance to obtain one of the most beloved images in the 20th century signed by the man himself. Comes with a certificate of authenticity from Carl Muscarello himself.

The seller circled the referenced birthmark on the sailor's right forearm. While very persuasive to the uninformed consumer, the mark is actually a dark patch of hair. Carl Muscarello has no such patch of hair on his arm. Carl has never made such a claim. Still, the improper information misguides those who seek to be enlightened about such matters or to purchase an actual piece of history. The adage "buyer beware" applies.

Misinformation aside, the autographed photo described above could be considered a bargain. In another advertised opportunity to "own a piece of history," an 11 x 14 photo of *V-J Day, 1945, Times Square*, signed by Carl Muscarello and Edith Shain was advertised at $2,799. The ad assured, "Although many men have claimed that they were the sailor in the picture, then-nurse Edith Shain identified Muscarello as the man who kissed her in Times Square to celebrate the victory over Japan, ending WWII." One wonders where all the money from such a sale goes, considering Muscarello is adamant that he earns no profits from signings.

Robert Hariman, professor of communication at Northwestern University, and John Louis Lucaites, an associate professor of communication and culture at Indiana University, probably would pay nothing for an autographed copy of *V-J Day, 1945, Times Square*. In their book, *No Caption Needed*, they present a historical, psychological, and sociological treatment of history's most recognized images. One of their chapters discusses Eisenstaedt's *V-J Day, 1945, Times Square*. Though they offer Eisenstaedt's most popular photograph much scholarly attention, both authors seem a bit befuddled by all the hoopla surrounding the kissing sailor's identity. At the same time, they recognize the pursuit to be important. Dr. Hariman writes, "It's sort of like claiming a lost lottery ticket, except you're not getting paid in cash but in media attention. It's one way to measure the significance of a photo; the lengths people will go to identify themselves with it."[17] Dr. John Louis Lucaites adds, "It never ceases to amaze us how entranced the culture is with 'who' the 'real' kissers are and the incredible lengths to which we go to make the determination."[18] It is incredible.

While Dr. Hariman and Dr. Lucaites have little interest in the kissing sailor's identity, that doesn't stop them from characterizing the anonymous couple: "The sailor and nurse probably come from lower—or lower middle-class backgrounds. . . . The sailor is exuberant because he has just been released from the probability of being killed or wounded in battle. The nurse has taken to the streets because she, too, wants to live without fear, separation, pain, and death."[19]

For not caring much about the kissers' identities, Hariman and Lucaites describe *V-J Day, 1945, Times Square*'s primary participants with incredible accuracy.

Others who did not attempt to determine the kissing sailor's identity (or ascertain what actually happened in *V-J Day, 1945, Times Square*) nevertheless expressed outrage about what they perceived to be going on in the photo. Rather than seeing a sailor and nurse celebrating joyously at the end of a long war, some saw an aggressor groping a victimized woman. Still others, like *The New Yorker* magazine, offered controversial portrayals of *V-J Day, 1945, Times Square*'s sailor and nurse. In its June 17, 1996, issue *The New Yorker* substituted for George and Greta a drawing of two homosexual men replicating the V-J Day, 1945, pose. The magazine article referenced Eisenstaedt's photo as an "eruption of lust."[20] Clearly, the writer did not interview Greta Friedman for her description of the event.

Even as Americans make their way through the early years of the twenty-first century, Eisenstaedt's iconic 1945 image continues to draw interest. Mel Levey, age twenty in 2005, took part in a Times Square Alliance sixtieth commemoration of the famous kiss. He concluded that the *V-J Day, 1945, Times Square* image is more famous than the event it commemorates.[21] Dr. Robert Hariman agrees: "The basic fact here is that 60 years later you've got a carnival going on in Times Square because of a photograph. Not because of the event, not because of V-J Day, but because someone caught it with a photograph."[22]

The interest in Eisenstaedt's picture approaches an almost cultish following, as admirers two and three generations removed from the end of World War II join older Americans and gaze in wonderment at the kissing sailor and nurse. Aaron

Rosenberg, a paralegal who first met Edith Shain at a conference on the 1940s, drove the celebrated nurse in a gay pride parade. He said of the experience, "It's amazing to drive her in the car. It's like the wave at Dodger Stadium. People are really passionate about that picture."[23] And some of those people were born several decades after the last day of World War II when a sailor struck a pose in Times Square for the ages. Accordingly, the picture adorns pocketbooks, helps sell mints, and continues to be hung in college dorm rooms by girls young enough to be the kissing sailor's great-granddaughter.

While the growing number of admirers may be a positive development, the circus' sideshow treatment is not. Consider the *New York Times* reporting of the Times Square Alliance's V-J Kiss commemoration in 2005:

A hot, angry mob of photographers stood pressed together yesterday on a platform in Times Square, shouting orders at a tiny old lady. "This way!" hollered one photographer. "One more time!" yelled another. "You got to kiss him on the lips!" "She doesn't want it!" said another. The woman, Edith Shain, 87, smiled politely but refused to grant the man by her side a kiss on the lips as she says she did 60 years earlier in the Alfred Eisenstaedt photograph that captured the euphoric end of World War II. In that picture, a sailor dips a nurse in an embrace that Mr. Eisenstaedt likened to "sculpture." But yesterday, each time Carl Muscarello, 78, pulled Ms. Shain in for a kiss, he got her cheek. The photographers moaned. The event organizers pleaded. The sun beat mercilessly down. Then, finally, Ms. Shain relented. A kiss was exchanged between the diminutive woman and the former New York police detective that held all the passion of brushing elbows. It was hardly the spontaneous picture of elation captured in 1945, but the cameras clicked and rolled, their operators satiated.[24]

Serious doubts about the couple's true identity added to the mayhem at the Times Square Alliance event. A comedy of errors existed. The Alliance invited George Mendonsa to be on hand at the celebration, but he refused when he learned that Edith

Shain accepted their invitation to be the nurse at the occasion. (George continues to maintain that she was a "fake.") Though Carl Muscarello willingly participated, shortly afterward he no longer partook in V-J Day commemorations with Shain owing to his discomfort with her handling of such events, as well as her rejection of his part in the famous photo.[25] Adding to the absurdity, the Time Square Alliance ventures no definitive opinion as to the kissing sailor's true identity, but extends invitations to claimants giving the impression that the one who accepts the invitation is indeed who they purport to be. Making matters more convoluted still, when a reporter at the 2005 reenactment of the *V-J Day, 1945, Times Square* kiss asked Edith Shain whether Muscarello is "the one," she replied, "I can't say he isn't. I just can't say he is. There is no way to tell."[26]

There is a way to tell. With the willingness of Time-Life and a team of historians, forensic anthropologists, photographic experts, and cutting edge technology, the means are at hand to recognize the participants in Alfred Eisenstaedt's beloved photograph. Even time remains an ally. The sailor and dental assistant continue to live among us. They anxiously wait to commemorate with all that day from more than a half-century ago when destiny drew them together for just an instant so that they might express what nearly everyone felt.

But time moves on. Eventually, the real kissing sailor, and the dental assistant he kissed, will be no more. These two national treasures will be lost to a world that never really got to cherish either one of them. Instead, a circus of claimed poses and clever posturing will bask in the limelight of a Leica's alleged flash. And a disputed mystery will forever overshadow the humble truth.

27

THE CURRENT

Even without *LIFE*'s recognition, George Mendonsa thought that the proof of his claim to the kissing sailor would propel him far ahead of his competitors. He was wrong. In 2011, a Google search for "the kissing sailor" puts forth twenty-four articles on Glenn McDuffie, Carl Muscarello, Edith Shain, or a general treatment of the V-J Day kiss before a single site makes George Mendonsa's case. When one types "The Kissing Sailor" as a Google image search, a photo of George Mendonsa does not show up on the screen until the searcher looks through seven pages of Glenn McDuffie, Carl Muscarello, and Edith Shain. Greta Friedman fares even worse. Her picture does not appear until page twelve. More people believe Glenn McDuffie or Carl Muscarello kissed a nurse in *V-J Day, 1945, Times Square* than they do George Mendonsa. Almost everyone thinks that one of the sailor claimants kissed Edith Shain. Most do not even know who Greta Freidman is. A review of the most recent *V-J Day, 1945, Times Square* news stories confirms this mindset.

Though Edith Shain never needed to worry about her competition, she campaigned for over thirty years as if she were in a close race. Though her campaign spread false information, Shain remained the media's darling. They accepted many of her claims as factual, and praised how she used her notoriety to honor veterans. Her calendar of scheduled appearances remained full up until the day she died. On November 11, 2008, she assumed the role of Grand Marshall of the New York Veteran's Day Parade. A day prior to the parade, Shain graced Broadway's *South Pacific* stage. The actors, who played World War II sailors, excitedly gathered to pose with the American icon. The assemblage created another irresistible photo opportunity. This time, the nurse made sure to look at the camera. The Associated Press was careful to properly identify her in the picture's caption.

Whenever news of Edith Shain quieted down, from 2005 onward it seemed Glenn McDuffie most often filled the information vacuum. In June 2009 people lined up at the Michael E. DeBakey VA Medical Center in Houston, Texas, to get McDuffie's autograph. During that signing he won the crowd over with quips about his role in the famous photo. Of the photographer, Alfred Eisenstaedt, McDuffie noted, "He took forever, and I just thought I kissed her enough."[1] The crowd burst into laughter. At another point he stood up and held out his arms to reenact the famous kiss. He offered, "And that nurse was standing in the middle of Times Square, she heard me, she turned around and held her arms out like this and that's when I went over and kissed her."[2] Women half his age looked on with maternal smiles, as if welcoming their returning war hero home. The long line of admirers loved him, this man who kissed the girl in that famous photo.

On August 14, 2009, another kissing sailor commemoration took place. For this ceremony Carl Muscarello was the kissing sailor. He arrived in style, seated in a 1936 K limo, a model whose passengers once included presidents Roosevelt, Truman, and Eisenhower. A Vietnam Brotherhood motorcycle convoy accompanied the limo to the Sarasota, Florida, bay front, by Seward Johnson's kissing sailor statue, "Unconditional Surrender." Over three hundred people congregated at the base of a twenty-five-foot tall sculpture to hear Muscarello speak.[3] During his speech, the former sailor turned NYPD detective turned American Express fraud investigator, turned golf instructor, revisited his footsteps from sixty-four years earlier. His story, as always, was a hit. Despite the controversy that surrounds the kissing sailor's identity, Muscarello remained diplomatic. The day prior he offered of other claimant kissing sailors, "Hey, I respect every one of those guys who thinks it was them. But I tell it like it is."[4] The reporter concluded of Muscarello, "His mind apparently is as agile as it was when he served as a NYPD detective and as a fraud investigator with American Express.... [He] can rebut his competitors' claims in convincing fashion."

As is normally the case when Muscarello speaks, he gained followers and admirers at the 2009 V-J Day commemoration. Terry Longpre, present during Muscarello's speech, later that day reflected in a blog:

> Today I can truly say that I met an icon . . . the sailor in the infamous picture of a sailor kissing a nurse on Aug 14, 1945 in Times Square. The picture appeared on the front page of Life magazine. For over fifty years "Moose" never identified himself to anyone as having been the Sailor in the picture.... It has been 64 years to the day since the picture was taken in Times Square. Even though he doesn't consider himself a hero, he is one of the best known icons from WWII and it was my pleasure not only to escort him to the base of the statue, but that have met him. What a guy—and he is ever so humble.[5]

Longpre joined Muscarello's cult following.

Though Glenn McDuffie, Carl Muscarello, and Edith Shain continue to be the most often referenced kissing sailor or nurse candidates, a counter-current has begun to push against the prevailing tide. The sailor from Portuguee Island and the dental assistant from Austria have begun to emerge from years of relative obscurity. In 2009 Raytheon Corporation invited George Mendonsa and Greta Friedman to appear on a float in the Bristol, Rhode Island, Fourth of July Parade, which is part of the nation's oldest Independence Day celebration. During that celebration, thousands of people stood, cheered, and followed the kissing sailor float as it passed by. Many who sought to see, touch, and talk with the kissing sailor were under thirty years old. They didn't see George and Greta as historical figures,

27-1. George and Greta appeared in 2009 at the Bristol, Rhode Island, 4th of July parade, the nation's oldest Independence Day celebration. As their float traveled down the two-mile parade route, adoring crowds sought to talk with the couple, touch them, and request their autographs. (*Photo taken by Lawrence Verria*)

or their kiss as a black-and-white ancient happening. That kiss remained relevant for even the youngest parade-goers. They knew George and Greta had a story to tell. And they wanted to hear it. So did many others.

In October 2010 a conference in Omaha, Nebraska focused on women's contributions on the World War II home front. Though the conference's organizers, *Patriot Productions*, initially invited Edith Shain to the event, upon investigating the identity of the nurse they opted to extend the invitation to Greta Friedman. The conference's organizers also invited George Mendonsa to speak. After Edith Shain passed away in June 2010, the organizers of the "Salute to Women on the Home Front" received phone calls complaining that the woman and man slated for the V-J Day kiss session were not the real kissing sailor and nurse. The event's planners encouraged the detractors to attend the conference and ask questions of the presenters. After the presentation on the V-J Day kiss, the crowd's

questions and comments demonstrated overwhelming support for Greta Friedman and George Mendonsa. The response
exceeded the organizers' expectations. Immediately following the session, conference-goers lined up to receive an autographed picture from both V-J Day kissers. And they sought
more than just George's and Greta's signatures. The long line
of conference attendees wanted to talk to the former sailor and
dental assistant, pose at their side, and let them both know
how much their picture meant to them, and how it made them
feel. Other sessions later that day had to be delayed to accom-
modate the extended time necessary for everyone to meet the
two American historical icons.

■ ■ ■ ■

Alfred Eisenstaedt's photo continues to strike a nerve throughout the United States and around the world. On August 14,
2010, the *Spirit of '45* paid tribute to the greatest generation.
Organizers of the nationwide program selected Times Square as
the *Spirit of '45*'s central location. In Times Square that morning, they conducted a kiss-in, where couples were encouraged
to mug it up as if Alfred Eisenstaedt were taking their picture.
To encourage the activity, *Spirit of '45* brought in the traveling
twenty-five-foot Seward Johnson sculpture, "Unconditional
Surrender." The statue stood for a few days in Times Square
within feet of the location of Alfred Eisenstaedt's famous V-J
Day picture from sixty-five years earlier. People of all ages and
from many countries, excitedly rushed down Times Square to
have their picture taken beside the sculpture of the unforgettable photographed kiss. Many replicated the photographed sailor
and nurse's pose. Almost no one walked by without stopping
and gazing up at Johnson's sculpture. Even sixty-five years after
the kiss, Alfred Eisenstaedt's *V-J Day, 1945, Times Square* and
Lt. Victor Jorgensen's *Kissing the War Goodbye* still captivate an
audience.

With almost seven decades separating *V-J Day, 1945, Times Square* from its present-day admirers, that photograph continues to communicate what the end of a long-fought and victorious war *felt* like. And even the greatest generation's children's children can't help but look on in awe. It is time to finally recognize the real sailor and dental assistant in that photo. The proof has been gathered. Experts in fields of photography, facial recognition, and forensic anthropology are prepared to speak to the evidence. And a publication, prized as much as its most popular picture, can now confidently share the story of its kissing sailor.

28

A LEICA'S NOTES

In 1980 *LIFE*'s kissing sailor returned to Times Square. George Mendonsa anticipated quite a homecoming. That didn't happen. Instead of embracing their progeny, *LIFE* assumed the role of an overwhelmed paternal figure who could not discern fact from fable. But the publication mogul did find the wherewithal to proudly dangle pictures of Alfred Eisenstaedt's V-J Day sailor in front of Time-Life book viewers. The reprinting contributed positively to their financial bottom line. The actual kissing sailor did not. He was expendable. As it turned out, sadly, so was *LIFE*.

In 2009 *LIFE* embarked on another publication pursuit, though this time in a different format from the past. This publishing effort utilized computer screens instead of paper. The new medium maintained some of *LIFE*'s original principles. Like the publication's prior versions, the picture continued to trump words. Digitally showcasing today's top photos, viewers can sign up as fans on Facebook, Twitter, and Tumblr. *LIFE* has reintroduced itself to a new generation of viewers.

Before the famous photo journal goes much further, they would do well to attend to some old unfinished business. Alfred Eisenstaedt's photo, *V-J Day, 1945, Times Square*, continues to remind a nation why they fought a terrible war seventy years ago, and what that victory felt like. The Show-Book of the World still needs to identify the couple that made their most beloved photo possible. They need not spend a whole issue doing so. That photo does not have to adorn the cover of their newly formatted digital publication. The original printing in August 1945 didn't. The article's title could read, simply, *A Leica's Notes*. They could cut to the chase. A quick read with a big black-and-white picture would suffice. They might write something like this:

On August 14, 1945, a dental assistant left her office at Lexington and 38th Street, heading west toward Times Square. She made the trek to read from the news ticker and learn if what she had heard all morning and afternoon really happened. Had the Japanese finally surrendered to the United States?

Though she walked quickly, keeping a brisk pace became increasingly difficult as she approached the crowded square. Bumps and other incidental contacts were apologized for or shrugged off. Neither deterred her from the mission. She just had to know. Was the war that had affected her life so personally and hurtfully finally over?

Before entering the square, she passed the 42nd Street subway station where people of every persuasion exited and bustled toward 43rd Street and beyond. Before she had a chance to look up at the news ticker, Greta got caught up with the flow of other eager pedestrians. She scampered into the middle of the square, not heeding those who crossed her path. Just before reaching tracks that made their way down the wide street's center, and shy of the 44th Street sign, the woman dressed in white stopped, turned, and looked up at the news ticker. She stood motionless, and read the moving type. The running text read, "VJ, VJ, VJ . . ." She thought that what she had heard all day must be true. Gazing at the news, Greta took in the moment fully.

Greta had arrived by herself, but she was not alone. Others in a crowded Times Square took notice of her. One such individual wore a dark, navy-blue uniform. That sailor, outpacing his trailing girlfriend, drew in on the dental assistant, whom he thought was a nurse. That mattered to him. The reasons need not be expounded upon here.

As the sailor swooped in, the dental assistant caught a quick glimpse of his approach. Before she could determine his intentions, the tall sailor overtook her, pinning her tapestry purse between them. Nearby, a photographer glanced in the sailor's direction. Without processing the moment before him, he turned around swiftly and snapped four pictures with his Leica camera.

Almost as quickly as the moment commenced, it ended. After the two kissers parted, the sailor turned to his girlfriend, who allowed, on this day only, her boyfriend's indiscretion. The woman in white hurried back to work. The photographer did not have the presence of mind to record the kissers' names, and went on to witness many more mugging couples that afternoon and evening. By day's end, no single shot stood out for his attention. Later, others would beg to differ.

The next day one of the photographer's processed negatives exposed for the ages the moment World War II ended. Owing to happenstance, the photographer's skill, and perhaps fate, Americans would forever know what it felt like when that horrible war was no more.

While the picture of the uniformed sailor and the dental assistant dressed in white appeared as a full-page visual in *LIFE* magazine on August, 27, 1945, neither of the picture's two subjects learned of the photograph for many years. And for decades, no one knew of them. Though the photographer did not consider *V-J Day, 1945, Times Square* one of his best photographs, nevertheless it became the most reproduced image in *LIFE* magazine's illustrious history, and one of the most beloved photos of all time.

Owing in part to the fact that no one took written notes at the time, over the years numerous former sailors and a few nurses attested to their part in the prized picture. For years, they, and others, argued about who kissed whom in Times Square on August 14, 1945.

Thankfully, what the photographer did not do, his Leica camera did. Without the use of written captions, the camera inscribed notes all over its photo. Facial structures, body markings, physical oddities, and height and body compositions lead to a definitive identification. Carl Muscarello, Ken McNeel, Glenn McDuffie, Edith Shain, Barbara Sokol, and many others who claimed a part in one of history's most endearing photos do not possess the traits required to hold claim to Alfred Eisenstaedt's kissing couple. Only one man and one woman do. They have an amazing story to tell.

George Mendonsa is the kissing sailor. His large tanned hands, dark patch of hair on the lower right arm, the faint "G" and "M" body marking, and a bump on his left forearm make for an unmistakable identity. Greta Friedman, with her twisted slim waist, tightly coiled hair, and long slender fingers clutched around her small purse, is the woman dressed in white so many people assume to be a nurse. Finally, he and she must be recognized.

Alfred Eisenstaedt, the Father of Photojournalism, may you rest in peace as your *V-J Day, 1945, Times Square* photograph lives on. George and Greta, may you be celebrated, long overdue, for a contribution that exceeds the capacity of a painter's brush to emulate.

With the publication of *A Leica's Notes*, and matters of the heart and soul at peace with the truth, we at *LIFE* are now clear to embark on the next phase of our proud history.

NOTES

Introduction

1. In November 2011, *75 Years: The Very Best of LIFE,* determined that the "proper title" for the magazine's most famous photo should be *V-J Day, Times Square, New York City, 1945.*

Chapter 2. The Place Where People Meet

1. Darcy Tell, *Times Square Spectacular: Lighting Up Broadway* (New York: Smithsonian Institution Press, 2007), 20.
2. Ibid., 42.
3. Ibid., 43.
4. Ibid., 44.
5. Ibid., 40.
6. Bill Harris, "Catching the World Series, 1919," in *The Century in Times Square*, edited by Merrill Perlman (New York: Bishop Books Inc., 1999), 25.
7. Tell, *Times Square Spectacular*, 174.
8. Ibid., 174.
9. Jill Stone, *Times Square: A Pictorial History* (New York: Macmillan Publishing Co., 1982), 113.
10. Tell, *Times Square Spectacular*, 120.
11. Ibid., 121.
12. Harris, "Catching the World Series, 1919," 77.
13. Anthony Bianco, *Ghosts of 42nd Street* (New York: HarperCollins, 2004), 120.
14. Stone, *Times Square*, 119.
15. Ibid., 119.
16. Tell, *Times Square Spectacular*, 122.
17. Ibid., 122.
18. Harris, "Catching the World Series, 1919," 56.

Chapter 3. The Publication

1. Wendy Kozol, *Life's America* (Philadelphia: Temple University Press, 1994), 8.
2. Alfred Eisenstaedt, *Eisenstaedt on Eisenstaedt* (New York: Abbeville Press Publications, 1985), 64.

3. John Loengard, *Life Photographers: What They Saw* (Boston: Little, Brown and Company, 1998), 10.

4. Ibid., 10.

5. Wendy Kozol, *Life's America*, 42.

6. Ibid., 29–30.

7. James L. Baughman, "Who Read Life? The Circulation of America's Favorite Magazine," in *Looking at LIFE Magazine*, edited by Erika Doss (Washington, D.C.: Smithsonian Institution Press, 2001), 46.

8. Kozol, *Life's America*, 35.

9. Baughman, "Who Read Life?" 46.

10. Ibid., 44.

11. Ibid., 45.

12. Ibid., 42.

13. Ibid., 42.

14. Peter Bacon Hales, "Imagining the Atomic Age," in *Looking at LIFE Magazine*, 105.

15. Erika Doss, "Rethinking America's Favorite Magazine, 1936–1972, in *Looking at LIFE Magazine*, 3.

16. Loudoun Wainwright, *Great American Magazine: An Inside History of LIFE* (New York: Alfred A. Knopf, 1986), 122.

17. "The Ten Years," *LIFE*, November 25, 1946, 117.

18. Baughman, "Who Read Life?" 44.

19. Kozol, *Life's America*, viii.

20. Baughman, "Who Read Life?" 44.

21. Doss, "Rethinking America's Favorite Magazine," 7.

22. Loengard, *Life Photographers*, 9.

23. Ibid.

24. Doss, "Rethinking America's Favorite Magazine," 18.

25. Wainwright, *Great American Magazine*, 122.

Chapter 4. The Duck from Portuguee Island

1. R. A. Scotti, *Sudden Sea: The Great Hurricane of 1938* (New York: Chapter & Verse, Ink., 2003), 98.

2. WPRI 12 Home Page, August 21, 2009, http://www.wpri.com/dpp/weather/local_wpri_hurricane_of_1938_retrospective_20090820_nek (accessed June 12, 2011).

3. R. A. Scotti's *Sudden Sea*, speaks in detail of the approach of the Long Island Express, also known as the Hurricane of '38, through personal accounts of those who witnessed the storm's quick arrival.

Those accounts echo George Mendonsa's memory of the most destructive hurricane to ever hit Rhode Island's coast.

4. Tom Clavin and Bob Drury, *Halsey's Typhoon* (New York: Atlantic Monthly Press, 2007), 66.

5. Ibid., 66.

6. Ibid., 152.

7. Charles Lilly, *Journal On Board USS "The Sullivans" DD537*, December 23, 1943–July 4, 1945, 68.

8. Clavin and Drury. *Halsey's Typhoon*, 106.

9. Ibid., 169.

10. Ibid., 77.

11. Ibid., 153.

12. Ibid., 169.

13. Ibid., 266.

14. Ibid., 51.

15. Ibid., 52.

16. Maxwell Taylor Kennedy. *Danger's Hour* (New York: Simon and Schuster, 2008), 294.

17. Ibid., 468.

18. NavSource Online: Aircraft Carrier Photo Archive, http://www.navsource.org/archives/02/17.htm (accessed June 18, 2011).

19. Kennedy, *Danger's Hour*, 275.

20. Ibid., 2.

21. Rich Lillie, survivor from burning *Bunker Hill*, phone interview by Lawrence Verria, November 19, 2009.

22. Kennedy, *Danger's Hour*, 342.

23. 2009 Lillie interview.

24. Pacific Wrecks, 1995, www.pacificwrecks.com/ships/usn/DD-537.html (accessed May 9, 2011).

25. Kennedy, *Danger's Hour*, 311.

Chapter 5. The Saved

1. Daniel Goldhagen, *Hitler's Willing Executioners: Ordinary Germans and the Holocaust*, 12th ed. (New York: Alfred E. Knopf, 1996), 286.

2. Lucy S. Dawidowicz, *The War Against the Jews 1933–1945*, 6th ed. (New York: Holt, Rinehart and Winston, 1975), 127.

3. "Broken Lives," *LIFE*, vol. 4, no. 113 (March 28, 1938), 23.

4. Goldhagen, *Hitler's Willing Executioners*, 286.

5. Ibid., 287.

6. Jewish Virtual Library, 2011, http://www.jewishvirtuallibrary.org/jsource/Holocaust/FloorScrub.html (accessed May 2, 2011).

7. Dawidowicz, *The War Against the Jews 1933–1945*, 507.

8. *New York Goes to War*, DVD, directed by Julie Cohen (New York: WLIW, 2007).

9. "Atoms Burst in Air to cut Loss of Life," *New York Times*, August 12, 1945, 28.

Chapter 6. The Model

1. David McCullough, *Truman* (New York: Simon and Schuster, 1992), 454.

2. Ibid., 459.

Chapter 7. The Father of Photojournalism

1. Bryan Holmes, "Introduction," in *Eisenstaedt Remembrances*, by Alfred Eisenstaedt and Doris O'Neil (Boston: Little, Brown and Company, 1990), ix.

2. John Loengard, *Life Photographers: What They Saw* (Boston: Little, Brown and Company, 1998), 13.

3. Alfred Eisenstaedt, *Eisenstaedt on Eisenstaedt* (New York: Abbeville Press Publications, 1985), 7

4. Loengard, *Life Photographers*, 23.

5. Ibid., 23.

6. Holmes, "Introduction," ix.

7. Ibid., x.

8. Eisenstaedt, *Eisenstaedt on Eisenstaedt*, 9.

9. Loengard, *Life Photographers*, 14.

10. Holmes, "Introduction," x.

11. Eisenstaedt and O'Neil, *Eisenstaedt Remembrances*, 26.

12. Eisenstaedt, *Eisenstaedt on Eisenstaedt*, 61.

13. Loengard, *Life Photographers*, 19.

14. Ibid., 19

15. Eisenstaedt, *Eisenstaedt on Eisenstaedt*, 40.

16. Ibid., 72.

Chapter 8. Morning, V-J Day, 1945

1. David McCullough, *Truman* (New York: Simon and Schuster, 1992), 459.

2. David Brinkley, *Washington Goes to War* (New York: Ballantine Books, 1988), 277.

3. Jan Morris, *Manhattan '45* (New York: Oxford University Press, 1987), 210.

Chapter 11. In Search of *the* Picture

1. Wendy Kozol, *Life's America* (Philadelphia: Temple University Press, 1994), 57.
2. Ibid., 56.

Chapter 13. Pictures from V-J Day

1. Paul D. Casadorph, *Let the Good Times Roll* (New York: Paragon House, 1989), 255.
2. Christopher Westhorp, ed., *VJ Day in Photographs* (London: Salamander Books, 1995), 20.
3. Peter Carlson, "The Happiest Day in American History," *American History* 45, no. 3 (August 2010), http://www.web.ebscohost.com/ehost/detail?sid=b5eddf6e-72af-447f-bedb-f6620e31e455%40sess ionmgr110vid=26&hid=110&bdata=JnNpdGU9Whvc3QtbG1Zq %3d%3d#db=f5h&AN=5161313 (accessed August 5, 2011).
4. *LIFE*, September 27, 1945, 32.
5. David Brinkley, *Washington Goes To War* (New York: Ballantine Books, 1988), 278.
6. Westhorp, *VJ Day in Photographs*, 29.
7. Brinkley, *Washington Goes To War*, 278.
8. Ray Hoopes, *Remember the Home Front* (New York: Hawthorne Books, Inc., 1977), 361.
9. Westhorp, *VJ Day in Photographs*, 18.
10. Carlson, "The Happiest Day in American History."
11. Alexander Feinberg, "All City Lets Go," *New York Times*, August 15, 1945.
12. Carlson, "The Happiest Day in American History."
13. Bill Rufty, "Lakeland Couple Shared Their Own Timeless Kiss on V-J Day," theledger.com (accessed August 14, 2007).
14. Gerard Meister, "It Was Nothing Like Eisenstaedt's," *American Heritage* (July 2005), 77.
15. Ibid., 77.
16. Carlson, "The Happiest Day in American History."
17. Ibid.
18. Ibid.
19. Feinberg, "All City Lets Go."
20. Carlson, "The Happiest Day in American History."

Chapter 14. No One Seemed to Notice

1. John Loengard, *Life Photographers:What They Saw* (Boston: Little, Brown and Company, 1998), 24.
2. James Sheridan, phone interview with Lawrence Verria, August 4, 2007.
3. "Ten Years Later," *LIFE,* November 25, 1946, 120.

Chapter 15. Eisenstaedt Names the Nurse

1. Many sources claim the photo was taken in September 1945. Of course, that is impossible because it first appeared in *LIFE* on August 27, 1945. Part of the confusion might stem from the fact that there were three V-J Days—August 14, August 15, and September 2 when the Japanese formally surrendered on board USS *Missouri.*
2. Bobbi Baker Burrows, interviewed by Lawrence Verria, Time-Life Building, New York, March 9, 2008.
3. Kristen Rothwell, "A Nurse's Iconic Kiss That Marked the End of World War II," 2005, Nursezone.com/include/PrintArticle.asp?art icleid=14241&Profile=Spotlight=on=nurses (accessed August 19, 2007).
4. Dean Lucas, *VJ Day Times Square Kiss*, May 2, 2007, http://www. famouspictures.org/mag/index.php?title=VJday_Times_Square_ Kiss (accessed August 19, 2007).
5. Ibid.
6. "Camera at Work," *LIFE* 3 (August 1980), 8.
7. Michael J. Kennedy, "Celebrating the V-J Day Kiss Seen 'Round the World,'" August 14, 2005, http://articles.latimes.com/2005/aug/14/ local/me-kiss14 (accessed November 10, 2008).
8. Ibid.
9. Rothwell, "A Nurse's Iconic Kiss That Marked the End of World War II."
10. Kennedy, "Celebrating the V-J Day Kiss Seen 'Round the World.'"
11. Edith Shain, phone interview by Lawrence Verria, December 9, 2008.
12. Rothwell, "A Nurse's Iconic Kiss That Marked the End of World War II."
13. 2008 Shain interview.
14. Ibid.
15. Rothwell, "A Nurse's Iconic Kiss That Marked the End of World War II."

16. "From Celebration to Circus, Caught Up in the March of Time," *Barista: Head Starters for the Hungry Mind*, August 17, 2005, http://barista.media2.org/?p=2085 (accessed August 19, 2007).

17. "Nurse Recalls Times Square Kiss 60 Years Later," in CTV.CA, 2007, http://www.ctv.ca/servlet/ArticleNews/print/CTVNews/20050812/famous_kiss-050812/?hub=CanadaAM&subhub+PrintStory (accessed August 19, 2007).

18. 2008 Shain interview.

19. Lucas, "VJ Day Times Square Kiss."

20. "Who Is the Kissing Sailor?" *LIFE* 3 (October 1980), 72.

21. Pat Milton, "Nurse Recalls Famous Times Square Kiss," August 14, 2005, News Herald .com (accessed August 7, 2007).

22. "Who Is the Kissing Sailor?"

23. "Nurse Recalls Times Square Kiss 60 Years Later."

24. Kennedy, "Celebrating the V-J Day Kiss Seen 'Round the World.'"

25. 2008 Shain interview.

26. "Our Special Guest—Edith Shain 2007," California Pioneers of Santa Clara County, 2007, http://www.californiapioneers.com/Edith%20Shain/Edith%20Shain.html (accessed October 13, 2008).

27. Emma Brown, "Anonymously World-Famous after WWII Photo, She Didn't Kiss and Tell," *Washington Post*, June 24, 2010, B5.

28. "The Nurse," LIFE.com, April 20, 2010, http://www.life.com/gallery/45081/a-ailor-nuse-a-legendary-kiss#index/3 (accessed July 25, 2011).

29. Lisa Huriash, "Kissing Sailor Remembers Nurse from WWII Photo 'Left Me Breathless,'" *Palm Beach Post*, June 24, 2010, http://www.palmbeachpost.com/news/state/kissing-sailor-remembers-nurse-from-wwii-photo-left-766334.html?printArticle+y (accessed January 27, 2011).

Chapter 16. *LIFE*'s Invitation

1. In a 1987 letter to George Mendonsa, Ann Morrel, a *LIFE* secretary, referenced the whole ordeal involving the search for the kissing sailor as "fun." As it turned out, the thirty-plus-year ordeal was not fun for either *LIFE* or Mendonsa.

2. Philip B. Kunhardt Jr., "Editor's Note," *LIFE* 3, no. 8 (August 1980), 4.

3. "Letters to the Editors," *LIFE*, vol. 19, no. 12 (September 11, 1945), 2

4. Bobbi Baker Burrows, phone interview by Lawrence Verria, July 22, 2011.

Chapter 17. I'm the Real Kissing Sailor

1. "Letters," *LIFE*, vol. 3, no. 12 (December 1980), 33.
2. Ibid.
3. Ibid.
4. "Who Is the Kissing Sailor?" *LIFE*, vol. 3, no. 10 (October 1980), 70.
5. Ibid.
6. Ibid.
7. Ibid.
8. Ibid.
9. Ibid.
10. Ibid.
11. Ibid.
12. George Byron Koch, "Letter to the Editor," *Wall Street Journal*, August 14, 1996, http://www.georgekoch.com/articles/sailor.htm (accessed July 10, 2011).
13. Koch, "Letter to the Editor."
14. Chris Palmer, "*Chris' Old Life Magazines*," http://www.kissingsailor. com (accessed October 10, 2007).
15. Ibid.
16. Carli Teproff, "WWII 'Kissing Sailor' Carl Muscarello Visits Fort Lauderdale School Kids," *Miami Herald*, October 15, 2010, http://articles.sun-sentinel.com/2010-10-14/news/fl-kissing-sailor-20101014_1_kiss-carl-muscarello-submarines (accessed January 22, 2011).
17. Carl Muscarello, phone interview by Lawrence Verria, July 19, 2011.
18. Ibid.
19. Andrea Elliot, "Carl and Edith Touch Lips Again," *New York Times*, October 16, 2005, http://www.theage.com.au/news/world/ carl-and-edith-touch-lips-again/2005/08/15/1123958007037. html?from=morestories (accessed August 19, 2007).
20. Lisa Huriash, "Kissing Sailor Remembers Nurse from WWII Photo 'Left Me Breathless,'" *South Florida Sun-Sentinel*, June 24, 2010, http:// www.palmbeachpost.com/news/state/kissing-sailor-remembers-nurse-from-wwii-photo-left-766334,html?printArticle=y (accessed January 27, 2011).
21. Carl Muscarello, phone interview by Lawrence Verria, March 4, 2008.
22. Huriash, "Kissing Sailor Remembers Nurse from WWII Photo."

23. Dean Lucas, *VJ Day Times Square Kiss*, May 2, 2007, http://www.famouspictures.org/mag/index.php?title=VJday_Times_Square_Kiss (accessed August 19, 2007).

24. Ibid.

25. Teproff, "WWII 'Kissing Sailor' Carl Muscarello Visits Fort Lauderdale School Kids."

26. 2008 Muscarello interview.

27. Ibid.

28. John Loengard, *Life Photographers: What They Saw* (Boston: Little Brown and Company, 1998), 24.

29. 2008 Muscarello interview.

30. Eugene Cunningham, letter provided Carl Muscarello, date unknown.

31. Flori Meeks, "Spring Resident Recounts 'THE KISS' that Signified the End of World War II," *Chronicle*, http://www.chron.com/disp/story.mpl/nb/spring/news/5130483.html (accessed March 14, 2010).

32. David Freelander, "Kiss Isn't just a Kiss for Times Square Sailor," http://www.amny.com/news/local/am-kiss0814,0,1019922,print.story (accessed January 24, 2008).

33. Flori Meeks, "Spring Resident recounts 'THE KISS' that signified the end of World War II," *Chronicle*, http://www.chron.com/disp/story.mpl/nb/spring/news/5130483.html (accessed March 14, 2010).

34. Glenn McDuffie, phone interview by Lawrence Verria, February 24, 2008.

35. Ruth Sheenan, "N.C. Boy Knew How to Celebrate," *News Observer*, http://www.newsobserver.com/news/sheehan/story/1130415.html (accessed July 7, 2008).

36. "Glenn McDuffie," *Good Moring America*, New York, August 14, 2007.

37. Archie Satterfield, "Mystery Kisser Identified?" Satterfield Newsletter, July 28, 2007, http://www.archiesatterfield.com/newletter.htm (accessed September 21, 2007).

38. Juan Lozano, "Sailor in Famous Photo Identified," Time.com, August 3, 2007, http://www.time.com/time/arts/article/0,8599,1649714.00.html (accessed August 19, 2007).

39. Emily Friedman, "Man Claims He's the Mystery Sailor in the 'The Kiss,'" *Good Morning America*, August 7, 2007, http://abcnews.go.com/GMA/OnlyinAmerica/story?id=3422191&page=1 (accessed August 15, 2007).

40. Meeks, "Spring Resident Recounts 'THE KISS.'"

41. Lois Gibson, "Homepage," 2005, http://www.loisgibson.com/kissing_sailor.asp (accessed October 9, 2007).

42. "Forensic Expert Identifies Mariner in Famed VJ New York Times Square Kiss," August 2007, http://www.andhranews.net/Intl/2007/August/13/Forensic-expert-identifies-11606.asp (accessed January 24, 2008).

43. Lois Gibson, "Comparison with a Scale," e-mail to Lawrence Verria, July 8, 2008.

Chapter 18. For Dissemination of News

1. Ronald R. Lagueux, "George Mendonsa, Plaintiff, v. Time Inc., Defendant C.A. No. 87-0371 L.," *United States District Court, Rhode Island*, February 23, 1988, http://nsulaw.nova.edu/faculty/documents/Mendonsa.htm (accessed August 3, 2010).

2. Ibid.

3. Ibid.

4. "Ex-Sailor Settles Lawsuit Over 1945 'Kiss' Photo," *Desert News Publishing Company*, October 16, 1988, http://www.desertnews.com/article/print/20765/Ex-SAILOR-SETTLES-LAWSUIT-OVER-1945-KISS-PHOTO.HTML (accessed July 28, 2011).

Chapter 20. You Want to Believe Them All

1. Dan Okrent, "Letter to the Editor," *Wall Street Journal*, August 20, 1996.

2. Edith Shain, "Letter to the Editor," *Wall Street Journal*, August 20, 1996.

3. Chris Palmer, *Chris' Old Life Magazines*, http://www.kissingsailor.com (accessed August 9, 2007).

4. Dirk Halstead, "Eisenstaedt," e-mail to Lawrence Verria, October 23, 2007.

5. Ken McNeel, phone interview by Lawrence Verria, February 23, 2008.

6. Alfred Eisenstaedt, *Eisenstaedt on Eisenstaedt* (New York: Abbeville Press Publications, 1985), 72.

7. "Kissing the War Good-Bye—The Real Kissing Sailor," OldLife Magazines.com, http://www.kissingsailor.com (accessed August 19, 2007).

8. Carl Muscarello, phone interview by Lawrence Verria, July 24, 2008.

9. 2008 Muscarello interview.

10. John Loengard, *Life Photographers: What They Saw* (Boston: Little, Brown and Company, 1998), 24.

11. Michael Kennedy, "Celebrating the V-J Day Kiss Seen 'Round the World,'" *Los Angeles Times* online, August 14, 2005, http://www.latimes.com/2005/aug/14/local/me-kiss14 (accessed November 10, 2008).

12. Edith Shain, phone interview by Lawrence Verria, December 9, 2008.

13. After looking at a picture of Carl Muscarello standing beside Edith Shain and learning that Muscarello claimed to be five feet eleven inches tall, Lois Gibson (Glenn McDuffie promoter) argued in an e-mail to the author, "Good grief, Carl Muscarello is practicing deception here. . . . You can tell from the scale he is taller than that! If he is just under 6', then Edith Shane must be 4', and it is a matter of record she is taller than that." Following Gibson's reasoning, Muscarello stands in at approximately six feet, eight inches.

14. Vincent Bugliosi, *Reclaiming History: The Assassination of President Kennedy* (New York: W.W. Norton & Company, 2007), 521n.

15. Gerald Posner, *Case Closed* (New York: Doubleday, 1994), 272.

16. Lois Gibson claims no other pictures of Glenn McDuffie exist from 1943 to 1946.

17. "Cambridgeshire: People Like You," *British Broadcasting Corporation*, http://www.bbc.co.uk/cambridgeshire/content/articles/2007/08/16/kiss_eisenstaedt_feature.shtml (accessed August 18, 2007).

18. David Freelander, "Kiss Isn't just a Kiss for Times Square Sailor," *AM New York*, August 14, 2007, http://www.amny.com/news/local/am-kiss0814,0,1019922.print.story (accessed January 24, 2008).

19. Eisenstaedt, *Eisenstaedt on Eisenstaedt*, 74.

20. Loengard, *Life Photographers*, 23.

21. Eisenstaedt, *Eisenstaedt on Eisenstaedt*, 74.

22. Archie Satterfield, "Mystery Kisser Identified?" Satterfield Newsletter, July 28, 2007, http://www.archiesatterfield.com/new letter.htm (accessed September 21, 2007).

23. "Kissing Sailor—Found at Last," Lois Gibson's Home Page, 2005, http://www.loisgibson.com/kissing_sailor.asp (accessed October 9, 2007).

24. Steve Martin, phone interview by Lawrence Verria, December 12, 2008.

25. James Sheridan, phone interview by Lawrence Verria, August 4, 2007.

26. Gerald O'Donnell, interviewed by Lawrence Verria, Middletown, Rhode Island, May 12, 2007.

27. Ibid.

28. "Kissing Sailor—Found at Last," Lois Gibson's home page.

29. "Ibid.

30. Ibid.

31. Satterfield, "Mystery Kisser Identified?"

32. Lois Gibson, "Black Triangle on Shoulder," e-mail to Lawrence Verria, September 7, 2008.

33. Ibid.

34. Richard Benson, phone interview by Lawrence Verria, September 13, 2008.

35. Emily Friedman, "Man Claims He's the Mystery Sailor in the 'The Kiss,'" *Good Morning America*, August 7, 2007, http://abcnews. go.com/GMA/OnlyinAmerica/story?id=3422191&page=1 (accessed August 15, 2007).

36. Juan Lozano, "Sailor in Famous Photo Identified," Time.com, 3 August 3, 2007, http://www.time.com/time/arts/article/0,8599,1649714.00. html (accessed August 19, 2007).

37. Glenn McDuffie, phone interview by Lawrence Verria, February 24, 2008.

38. Satterfield, "Mystery Kisser Identified?"

39. Jacqui Goodard, "A Kiss is Just a Kiss . . . But This One Was Mine," Timesonline, August 13, 2007 timesonline.com (accessed September 26, 2007).

40. Freelander, "Kiss Isn't just a Kiss for Times Square Sailor."

41. Ibid.

42. 2008 McDuffie interview.

Chapter 21. More Plot Than Proof

1. "The Kissers," *America in World War II*, http://www.americainwwii. com (accessed August 19, 2007).

2. Tom Huntington, "The Kissers," *America in World War II*, December 2005, http://www.americaiinwwii.com/stories/kissers.htm (August 19, 2007).

3. Gerald O'Donnell, interviewed by Lawrence Verria, Middletown, Rhode Island, May 12, 2007.

Chapter 22. Considerations

1. George Mendonsa's lawyer hired John Hopf to take photos of George's arms, hands, and face for use in a 1987 lawsuit against Time Inc. George brought the case against Time Inc. for the use of his likeness for their profit. The specifics of that case are discussed in Chapter 24.

2. John Loengard, *Life Photographers: What They Saw* (Boston: Little, Brown and Company, 1998), 24.

3. Ibid.

4. Alexander Feinberg, "All City 'Lets Go,'" *New York Times*, August 15, 1945, 1.

5. Christopher Westhorp, ed., *V-J Day in Photographs* (London: Salamander Books, 1995), 25.

6. Loengard, *Life Photographers*, 24.

7. Ibid.

8. Richard Benson, *The Benson Report*, Newport, Rhode Island, 1987.

Chapter 23. A Mountain of Evidence

1. George Mendonsa, *Plaintiff vs. Time, Incorporated Defendant* is discussed in considerable detail in Chapter Eighteen.

2. Richard Benson, The Benson Report, Newport, Rhode Island, 1987.

3. Ibid.

4. Ibid.

5. Ibid.

6. Ibid.

7. Lois Gibson claims that she determined that McDuffie's hands are the same exact size as the kissing sailor's.

8. Benson, The Benson Report.

9. Ibid.

10. Ibid.

11. Gerald O'Donnell, interviewed by Lawrence Verria, Middletown, Rhode Island, May 12, 2007.

12. "VJ Day Sailor," Navy War College Museum, 2006, http://www.nwc.navy.mil/museum/VJDaySailor/ (accessed September 24, 2006).

13. Ibid.

14. Baback Moghaddam, Hanspeter Pfister, Jinho Lee, "3D Facial Modeling & Synthesis of the Sailor in Alfred Eisenstaedt's 'VJ-Day Kiss' Photo," *Mitsubishi Electric Research Laboratories*, 2005, http://www.merl.com/people/baback/vj/ (accessed April 3 2007).

15. "VJ Day Sailor."

16. Mark D. Faram, "The Kiss Heard 'Round the World," *Navy Times* (October 24, 2005), 16.

17. "60 Year-Old Mystery Solved—MERL IDs 'Kissing Sailor' of WWII," *CONNECTions*, vol. 5, no. 2 (Winter 2006), 2.

18. In his 1987 study, Richard Benson of Yale University determined the dark spot on the kissing sailor's arm was a dark and thick patch of hair. Benson found that this thicker patch of hair is also present on George Mendonsa's arm, as evidenced in a photo taken by John Hopf in 1987.

19. Norman Sauer, KS Inclusions, e-mail to Lawrence Verria, May 27, 2009.

20. Ibid.

Chapter 24. Indisputable? The Case for Greta

1. Edith Shain, "Letter to the Editor," *Wall Street Journal*, August 20, 1996.

2. "Camera At Work," *LIFE*, vol. 3, no. 8 (August 1980), 7.

3. "Who Is the Kissing Sailor?" *LIFE*, vol. 3, no. 10 (October 1980), 69.

4. Bobbi Baker Burrows, "In Appreciation of Eisie," *The Digital Journalist*, http://digitaljournalist.org/issue9911/burrows.htm (accessed September 29, 2007).

5. Bobbi Baker Burrows, interviewed by Lawrence Verria, Time-Life Building, New York City, March 27, 2008.

6. "Nurse in Times Square War Photo Reunites with Navy," *NPR*, http://www.npr.org/templates/story.php?storyId=96801284 (accessed November 10, 2008).

7. Edith Shain, phone interview by Lawrence Verria, December 9, 2008.

8. Kristin Rothwell, "A Nurse's Iconic Kiss That Marked the End of World War II," *Nurse Zone*, 2005, Nursezone.com (accessed August 19, 2007).

9. "Who Is the Kissing Sailor?" 72.

10. Pat Milton, *Nurse Recalls Famous Times Square Kiss*, August 14, 2005, News Herald .com (accessed August 7, 2007).

11. Richard Goldstein, "Edith Shain, Who Said Famous Kiss Came Her Way, Dies at 91," *New York Times*, June 24, 2010, http://www.nytimes.com/2010/06/24/nyregion/24shain.html?pagewanted=print (accessed November 24, 2010).

12. Greta Friedman, phone interview by Lawrence Verria, August 24, 2008.

Chapter 25. The Carnival

1. John Loengard, *Life Photographers: What They Saw* (Boston: Little, Brown and Company, 1998), 24.

2. Philip Kunhardt's inaccurate date reference was interpreted by claimant kissing sailor Glenn McDuffie as an attempt to deny him his due. McDuffie claimed to have kissed the nurse on August 14, 1945.

3. Philip B. Kunhardt Jr., "Editor's Note," *LIFE*, vol. 3, no. 8 (August 1980), 4.

4. George Mendonsa, interview by Lawrence Verria, September 21, 2008.

5. Bobbi Baker Burrows, phone interview by Lawrence Verria, July 22, 2011.

6. "From Celebration to Circus, Caught Up in the March of Time," *New York Times*, August 17, 2005, http://barista.media2org//p=2085 (accessed August 19, 2007).

7. Greta Friedman, letter to Dr. Guido Knopp and Ullrich Lenze, June 1, 1991.

Chapter 26. The Circus

1. David Kindred, "It Started with a Kiss," *Golf Digest*, January 2007, 77.

2. "Kissing Sailor, 80, Fells Burglar," *CBS News*, September 18, 2006, http://www.cbsnews.com/stories/2006/09/18/national/main201892.shtml (accessed September 24, 2006).

3. Ibid.

4. "Kissing Sailor Debate," *Brandemeier in the Morning* on WLUP (Chicago), August 2007.

5. "Life Magazine Sailor Nurs—Kiss and Did Not Make Up," *JB1TV*, June 23, 2010, http://www.youtube.com/user/JB1TV? blend=22&ob=5 (accessed July 24, 2011).

6. "Kissing Sailor Debate."

7. Ibid.

8. Ibid.

9. "Life Magazine Sailor Nurse."

10. Mike Saewitz, "Sculptor at Center of Copyright Infringement Case," *Herald Tribune*, May 9, 2006, http://www.heraldtribune.com/apps/pbcs.dll/article?AID=/20060509/NEWS/605090464 (accessed November 11, 2007).

11. Ibid.

12. Juan Lozano, "Sailor in Famous Photo Identified," Time.com, August 3, 2007 http:www.time.com/time/arts/article/0,8599,1649714.00. html (accessed August 19, 2007).

13. Guy Fletcher, "A Kiss For the Ages," *Frederick* 291 (September 9, 2009), 55.

14. "Marshall Berman, Everyman in Times Square," *Columbia College Today* (excerpt from Berman's *On the Town*), http://www.college.columbia. edu/cct_archive/mar_apr07/forum.php (accessed September 3, 2008).

15. Natalie Andrews, "The Other Woman in the WWII 'Kiss' Photo," *Daily Herald*, November 11, 2006, http://www.heraldextra.com/ content/ view/199837/ (accesed October 4, 2007).

16. Recollections of Gloria Delaney, believed to be the Nurse in the Background of Lt. Victor Jorgensen's V-J Day Photo (see Andy Newman's "Nurse's Tale of Storied Kiss. No, Not That Nurse," on the front page of the *New York Times*, August 14, 2010), indicate that Eisenstaedt's picture was taken during the afternoon well before 7:00 p.m.

17. Sewell Chan, "62 Years Later, a Kiss That Can't Be Forgotten," *New York Times City Room*, August 14, 2007, http://cityroom.blogs. nytimes.com/2007/08/14/62-years-later-a-kiss-that-cant-be-forgotten (accessed November 28, 2008).

18. John Louis Lucaites, "CSI Expert Determines Famous Times Square Kisser," *No Caption Needed,* August 4, 2007, http://www. nocaptionneeded.com/?p-150 (accessed January 24, 2008).

19. Chan, "62 Years Later, a Kiss That Can't Be Forgotten"

20. Erin Overbay, "Remembering that Immortalized Kiss," *The New Yorker*, June 24, 2010, newyorker.com/online/blogs/backissues/ 2010/06/back-issues-edith-shain.html (accessed July 17, 2011).

21. "From Celebration to Circus, Caught Up in the March of Time," *New York Times*, August 17, 2005, http://barista.media2org// p=2085 (accessed August19, 2007).

22. Chan, "62 Years Later, a Kiss That Can't Be Forgotten."

23. Michael Kennedy, "Celebrating the V-J Day Kiss Seen 'Round the World'" *Los Angeles Times online*, August 14, 2005, http://www.latimes. com/2005/aug/14/local/me-kiss14 (accessed November 10, 2008).

24. "From Celebration to Circus, Caught Up in the March of Time."

25. Carl Muscarello grew uncomfortable with Edith Shain "using" the V-J Day Kiss for profit. At one point he thought Edith Shain hired an agent to book engagements involving her part in Alfred Eisenstaedt's photo. Edith Shain denied the employment of an agent to handle any of her affairs.

26. "From Celebration to Circus, Caught Up in the March of Time."

Chapter 27. The Current

1. "Sailor Donates Famous Poster," *Houston News*, June 16, 2009, http://www.click2houston.com/news/19769326/detail.html (accessed June 2, 2011).

2. "The Kissing Sailor," *Pentagon Channel*, 2009, youtube.com/watch?v=POPAL-AzryE (accessed June 21, 2011).

3. Halle Stockton, "Big Kiss Looms Large over Anniversary," *Herald Tribune*, August 16, 2009, http://www.heraldtribune.com/article/20090816/ARTICLE/908161041?template=printpicart (accessed July 13, 2011).

4. Billy Cox, "One Half of an Immortal Kiss?" *Herald Tribune*, August 14, 2009, http://www.heraldtribune.com/article2009081/ARTICLE/9081410114?p=1&tc=pg (accessed July 14, 2011).

5. "The Kiss of a Generation," *Manatee's Military Moms*, August 16, 2009, http://manateesmilitarymoms.blogspot.com/search/label Terry%20Longpre (accessed July 12, 2011).

BIBLIOGRAPHY

BOOKS

Berman, Marshall. *On the Town: One Hundred Years of Spectacle on Times Square*. New York: Random House, 2006.

Bianco, Anthony. *Ghosts of 42nd Street*. New York, HarperCollins, 2004.

Bradley, James. *Flags of Our Fathers*. New York: Bantam House, 2000.

Brinkley, David. *Washington Goes to War*. New York: Ballantine Books, 1988.

Callahan, M. Catherine. *Born Newporters*. Newport, R.I.: Kathryn Whitney Lucey Photography, 2002.

Casdorph, Paul D. *Let the Good Times Roll: Life at Home in America During WWII*. New York: Paragon House, 1989.

Clavin, Tom, and Bob Drury. *Halsey's Typhoon*. New York: Atlantic Monthly Press, 2007.

Decade of Triumph: The 1940's. Alexandria, Virginia: Time-Life Books, 1990.

Dawidowicz, Lucy S. *The War Against the Jews 1933–1945*, sixth ed. New York: Holt, Rinehart and Winston, 1975.

Eisenstaedt, Alfred. *Eisenstaedt on Eisenstaedt*. New York: Abbeville Press Publishers, 1985.

——. *Eisenstaedt's Guide to Photography*. Middlesex, England: Viking Press, 1978.

——. *Witness to Our Time*. New York: Viking Press, 1966.

——, and Doris O'Neil. *Eisenstaedt Remembrances*. Boston: Little, Brown and Company, 1990.

Garner, Joe. *We Interrupt this Broadcast*. New York: Sourcebooks MediaFusion, 1998.

Goldhagen, Daniel. *Hitler's Willing Executioners: Ordinary Germans and the Holocaust*, second ed. New York: Alfred E. Knopf, 1996.

Harriman, Robert, and John Louis Lucaites. *No Caption Needed: Iconic Photographs, Public Culture, and Liberal Democracy*. Chicago: University of Chicago Press, 2007.

History of World War II. New York, Marshall Cavandish Corp., 2005.

Hoopes, Roy. *Americans Remember the Home Front*. New York: Hawthorne Books, 1977.

Hornfischer, James D. *The Last Stand of the Tin Can Sailors*. New York: Bantam Dell,2004.

Kennedy, Maxwell Taylor. *Danger's Hour*. New York: Simon and Schuster, 2008.

Kozol, Wendy. *Life's America*. Philadelphia: Temple University Press, 1994.

Lacayo, Richard, and George Russel. *Eyewitness: 150 Years of Photojournalism*. New York: Time Inc., 1995.

Loengard, John. *Life Photographers: What They Saw*. Boston: Little, Brown and Company, 1998.

Manchester, William. *The Glory and the Dream*. New York: Bantam, 1984.

McCullough, David. *Truman*. New York: Simon and Schuster, 1992.

Morris, Jan. *Manhattan '45*. New York: Oxford University Press, 1987.

The Century in Times Square, edited by Merrill Perlman. New York: Bishop Books Inc., 1999.

Scotti, R. A. *Sudden Sea: The Great Hurricane of 1938*. New York: Chapter & Verse, Ink., 2003.

Stone, Jill. *Times Square; A Pictorial History*. New York: Macmillan Publishing Co., 1982.

Sullivan, Robert, ed. *75 Years: The Very Best of LIFE*. New York: Time Home Entertainment Inc., 2011.

———. *The Classic Collection*. New York: LIFE Books, 2008.

Tell, Darcy. *Times Square Spectacular: Lighting Up Broadway*. Washington, D.C.: Smithsonian Institution Press, 2007.

Wainwright, Loudoun. *Great American Magazine: An Inside History of LIFE*. New York: Alfred A. Knopf, 1986.

Westhorp, Christopher, ed. *VJ Day in Photographs*. London: Salamander Books, 1995.

ARTICLES

"Atoms Blast in Air to Cut Loss of Life." *New York Times*. August 12, 1945, 28.

Baughman, James L. "Who Read Life? The Circulation of America's Favorite Magazine." In *Looking at LIFE Magazine*, edited by Erika Doss. Washington, D.C.: Smithsonian Institution Press, 2001.

Brown, Emma. "Anonymously World-Famous after WWII Photo, She Didn't Kiss and Tell." *Washington Post*, June 24, 2010, B5.

Busch, Noel F. "Week the War Ended." *LIFE*, August 27, 1945, 29–33.

"Camera at Work." *LIFE*, vol. 3 (August 1980), 8.

Doss, Erika. "Rethinking America's Favorite Magazine, 1936–1972." In *Looking at LIFE Magazine*, edited by Erika Doss. Washington, D.C.: Smithsonian Institution Press, 2001.

Ewers, Justin. "The Kiss That Wasn't Just a Kiss: Half of a Famous Pair Identified at Last." *WWII Today*, December 1, 2007.

Faram, Mark. "The Kiss Heard 'Round the World.'" *Navy Times*. October 24, 2006, 16.

Feinberg, Alexander. "All City 'Lets Go.'" *New York Times*, August 15, 1945, 1.

Field, James A., Jr. "Tokyo, 1945." *American Heritage*, July 2005.

Fletcher, Guy. "A Kiss for the Ages." *Frederick: Life in Mid-Maryland*, September 2009, 46–55.

Haberman, Clyde. "The Crossroads." In *The Century in Times Square*, edited by Merrill Perlman. New York: Bishop Books Inc., 1999.

Hales, Peter Bacon. "Imagining the Atomic Age." In *Looking at LIFE Magazine*, edited by Erika Doss. Washington, D.C.: Smithsonian Institution Press, 2001.

Holme, Bryan. "Introduction." In *Eisenstaedt Remembrances*, by Alfred Eisenstaedt, ix–xvii. Boston: Little, Brown and Company, 1990.

"'An Imperial Message Is Forthcoming Soon' Official News Agency Reports in Broadcast at 1:49 A.M." *New York Times*, August 14, 1945, 1.

Kindred, David. "It Started with a Kiss." *Golf Digest*, January 2007.

Kunhardt, Philip B., Jr. "Editor's Note." *LIFE*, vol. 3, no. 8 (August 1980), 4.

"Letter to the Editor." *LIFE*, vol. 19, no. 9 (September 17, 1945), 2–4.

"Letter to the Editor." *LIFE*, vol. 3, no. 8 (October 1980), 12.

"Letters." *LIFE*, vol. 3, no.10 (December 1980), 12.

Meister, Gerard. "My VJ Day: It Was Nothing Like Eisenstaedt's." *American Heritage*, July 2005.

Mendonsa, George. "Letter to Editor." *Newport Daily News*, April 13, 1989.

Murray, Jennifer. "George Mendonsa: Newport Trap Fisherman." *Newport History: Bulletin of the Newport Historical Society*, 1991, 1–54.

Newman, Cathy. "A Life Revealed." *National Geographic*, April 2002.

Okrent, Daniel. "V-J Day Sailor Remains a Mystery." *Wall Street Journal*, August 26, 1996.

Patterson, Neal. "Peace—It's Wonderfully Noisy." *Daily News*, August 15, 1945, 3.

"Sailor's Sailor." *East Bay Life*, July 1–3, 2009, 1–5.

"Truman Message Due After 9 A.M." *New York Times*, August 14, 1945, 1.

"Victory Celebrations." *LIFE*, August 27, 1945, 21–29.
"Where Art They Now?" *LIFE*, November 25, 1946, 140–152.
"Who Is the Kissing Sailor?" *LIFE*, October 1980, 69–72.

INTERVIEWS

Benson, Richard. Phone interview by Lawrence Verria. September 13, 2008.

Burrows, Barbara Baker. Interview by Lawrence Verria. New York City, March 27, 2008.

——. Phone interview by Lawrence Verria. July 22, 2011.

Brown, Marvin. Phone interview by Lawrence Verria. July 19, 2008.

Bucolo, Anthony. Phone interview by Lawrence Verria. May 10, 2007.

Friedman, Greta. Interview by Patricia Redmond. *Greta Freidman Collection*. Library of Congress, May 26, 2006. http://Icweb2.loc.gov/diglib/vhp/bib/42863. Accessed June 24, 2008.

——. Phone interview by Lawrence Verria. August 24, 2008.

——. Phone interview by Lawrence Verria. November 23, 2008.

——. Interview by Lawrence Verria. Bristol, Rhode Island. 4 July 2009.

Lillie, Rich. Phone interview by Lawrence Verria. November 14, 2009.

Martin, Steve. Phone interview by Lawrence Verria. December 17, 2008.

McNeel, Ken. Phone interview by Lawrence Verria. February 23, 2008.

McDuffie, Glenn. Phone interview by Lawrence Verria. February 24, 2008.

Mendonsa, George. Interview by Middletown High School Teacher. Middletown High School, Middletown, Rhode Island. 1992.

——. Interview by Dr. Evelyn M. Cherpak. Navy War College in Newport, Rhode Island. November 8, 2005.

——. Interview by Lawrence Verria. Middletown, Rhode Island. April 10, 2007.

——. Interview by Lawrence Verria. Middletown, Rhode Island. May 10, 2007.

——. Interview by Patricia Redmond. *George Mendonsa Collection*. Library of Congress, May 29, 2007. http://Icweb2.loc.gov/diglib/vhp/bib/42868. Accessed June 24, 2008.

——. Interview by Lawrence Verria. Middletown, Rhode Island. August 18, 2007.

——. Interview by Lawrence Verria. Middletown, Rhode Island. September 21, 2008.

——. Interview by Charles Berlutti. September 2009.

——. Interview by Lawrence Verria. Middletown, Rhode Island. July 1, 2010.

Mendonsa, Rita. Interview by Lawrence Verria. Middletown, Rhode Island. May 3, 2007.

McNeel, Ken. Phone interview by Lawrence Verria. February 23, 2008.

McDuffie, Glenn. Phone interview by Lawrence Verria. February 24, 2008.

Muscarello, Carl. Phone interview by Lawrence Verria. March 4, 2008.

——. Phone interview by Lawrence Verria. July 24, 2008.

O'Donnell, Jerry. Interview by Lawrence Verria. Middletown, Rhode Island. April 17, 2007.

Shain, Edith. Phone interview by Lawrence Verria. December 9, 2008.

Sheridan, James E. Phone interview by Lawrence Verria. August 4, 2007.

CORRESPONDENCE

Cunningham, Eugene C. Letter to Carl Muscarello. Date unknown.

Friedman, Greta. Letter to Ullrich Lenze and Dr. Guida Knopp. June 1, 1991.

——. Letter to Bryant Gumbel. August 11, 1995.

——. Letter to Jeff Zucker. October 26, 1995.

——. Letter to Lawrence Verria. October 14, 2009.

——. Letter to Lawrence Verria. April 12, 2011.

Gibson, Lois. "Kissing Sailor." E-mail to Lawrence Verria. February 5, 2008.

——. "My Research." E-mail to Lawrence Verria. February 5, 2008.

——. "Comparison with a Scale." E-mail to Lawerence Verria. July 8, 2008.

——. "Black Triangle on Shoulder." E-mail to Lawrence Verria. September 7, 2008.

——. "Answers to Kissing Sailor Questions." E-mail to Lawrence Verria. September 9, 2008.

——. No Subject. E-mail to Lawrence Verria. September 9, 2008.

Halstead, Dirk. "Eisenstaedt." E-mail to Lawrence Verria. October 23, 2007.

Kunhardt, Peter. Letter to George Mendonsa. October 17, 1980.

——. Letter to George Mendonsa. 1981.

Mendonsa, George. Letter to Donald Morrison. November 1, 1989.

——. Letter to Mary Stienbauer. Middletown, Rhode Island. February 6, 1991.

——. Letter to Carl Muscarello. October 3, 1995.

McAdams, John. "3 Tramps at Dealey Plaza." E-mail to Lawrence Verria. February 26, 2008.

Morrell, Ann. Letter to George Mendonsa. January 15, 1987.

Muscarello, Carl. Letter to George Mendonsa. October 27, 1995.

——. Letter to Lawrence Verria. March 5, 2008.

——. Letter to Lawrence Verria. July 24, 2008.

O'Donnell, Jerry. Letter to Diana Francis. March 4, 2007.

Sauer, Norman, PhD. Letter to Lawrence Verria. April 23, 2009.

——. " Kissing Sailor Inclusions." E-mail to Lawrence Verria. May 27, 2009.

WEB

"Alfred Eisenstaedt Biography." *LIFE.* http//www.life.com. Accessed August 19, 2007.

Burrows, Bobbie Baker. "In Appreciation of Eisie." *Digital Journalist.* http://www.Digitaljournalist.org. Accessed September 7, 2008.

"Cambridgeshire: People Like You." British Broadcasting Corporation. http://www.bbc.co.uk/cambridgeshire/content/articles/2007/08/16/kiss_eisenstaedt_feature.shtml. Accessed August 18, 2007.

"Carl Muscarello the Kissing Sailor Signed Photo COA." ebay.com. Accessed July 16, 2008.

Carlson, Peter. "The Happiest Day in American History." *American History*, 45 no. 3, August 2010. http://www.web.ebscohost.com/ehost/detail?sid=b5eddf6e-72af-447f-bedb f6620e31e455%40sessionmgr110vid=26&hid=110&bdata =JnNpdGU9Whvc3QtbG1Zq%3d%3d#db=f5h&AN=5161313. Accessed August 5, 2011.

"Con 'Artist' Catches Crooks." *Time.* January 20, 2001. http://www.time.com. Accessed August 19, 2007.

"CSI Reveals 'Kiss' Identity. *ABC News.* August 7, 2007. http://abcnews.go.com/Technology/Video/videoLogin?id=3454648. Accessed August 3, 2011.

Eckhart, Robert. "The Case Against One Sarasota Statue." *Herald Tribune.*www.heraldtribune.com/apps/pbcs.dll/article?AID= /20100201/ARTICLE/2011030/24. Accessed February 1, 2010.

Eisman, Dale. "The Times Square Kiss Mystery Lingers, Deliciously." November 11, 2005. http://www.Content.hamptonroads.com. Accessed August 19, 2007.

Elliot, Andrea. "V-J Day Is Replayed, but the Lip-Lock's Tamer This Time." *New York Times*, August 15, 2008. http://www.Nytimes.com. Accessed September 3, 2008.

Everyman in Times Square. April 2007. http://www.college.columbia.edu. Accessed September 3, 2008.

Freelander, David. "Kiss Isn't just a Kiss for Times Square Sailor." August 14, 2007. http://www.amny.com. Accessed January 24, 2008.

Friedman, Emily. "Man Claims He's the Mystery Sailor in 'The Kiss.'" August 7, 2007. http://www.abcnews.go.com/US/story?id=3422191&page=1. Accessed August 15, 2007.

"From Celebration to Circus, Caught Up in the March of Time." http://www.Barista.media2.org. Accessed August 19, 2007.

Gibson, Lois. Homepage. http://www.Loisgibson.com. Accessed August 19, 2007.

Goddard, Jacqui. "A Kiss Is Just a Kiss . . . But This Famous One Was Mine." August 13, 2007. http://www.Timesonline.com. Accessed September 26, 2007.

Harimann, Robert, and John Louis Lucaites. "The Times Square Kiss: Iconic Photography and Civic Renewal in U.S. Public Culture." June 2007. http://www.Historycooperative.org. Accessed August 20, 2007.

Huntington, Tom. "*The Kissers*." americainwwii.com. Accessed August 19, 2007.

"Instructor Helps Identify Sailor in Famous Photograph." 2006. http://www.Dce.Harvard.edu/pubs/alum/2006/03.html. Accessed August 19, 2007.

Jewish Virtual Library. 2011. http://www.jewishvirtuallibrary.org/jsource/Holocaust/FloorScrub.html. Accessed May 2, 2011.

Kennedy, Michael J. "Celebrating the V-J Day Kiss Seen 'Round the World.'" *Los Angeles Times*. August 14, 2005. http://articles.latimes.com/2005/aug/14/local/me-kiss14. Accessed November 10, 2008.

Kuffner, Alex. "Famed Kissing Sailor Has More Proof." *Providence Journal*. August 5, 2005. http://www.Projo.com. Accessed August 19, 2007.

Lagueux, Ronald R. "George Mendonsa, Plaintiff, v. Time Inc., Defendant C.A. No. 87-0371 L." United States District Court, Rhode Island. February 23, 1988. http://nsulaw.nova.edu/faculty/documents/Mendonsa.htm. Accessed August 3, 2010.

"LIFE Magazine Sailor Nurse—Kiss and Did not Make Up." *JB1TV*. June 23, 2010. http://www.youtube.com/user/JB1TV?blend=22&ob=5. Accessed July 24, 2011.

Lozano, Juan A. "Sailor in Famous Photo Identified." *Time*. August 3, 2007. time.com. Accessed August 19, 2007.

Lucas, Dean. "VJ day Times Square Kiss." May 2, 2007. http://www.famouspictures.org/mag/index.php?title=VJday_Times_Square_Kiss. Accessed August 19, 2007.

Milton, Pat. "Nurse Recalls Famous Times Square Kiss." August 14, 2005. News-herald.com. Accessed August 7, 2007.

Mullins, Nelson. Home Page. nelsonmullins.com. Accessed August 18, 2008.

"Nurse Recalls Times Square Kiss 60 Years Later." August 12, 2005. ctv.ca. Accessed August 19, 2007.

"Nurse in Times Square War Photo Reunites with Navy." *NPR*. November 10, 2008. http://www.NPR.org. Accessed November 10, 2008.

"Our Special Guest—Edith Shain 2007." *California Pioneers*. 2007. http://www.Californiapioneers.com. Accessed October 13, 2008.

"Pacific Wrecks." 1995. www.pacificwrecks.com/ships/usn/DD-537.html. Accessed May 9, 2011.

"R.I. Last State Still Marking V-J Day." CBS News. August 13, 2006. www.cbsnews.com/stories/2006/08/13/ap/natinoal/printable D8JFMSRGO.shtml. Accessed May 26, 2009.

Rothwell, Kristen. "A Nurse's Iconic Kiss That Marked the End of World War II." *Nurse Zone*. 2005. Nursezone.com. Accessed August 19, 2007.

Rufty, Bill. "Lakeland Couple Shared Their Own Timeless Kiss on V-J Day." August 14,
  2007. http://www.theledger.com. Accessed October 11, 2007.

Saewitz, Mike. "Sculptor at Center of Copyright Infringement Case." *Herald Tribune*. http://www.heraldtribune.com. Accessed February 12, 2009.

Sanders, Glenda. "One of V-J Day's Most Famous Celebrants Recalls Joy, Sadness." July 30, 2007. thevillagedailysun.com. Accessed August 19, 2007.

Satterfield, Archie. "Mystery Kisser Identified?" http://www.Archiesatterfield.com. Accessed September 26, 2007.

Sheehan, Ruth. "N.C. Boy Knew How To Celebrate." July 4, 2008. http://www.newsobserver.com. Accessed July 7, 2008.

"Times Square Kiss-In." August 14, 2007. http:www.timessquarenyc.org. Accessed August 19, 2007.

"V-J Day Kiss (Carl Muscarello)." ebay.com. Accessed August 1, 2008.

WPRI 12 Home Page. August 21, 2009. http://www.wpri.com/dpp/weather/local_wpri_hurricane_of_1938_retrospective_20090820_nek. Accessed June 12, 2011.

MULTIMEDIA

"Kissing Sailor Debate." *Brandmier in the Morning* recording. 97.9 *WLUP,* Chicago. August 2007.

Koppel, Ted, Peter Jennings, and Pete Simmons. "45/85: America and the World Since 1985." New York: American Broadcasting Companies, 1985.

New York Goes to War. DVD. Directed by Julie Cohen. New York: WLIW, 2007.

"Who Is the Kissing Sailor?" *20/20.* New York, 1980.

MISCELLANEOUS

Benson, George. The Benson Report. Newport, Rhode Island, 1987.

Lee, Jinho, Baback Moghaddam, and Hanspeter Pfister. "3D Facial Modeling and Synthesis of the Sailor in Alfred Eisenstaedt's 'VJ -Day Kiss' Photo." *Mitsubishi Electric Reasearch Lab*, 1995.

Lilly, Charles H. "Journal on Board USS 'The Sullivans' DD537." December 23, 1943–July 4, 1945.

Manhattan New York City Telephone Directory. New York Telephone Company. Summer / Fall 1945.

Sauer, Norman, PhD, Amy Michael, Jamie Minns, and Megan Moreau. "Kissing Sailor Identification Slide Show." Michigan State University. April 29, 2009.

INDEX

Page numbers in *italics* indicate illustrations. Page numbers followed by an "n" indicate endnotes.

AUTHORS

LAWRENCE VERRIA (lawrenceverria.com) serves as the North Kingstown (RI) High School Social Studies Department Chair. His teaching career spans forty years. His professional recognitions include the 2000 Rhode Island Teacher of the Year, the 2008 Susan B. Wilson Civic Education Award, and the 2022 Gilder Lehrman Institute of American History Rhode Island Teaching Award. In 2022 Verria published his second book, *The Cool Moose: Robert J. Healey, Jr. Beyond the Beard*. He and his wife, Celeste Verria, live in Bristol, Rhode Island, where they raised their three daughters.

GEORGE GALDORISI is Director of Strategic Assessments and Technical Futures for the Naval Information Warfare Center Pacific. Prior to joining NIWC Pacific, he completed a thirty-year career as a naval aviator, culminating in fourteen years of consecutive service as executive officer, commanding officer, commodore, and chief of staff. He enjoys writing, especially speculative fiction about the future of warfare. He is the author of fifteen books, including four consecutive New York Times bestsellers. He is co-editor of the 2021 Naval Institute Press book *AI at War: How Big Data, Artificial Intelligence, and Machine Learning Are Changing Naval Warfare*.